THE NEW
LIBERALISM

THE NEW LIBERALISM

The Rising Power of Citizen Groups

JEFFREY M. BERRY

BROOKINGS INSTITUTION PRESS

Washington, D.C.

Copyright © 1999 by
THE BROOKINGS INSTITUTION
1775 Massachusetts Ave. N.W.
Washington, D.C. 20036
www.brookings.edu

Library of Congress Cataloging-in-Publication data

Berry, Jeffrey M., 1948-
    The new liberalism : the rising power of citizen groups / Jeffrey M. Berry.
        p. cm.
    Includes bibliographical references and index.

    ISBN 0-8157-0908-0 (cloth : alk. paper)
    ISBN 0-8157-0907-2 pbk : alk. paper)
    1. Pressure groups--United States. 2. Lobbying--United States. 3.
Political participation--United States. 4. Political
planning--United States. 5. Liberalism--United States. I. Title.
    JK1118 .B43 1999
    322.4'3'0973--dc21   98-40249
                                                                            CIP

First softcover printing, August 2000

Digital printing

The paper used in this publication meets the minimum requirements of the American National Standard for Information Sciences—Permanence of Paper for Printed Library Materials, ANSI Z39.48-1984

Typeset in Palatino

Composition by Oakland Street Publishing
Arlington, Virginia

Acknowledgments

AS READERS WILL quickly discover, this book is built on a large data base—one that I could not have compiled entirely on my own. It was my good fortune to have Seth Aframe, Russell Reiter, Jennifer Rich, Deborah Schildkraut, and Tracy Turner assist me with the research. Their dogged, painstaking work made this book possible, and I will forever be in their debt.

At a preliminary stage of the project, Maria Figueroa was instrumental in collecting material that allowed me to refine the research design. Toward the end, Lori Brainard helped me to track down some final pieces of the puzzle.

My colleague, Kent Portney, let me badger him with a thousand questions about the research design for this project. At later stages, completed drafts were read by Frank Baumgartner, Bill Browne, Jim Glaser, Kent Portney, Kay Lehman Schlozman, Rick Valelly, David Vogel, and Kent Weaver. Their detailed comments were invaluable to me as I prepared the final version of the manuscript. Thanks to all these fine scholars for their efforts and their insights.

Frank Baumgartner was kind enough to use a draft of this book in two of his classes at Texas A&M University and then to invite me to campus to discuss it with his students. I hope the A&M students in PS 314-H and PS 672 enjoyed reading this work. I suspect they didn't enjoy writing the paper that was assigned, but I certainly enjoyed reading their critiques.

Rick Valelly also used a draft in one of his courses at Swarthmore. The Department of Political Science at Boston College was kind enough to invite me to spend the day on campus talking to groups of students and to give a presentation to faculty and graduate students. Thanks to the chair, Dennis Hale, and all members of the department for their gracious hospitality and for the stimulating discussions about citizen groups in national politics.

A paper stemming from this project, "The Changing Face of American Liberalism," was presented at the conference on The Politics of Inequality in the Twentieth Century at the Kennedy School of Government, Harvard University. The conference was expertly organized by John Gerring and David Hart. Ulrich Willems and Thomas Von Winter brought me to Hamburg to speak on "America in the Age of Postmaterialism" to the scholars gathered for the Conference on Political Representation of Minority Interests. The meeting was held under the auspices of the Study Group on Organized Interests of the German Political Science Association. I couldn't have had nicer hosts. Another opportunity to test ideas came at the conference on Civic Engagement in American Democracy in Portland, Maine. The conference was sponsored by the Harvard University Department of Government and the Russell Sage Foundation. Thanks to the organizers, Morris Fiorina and Theda Skocpol, for including my paper, "The Rise of Citizen Groups." The conference on American Democracy Entering the 21st Century was held as part of Northeastern University's centennial celebration. I appreciate Bill Crotty's invitation to participate and to give a talk, "Christians and Environmentalists in the 104th Congress." Another paper, "The Rise of Postmaterialism in American Politics," was delivered at the annual meeting of the American Political Science Association in 1996.

Nancy Davidson, acquisitions editor at the Brookings Institution Press, went far beyond the call of duty in helping to bring this book to fruition. She was a constant source of good advice and suggestions and was always encouraging. I am also grateful to Theresa Walker for editing the manuscript, Carlotta Ribar for proofreading it, and Julia Petrakis for constructing the index. The views expressed here are entirely my own and do not represent those of the Brookings Institution, its trustees, officers, staff members, or the organizations that support its research.

To Lori

Contents

Tables

CHAPTER ONE

Not Dead

ONE OF THE truisms about American politics is that liberalism is dead. Labor is weak; the welfare state has collapsed; conservatives dominated Congress even before the Republicans formally took control in 1995; and Bill Clinton could win re-election in 1996 only by running on Republican issues. Liberals are seen as a sad lot, still trying to figure out what happened. They almost have a nostalgic quality about them, sort of like the bell bottoms stuck in the back of the closet.

But liberalism is not dead. Indeed, it's thriving.

Liberalism has, however, changed its stripes. Today American liberalism stresses culture, status, life-style, morality, and rights—postmaterialism. Traditional liberalism, concerned with issues of economic equality and promoted primarily by unions and groups sympathetic to the poor, is in retreat. Although groups on both the right and the left advocate postmaterialism, liberal groups have been most successful in getting government to respond to their priorities. Citizen lobbying groups are the moving force behind modern liberalism.

The Liberals' Agenda

This argument about contemporary liberalism is not based on revisionist history, a deconstruction of what the terms *liberal* and *conservative* actually mean, a novel interpretation of current social policy, or a new research methodology for studying American politics. Instead it rests on a rather

1

conventional analysis of the congressional agenda. I looked at what Congress actually did in three separate sessions and recorded basic information about the types of policies Congress acted on and which kinds of interest groups were involved. It is important to emphasize that this study is restricted to policymaking in Congress. Thus, the argument about liberal postmaterialism is an argument only about how it has fared there. Research on the federal courts or on state-level politics or on public opinion might reveal different patterns; the mix of issues and advocacy may be significantly different outside of Congress. Still, Congress is at the center of American national politics, and the policies it considers and acts on shape the lives of Americans in direct and fundamental ways.

The major findings of my analysis can be stated succinctly:

First, since the early 1960s the agenda of American politics has shifted from a preoccupation with issues that are exclusively material in orientation to a focus on issues that involve quality-of-life concerns. In simple terms, policy decisions in Congress have moved from questions on how to increase the economic pie to questions about how to balance economic growth with the need to enhance the environment, protect consumers, or improve personal well-being. The change has been dramatic and enduring, and the rise of postmaterialism has profound consequences for whose interests are represented in the legislative process.

Second, citizen groups have been the primary political force behind this trend. Citizen groups of the left are most responsible for causing this change. Despite the prominence of conservative citizen groups and their success in attracting members, they have been marginal players in the legislative process. (By *citizen groups* I mean lobbying organizations that mobilize members, donors, or activists around interests other than their vocation or profession.)[1]

Although the liberal citizen groups are only a small proportion of the thousands and thousands of lobbies in Washington, the analysis in this book shows that they have been remarkably successful in influencing public policy. Regardless of their impact, though, they are important to study because for millions of Americans, these organizations are the means by which they support advocacy on the political issues they care the most about. For many people an identity as a Republican or a Democrat is superficial—-if they have any partisan identity at all. A more intensely held identity is often that of a feminist, an evangelical Christian, or an environmentalist. If so, people will feel more affinity for the National Organization for Women, the Christian Coalition, or the Sierra Club than they do for any political party.

Americans are not only able to find groups that work in the broad area they are concerned about, but the competition between these lobbies for members creates an incentive for these organizations to develop a policy niche. Is your interest in the environment mostly a concern for endangered species, toxic wastes, national parks, or wilderness? There are groups that specialize in each. Christian social conservatives can choose from the Christian Coalition, Concerned Women for America, the Eagle Forum, the Family Research Council, the National Right to Life Committee, and many other organizations. If we want someone in Washington to stand up for us, to speak passionately, and to aggressively advocate the policies that matter most to us, then a citizen lobby is the most obvious vehicle to serve as our representative in the policy-making process.

Citizen groups are immensely popular, and many have memberships in the six figures. These groups do not represent a cross-section of America, though that's true of all interest groups. They have earned the grudging respect of bureaucrats who understand that such groups cannot be dismissed as outsiders or irritating troublemakers. Legislators actively pursue the support of citizen groups, even though relatively few of these groups are directly involved in the electoral process. Legislators know the activists in the organization will get the word out about who their friends are.

Citizen groups have not only been widely accepted by the public but have also been embraced by the media. Again, though, the liberal groups have enjoyed the greatest success in gaining the trust of journalists. Even business, with its immense resources, is no match for citizen groups when it comes to media coverage. The Alar scare is illustrative.[2] In 1989 the Environmental Protection Agency (EPA) issued a report indicating that daminozide, a ripening agent used for red apples, could cause cancer in 5 out of 100,000 individuals who had some exposure over a seventy-year period. At the same time, EPA announced that Alar, the commercial product using daminozide, wouldn't be barred from the market for another eighteen months. The Natural Resources Defense Council (NRDC), outraged at what they regarded as EPA's cowardly stance, issued its own report a few days later indicating that 5 out of every 20,000 children could get cancer from their exposure to chemical residues in fruits and vegetables. The NRDC also hired a public relations firm that pitched the report to CBS's "60 Minutes." The popular TV news magazine soon ran a story describing Alar as "the most potent cancer causing agent in the food supply today."[3] Later Consumers Union reported that its tests showed that 75 percent of apple juice samples contained Alar.

However, substantial scientific evidence indicated the contrary about Alar. Despite rebuttals by independent scientists and the trade groups representing growers and juice processors, the charges about Alar stuck to the apples. The Processed Apple Institute claimed that its tests showed that less than 1 percent of commercially sold juice had traces of Alar. Their research was to no avail; there was almost no way of effectively rebutting Consumers Union. The industry suffered an estimated $125 million in lost sales, and the market did not return to normal until 1992.[4] Stories about carcinogenic agents are almost always newsworthy, but the charges against Alar acquired additional credibility because NRDC and Consumers Union, two highly respected citizen groups, jumped into the fray after EPA took its equivocal stand.

In their studies of Washington lobbies, political scientists have traditionally focused on corporations, industry trade groups, and professional associations. These groups long dominated Washington interest group politics, and academics have dwelt on how the political system is biased in favor of business. Most of the interest group scholarship in the twentieth century can be summed up in E. E. Schattschneider's memorable observation that "the flaw in the pluralist heaven is that the heavenly chorus sings with a strong upper-class accent."[5] Yet a growing body of literature suggests a broader, more diverse interest group system. Citizen groups have emerged in many policy areas and are active participants in policymaking.[6]

What has not arisen out of this newer literature on citizen groups is a clear sense of how citizen groups have fared compared with the corporations and trade groups they contend with.[7] The theoretical work on interest groups emphasizes that the advantages of business extend far beyond the lobbying arena to the broader values of society.[8] The enthusiasm political scientists have shown for documenting the advantages of business has not been matched by an inclination to study ways in which that bias might be decreasing over time. The real question, then, is how to measure political change. What constitutes a shift in power among all the different types of groups working to influence public policy? What tools can be used to determine the answers to these questions?

This study uses several different approaches to measure the impact of interest groups on public policy, but first the work must be situated within the larger context of interest group research. In measuring the influence of citizen lobbies and accounting for political change, three areas of scholarship are especially helpful.

First, citizen group advocacy represents the political consequences of the public's changing constellation of values. Because interest group scholarship has concentrated on business, most studies examine the pursuit of material goods, such as greater profits, regulatory advantages, better wages and benefits, and tax reductions. The lobbies pursuing these goals come to Congress and ask for these policies on the grounds that they will benefit the public good by expanding economic activity (business) or by more fairly allocating the wealth of the nation (labor). The basic value is not that the pursuit of wealth is of paramount importance but that increasing wealth is a means to other ends. Expanding wealth adds to national security, nurtures freedom by encouraging people to pursue their dreams, and frees families to enjoy more leisure time together. The greater the size of the economic pie, the more there is left to contribute to churches, colleges, symphonies, and museums—the institutions that enrich our lives.

Those with postmaterialist values have a fundamentally different view of what is important in life. Postmaterialist groups often ask that business be restricted in its pursuit of greater wealth. These citizen lobbies do not view the greatest degree of economic growth as optimum. Postmaterialists say, in effect, let's trade in some of that potential economic return and maintain our wilderness, clean the air that we breathe, and preserve the integrity and safety of consumer markets. "Enough already" is the cry of postmaterialists: above a certain level, more wealth will not make us a better society or make life more fulfilling.

Another strand of postmaterialism is unrelated to the trade-off of economic growth and consumer and environmental protection. This second focus is on rights and status. As such, these lobbies actively pursue civil rights for minorities and push for what they see as inalienable rights, like a fetus's right to life or, conversely, the right to control one's own body and have an abortion.

The nature of postmaterialism will be developed more thoroughly in chapter 3, but our concern here is its utility in the analysis of political change. University of Michigan political scientist Ronald Inglehart has measured material and postmaterial attitudes over time and finds increasing support for postmaterialist values in affluent, postindustrial societies.[9] Attitudes, however, are one thing, policies another. If citizen groups are successful agents of change, we should see some manifestation of that in what Congress considers and in what is eventually enacted into law. Citizen groups are certainly not the only force behind postmaterialist policies, but they are the primary means of political mobilization for those who hold these values.

A second perspective on political change—or lack thereof—focuses on lobbies and advocacy, especially the role of business in politics. As already noted, most of those who have studied interest groups have concluded that there is a persistent dominance by business. More broadly, they see the role of business as proof that the political system protects the status quo and is resistant to change.[10] One of the most prominent exponents of this view is Charles Lindblom, who makes a compelling case that business gets most of what it wants from government because without continuing prosperity, elected officials stand a greater risk of electoral defeat.[11] Business provides jobs and wages, and when an industry tells government it needs help, it behooves government to listen and then to act.

The most vociferous critics of this view would probably be business lobbyists in Washington. They would want to know why social scientists consider business one big happy family, united around a common agenda of goodies they want from the federal government. They might ask, for example, which set of telecommunications lobbies always wins? The hundreds of interest groups in that field are perpetually divided. The same would be true of health care or financial services, where there are many different sides to the industry and where conflict is endemic.

Those who view business as a dominant elite would not be persuaded by this counterargument. That industries are sometimes divided does not negate the deep and enduring support for the business sector by government. Individual policy conflicts are modest concerns; what is really significant is what Lindblom calls the "privileged position" of business.[12] The views of business are anticipated by policymakers, and influence is felt without business having to do anything. Business leaders are always consulted by government officials, and it is not individual policy decisions for industries but the general business climate that is critical. When President Clinton was elected, he envisioned quick congressional action on a range of important social policy initiatives. After he met with business leaders before his inauguration and got an earful about what his administration needed to do, he made budget deficit reduction his top priority. An exasperated and despairing Clinton told his aides that they'd all become "Eisenhower Republicans."[13]

If business is truly privileged, it stands to reason that it should have little trouble prevailing over citizen groups. Direct conflicts between business and citizen groups cannot be dismissed as incidental to the larger question of business dominance. Dismissing the outcomes of major policy disputes affecting business as not pertinent to the question of the status quo versus fundamental change is to claim that public policy is somehow irrelevant to understanding politics. Can one understand a war without studying any of the battles? This study examines important issues on which citizen groups want to restrict what business can do and asks, "who wins?"

Third, political change stimulated by rising citizen activism is often associated with social movements. Social movements challenge the existing political order by making demands on policymakers on behalf of traditionally marginalized constituencies. Most of the organizations studied fall into one movement or another, such as the women's movement, the environmental movement, the consumer movement, the evangelical Christian movement, or the civil rights movement. References to such "movements" often follow colloquial language rather than any strict definition used by sociologists, but the advocacy organizations in these policy areas have, in fact, mobilized groups previously underrepresented in the public policymaking process.[14]

One view of social movements is that although they initially challenge those who hold power in America, over time those movements with significant popular support drop their radical edge as they are co-opted into more conventional forms of political participation. The fluid and loosely knit organizations providing leadership to a movement mature into Washington lobbies. Also, one of the two major parties may move closer to the movement and make an open and concerted effort to mobilize the movement's followers on its behalf. In this sense, a movement becomes institutionalized as part of normal interest group and party politics.

This is a very positive conception of social movements, as a safety valve that channels dissent into constructive and peaceful political change. The civil rights movement gathered steam with its marches and protests, some of them ending in wrenching confrontations with southern law enforcement officials. Over time civil rights advocacy turned more decidedly to Washington lobbying aimed at all three branches of government. The Democratic Party firmly embraced the movement, and African Americans became an increasingly important component of the party's coalition.

A different view is that social movements are usually transitory or episodic and are not effectively institutionalized into public policymaking. Government officials may largely ignore the newly emerging activism, and since it is difficult to keep supporters engaged over the long term, the movement will decline into insignificance. There is no denying that some movements gain concessions from government, but many contemporary scholars believe that movements participate in the policymaking process only to the degree that the political establishment permits them. Typically, government makes concessions to defuse some of the pressure applied, but after creating opportunities for activists and organizations representing a movement to take part in government deliberations, it then closes off those opportunities when the pressure eases.[15] Government giveth, and government taketh away.

Do citizen groups follow this political opportunity model of social movements? Since my analysis begins in the early 1960s and ends in the early 1990s, we should expect to find such a trajectory if in fact these citizen groups reflect social movement politics. Over time, how do these groups fare in longevity, vitality, and resources? In terms of their participation in the governmental process, are they *given* opportunity by the state, or do they create their own opportunities?

Change or Stability?

All the questions posed or implied ask how interest group politics has changed over the years. For interest group scholars it's hard to see the landmarks. Unlike the study of political parties, where elections can signal important shifts, no political events tell us when the torch is passed among different sectors of the interest group community.

For those who believe that business rules, there should be no expectation that such important changes ever take place. Even for those who believe that the interest group system is more dynamic, no accepted measurements exist of how levels of change might be determined. The challenge of this study was developing a research design that would be sensitive to the mix of interest groups and the types of public policies that characterize the legislative process at different points in time.

To answer these questions as concretely as possible, the research documented the efforts of interest groups to influence the legislative process. For three different sessions of Congress, 1963, 1979, and 1991, we identified which lobbies worked on which issues and tried to determine how interest group politics and legislative policymaking changed over time. For each year, all domestic social and domestic economic issues that were the subject of a congressional hearing and received at least minimal coverage in the press were examined. For the three sessions combined, 205 separate policy issues taken up by Congress met these criteria. Legislative case histories were prepared for each of these 205 issues. These case studies form the primary data base for this book. (See appendix A for a detailed explanation of the research methodology and appendix B for a list of the cases.)

At the outset two central issues were how far back could the research go and what years should be chosen for study. The first year chosen would serve as a baseline against which change could be measured. This may seem to be a rather arbitrary decision since there is no consensus on a year or period that represents anything emblematic of interest group politics. There is, however, a realistic limitation in how far into the past this type of research can go. Just as attitudinal studies can only reach back as far as the first sophisticated public opinion polls, studying interest groups across a broad range of issues is also limited to the period in which the appropriate resources are available. In practical terms, the need for sufficient newspaper coverage of an entire set of issues before Congress in any one year, and the development of *Congressional Quarterly Weekly Report* into a relatively comprehensive record of what goes on in Congress, limited the kind of historical research conducted to sessions since the early 1960s.

Yet this limitation hardly seems problematic. To go back much further is to invite comparisons with times so different (World War II, the Depression, the Roaring Twenties) that the longer-term comparisons of interest groups would be discounted anyway in favor of analysis of more recent times. Even if it weren't for the practical limitations, it seems best to compare the system we have now with its direct antecedents rather than searching far back into the earlier part of the twentieth century.

In considering citizen groups and Congress in the postwar era, three periods appear as distinct historical phases. The first was defined as 1948 to 1963. This is a time frame when we should expect to find only limited citizen group advocacy. The scholarly literature on interest groups from that period reveals almost no coverage of lobbying by citizen groups.[16] The literature emphasizes that the 1950s were a period when "iron triangles" and "subgovernments" were said to typify the policymaking process. This model couldn't be more simple: the head lobbyist from the leading trade group, congressional committee or subcommittee chairmen, and a top bureaucrat or two would work together to settle the questions at hand in a particular policy area. Iron triangles operated in a friendly, consensual fashion, but participation was rigidly controlled and outsiders found these subsystems impenetrable.[17]

Scholars have never determined just how prevalent iron triangles were, and in chapter 4 this model will be tested with the data that have been gathered. Clearly, during this period political scientists considered business, farm, and labor to be active and important participants in public policymaking, while regarding citizen groups as marginal actors. To be sure, there was some citizen advocacy. An important episode in the history of citizen advocacy came with the fight at the 1948 Democratic national convention, when the Americans for Democratic Action (ADA) spearheaded a fight for a more liberal civil rights plank in the party platform. Even though Harry Truman called the ADA faction "crackpots," the liberal plank was adopted over the objections of party bosses and southern delegations.[18] Civil rights groups continued to be active during this entire period, and a modest amount of environmental advocacy existed as well.

In the second period, which stretches from the Johnson years through the Carter administration (1964–80), many new liberal citizen advocacy groups were formed. Previous research has shown that a surge of new citizen groups started during this time as entrepreneurs cultivated funding sources from foundations, government agencies, large donors, and individuals.[19] Most of these new citizen lobbies promoted liberal causes. The civil rights movement gathered momentum at the beginning of this period, and its effectiveness was a major stimulus to organizing in other areas. A number of environmental and consumer groups were started then, and the emergence of Ralph Nader, Common Cause, and new public interest law firms suggested that important changes were taking place in interest group politics. Notoriety, however, is not the same as influence, and whether this apparent new force in American politics had any long-term impact remains to be seen.

The election of Ronald Reagan was widely interpreted as a sea change in American politics, and the third period encompasses the twelve years of the Reagan and Bush administrations (1981–92). Reagan's campaign and election spurred organizers on, and the efforts to mobilize the right were emboldened by the lofty ambitions of his principled conservatism.

Numerous citizen groups on the right already existed, some forming in reaction to the Supreme Court's *Roe* v. *Wade* decision in 1973 or to the proposed Equal Rights amendment. The visibility of conservative organizing was heightened by the emergence of two controversial citizen groups. The National Conservative Political Action Committee (NCPAC) targeted liberal Democratic senators running for reelection in 1980 and ran independent expenditure campaigns against them. The committee ran ads in South Dakota, for example, that told voters there, "While the energy crisis was brewing, George McGovern was touring Cuba with Fidel Castro."[20] Whether these senators would have lost anyway in what was a strong Republican tide cannot be determined, but what was important was that NCPAC was popularly awarded the credit for dispatching paragons of American liberalism like McGovern and Frank Church.

The second conservative group, the Moral Majority, was founded in 1979 and quickly established a symbiotic relationship with the Reagan administration. With an avowed purpose of trying to anchor public policy with traditional Christian values, it represented an effort by its leader, the Reverend Jerry Falwell, to enhance the influence of evangelical Christians in American political life. Like NCPAC, the Moral Majority didn't last long, but it was succeeded by the Christian Coalition, a much more politically savvy organization. The Reagan-Bush years were ones of great ferment on the right, and a variety of citizen groups took it upon themselves to try to advance the agenda of those administrations, while at the same time pressuring Reagan and Bush to maintain a firm, conservative stance. If these conservative groups succeeded in their goal of becoming "players" in national policymaking, evidence of this activity should show up during this time.

The political world is a messy place, and there is no assumption that everything was held constant in these three separate years except for the changing advocacy of citizen groups. Still, there is constancy in a few key respects. Each of the three years, 1963, 1979, and 1991, was the third year of a first-term president. The third year was chosen to avoid both the honeymoon of the first months of a new presidency and the exigencies of election-year politics in Congress. The Democrats controlled Congress in the three different years studied. The White House was controlled by Democrats in 1963 and 1979, and by the Republicans in 1991. Finally, the intervals between the data points are roughly equivalent, and each of these three years falls toward the end of the selected periods.

Since the data analysis focuses on change over time, it is important to ask if one or more of these three years was particularly unusual. If one of the three sessions of Congress was atypical, interpretations of the data could be misleading. As there is no agreement on what a typical session of Congress looks like, it may seem like there is no way of knowing if any of these years are highly unrepresentative. Yet there are some straightforward ways of comparing these sessions of Congress to others. First, for any of these three years was there an unusual movement in a particular policy direction, as there was with the Great Society in 1965 or the Reagan Revolution in 1981? For these three years the answer is clearly no. Second, was there an unusual congressional election directly preceding these sessions, such as the Republican landslide in 1966 or the Democratic sweep in 1974? Again, the answer is no. Third, were there any outside events or conditions that seemed to have an unusual and significant impact on the Congress in those three years? None is apparent.[21]

The scholarly research in the areas emphasized in this study also suggests that the findings are unlikely to have been compromised by the selection of these particular years. Research on interest group populations indicates that different types of lobbies may rise and fall over time, but no evidence shows that they change rapidly from year to year.[22] What political scientists know about agenda building indicates that it is difficult to move agendas decisively one way or the other. For various reasons individual issues can suddenly gain momentum after languishing for years, but there are also strong forces that push the congressional agenda toward the status quo.[23] Agendas are not ephemeral, episodic creations of each Congress. Rather, they are cumulative, incremental products reflecting years of laborious advocacy by legislators and lobbyists alike.

Another important decision was how to define the set of issues to study. Thousands of bills are introduced into each Congress, many of them trivial and largely duplicative of other bills. Researchers studying legislative policymaking must use some filter to distinguish the bills that are significant enough to merit inclusion in their data.[24] Since a primary focus of this research is on agenda building, it made sense to select issues that congressional committees were holding hearings on. Hearings are traditionally the first serious, formal step in considering new legislation. As legislators become aware of new problems, hearings offer a way to study the issue, ponder the alternatives, and demonstrate that they are concerned (even if the committee fails to report a bill to the full chamber). Political power can be exercised in ways that keep issues off the political agenda, and the methodology used does not solve the difficult (if not intractable) problem of measuring influence that is not directly observable.[25] Nevertheless, this approach has the virtue of allowing us to determine which groups are at least successful in having their problems defined as political issues and to have gained enough support for at least some in the Congress to take up their cause.[26] Of all the problems we face as a society, Congress takes up only some of them. Whose problems are they? And how does this decision change over time?

Although the issue purview extends to all domestic social and economic policy, it excludes appropriations (which largely parallel statutory authorizations), oversight hearings, nominations, and foreign and defense policy. (Foreign trade, however, is included because it is usually no less a domestic economic issue than a foreign policy problem.) If both the House and Senate held hearings on a bill, only the hearings in one house were used and only one case study was developed. A yearly index of all hearings published by the Congressional Information Service (CIS) provided the comprehensive list of hearings to investigate. For each entry in the index we conducted a preliminary investigation to see if there was enough information to undertake a legislative history. (We used a randomization process so that House and Senate hearings had an equal chance of being selected first.) We drew data from five sources: *Congressional Quarterly Weekly Report*, the *New York Times*, the *Wall Street Journal*, published congressional hearings, and summaries in the CIS index itself. The process continued until all possible cases were reviewed.[27] Consequently, the cases for each of the three data points form a complete record of all important domestic issues on the congressional agenda for those years.

Each of these case studies includes information about the nature of the legislation and a chronicle of what happened to the bill as it went through the legislative process. (It did not have to pass or even get out of committee.) We tracked each case through the end of each Congress; thus for bills that had hearings in 1991, any progress those bills made before the end of 1992 was recorded. The data base also contains extensive information on interest group participation, the nature of interest group coalitions, the press coverage given to participating groups, and a determination of who won and who lost in the final resolution of the bill.

The 205 case studies provide the evidence used in most of what follows. In other parts of the study, the focus switches to two other data sets. One is on media coverage of interest groups in 1995; the other is on the relative effectiveness of liberal and conservative citizen groups in the Republican-led 104th Congress. Information about these two additional sources of data is contained in the pertinent text and in appendix A.

Participation and Efficacy

The research was designed to answer a long list of questions about citizen groups in national politics. In general terms, though, the chapters that follow concentrate on the participation of different kinds of advocacy organizations in the legislative process and their efficacy in influencing public policy. Chapter 2 puts forth a population baseline to gauge group participation against and then develops some measures of involvement by groups in congressional policymaking.

Chapter 3 looks at the congressional agenda and calculates the proportion of issues incorporating a postmaterial side at each of the three points in time. It also looks at issues relating to economic equality and tries to determine whether or not there is common ground on which traditional liberals and postmaterial liberals can work together.

Chapter 4 builds on the previous two by linking citizen group advocacy with the trend toward increasing postmaterialism. The analysis moves from agenda building to issue outcomes, including data on which groups won and lost in each of these three sessions of Congress. Issues on which business was in direct conflict with citizen groups working on behalf of environmental, consumer, or other postmaterial causes are emphasized.

In chapter 5 the participation rates of liberal citizen groups are compared with those of conservative groups. Since it is possible that the liberal groups have fared particularly well because of the Democrats' control of the Congress during the three years examined, this chapter also provides an analysis of the 104th Congress (1995–96). Did the Republican takeover of the House and Senate seriously alter the relative level of success of liberal and conservative citizen groups?

Chapter 6 examines citizen group resources, including the attention that journalists pay to these organizations. Liberal and conservative groups are compared in terms of media coverage across a range of tests. Patterns of resource allocation are discussed, and the ways in which these groups differ in organizational behavior are considered in detail.

The conclusion, chapter 7, returns to a comparison of postmaterial liberalism and traditional, economic equality liberalism. The future seems bright for liberal postmaterialists and the lobbies that represent them. Although both liberal and conservative citizen groups embody enduring values in American life, the liberal lobbies have proved more adept at mobilizing resources and converting those resources into effective political advocacy.

Ultimately, the findings are important not because they improve our understanding of contemporary interest group politics but because they bear upon the level of representation that various constituencies receive in Washington. Interest groups are popularly viewed as organizations that do their best to subvert democracy. They are blamed for persuading Congress to pass too much "special interest" legislation and blamed for not letting Congress pass enough legislation (gridlock). Their campaign donations are said to undermine democratic government and to degrade our electoral system. For all their faults, however, interest groups link citizens to government. They empower people by organizing those citizens with similar interests and expressing those interests to policymakers. In this regard, the growth of citizen groups reflects an expansion of organizing around interests that have too often received too little attention in Washington.

CHAPTER TWO

The Rise of
Citizen Groups

AMONG ALL DEMOCRACIES the United States is unique in the degree to which people organize into lobbying groups. In Europe, organizing to push for some of the same concerns pursued by American citizen groups has increased. However, these interests have been aggregated in a much different way. In a number of European countries green parties emerged from social movements championing environmental protection.[1] In the United States, green parties have never amounted to much, but environmental lobbies are immensely successful.

The way in which political interests are organized and articulated depends on many different structures. In the United States, the most obvious influence is a two-party system that eschews proportional representation and relies on single-member districts and plurality-based elections. The last new political party to capture the presidency was the Republican Party in 1860. In the postwar era the House of Representatives has never had more than a few members who were neither Republicans nor Democrats. Although many Americans are critical of our two parties and would like more choice, the system is stacked against third parties.

The structure of our political system is much more conducive to the formation of interest groups than to new political parties. The two parties are vote maximizers, extending far and wide to try to build an electoral majority. By contrast, interest groups are policy maximizers.

Whereas the two parties will often dilute their policy stands so as not to offend potential supporters, interest groups profit from tailoring their appeals to narrow audiences with bold, emphatic, and unyielding policy stands. They are much like cable TV channels, which can make money by finding a small but faithful audience.[2]

The staggering rise in the numbers of interest groups active in Washington is persuasive evidence of the fertility of our system in propagating interest groups.[3] Thus, it may seem unremarkable that so many new citizen groups have formed since the 1960s: the last three decades have been a great bull market for lobbying groups. Yet bull markets on Wall Street do not favor the stocks of all sectors of the economy equally. The same may be true for interest groups. The first task here is to determine if the growth of citizen group lobbying is distinctive. That is, has citizen group advocacy grown at a significantly greater rate than that of other interest group sectors?

The data gathered from the legislative case histories allow us to measure political change from our three sessions of Congress in 1963, 1979, and 1991. The findings suggest that the growth of citizen group advocacy reflects something more than the general growth of interest groups. Citizen groups are different; they are not just a bellwether of general interest group prosperity. The underlying question is, why have citizen groups flourished as never before? The answer is not so simple. It is necessary to look beyond the case histories collected for this study to the larger history of America since the 1960s. Interest groups do not just pop up because some constituency would benefit from greater representation in Washington. To understand the changing mix of interest groups in national politics, one must examine how the structure of the American political system has evolved. Besides concerned citizens and skillful leaders who can exploit those concerns, the development of new groups requires available resources and opportunities to participate in the political process.

The first part of this chapter offers some data on the participation of citizen groups in the legislative process. I compare how their participation changed over time against a population baseline for interest groups of all types. The next step is to stand back from the growth of citizen group advocacy and ask where it all came from. If the development of citizen groups does not simply reflect the general growth of interest group politics, what are the sources of its distinctiveness? Finally, how has the growth of citizen group advocacy been aided by changes in the structure of government and by broader changes in interest group politics?

The Representation of Citizen Groups

Unfortunately for scholars studying interest groups, there is no standard data base to measure the population of lobbying organizations over time. The government in Washington doesn't keep track of the number or names of groups that lobby there. Although Congress passed a law in 1946 to require that lobbyists register with it, it was a toothless piece of legislation, and interest groups widely ignored it. In 1995 a new lobbying registration law was passed, which may help scholars in the future.[4] Even measuring the participation of groups in a single year is difficult. There are no official lists of who participates in individual policy conflicts. Scholars don't even agree on what an interest group is. Some study only voluntary organizations, thereby excluding corporations and other institutions that lobby.

The single best study of the contours of the interest group community is Kay Lehman Schlozman and John Tierney's *Organized Interests and American Democracy*.[5] Drawing on a commercially published directory, *Washington Representatives*, Schlozman and Tierney examined each entry in the 1981 edition and classified the roughly 7,000 organizations listed into twelve basic types of interest groups.[6] Although surely groups were missing from the directory, Schlozman and Tierney's study is carefully crafted, and there is no reason to doubt the basic patterns that emerge from their data. Luckily, the year they chose to study, 1981, corresponds closely to the middle year of this study (1979), so some direct comparisons can be made with the case history data. When some of their categories are combined to approximate the definition of citizen group used in this study, the Schlozman and Tierney data show that roughly 7 percent of all interest groups having some representation in Washington in 1981 were citizen groups.[7] This representation could mean an organization either has its own lobbying office in Washington or hires lobbyists from law firms or public relations firms to represent it. Schlozman and Tierney also use a second measure restricted to organizations that have their own lobbying office. The proportion of citizen groups rises to about 14 percent since most of the interest groups using lobbyists from law firms and public relations firms are corporations that find it more economical to hire lobbyists as the need dictates rather than funding a Washington office of their own. The first measure is the more comprehensive one as it recognizes the different forms that Washington representation can take, while the second measure restricted to organizational offices sharply underestimates business representation.[8]

Who Participates?

Schlozman and Tierney's 1981 data set is important because it offers a rigorous measurement of who is represented in interest group politics. Being represented in Washington is a critical step toward influencing public policy. For an interest group, just being informed about what is going on in certain policy areas and having the capability to monitor events so that organizational leaders are well informed is a crucial advantage in the policymaking process.[9]

To actually exert influence, however, groups must act on the information that their representatives collect. A beginning point for studying influence is to see which groups actually participate. To measure participation, we reviewed each of the congressional hearings for the 205 cases in this study to see which groups testified. Although some groups participate in the legislative process without making an attempt to testify, there is reason to believe that hearings capture much of the overall roster of lobbying participants. Testifying at hearings helps to legitimize a group's participation in the policymaking that follows. Lobbyists like to use the opportunity that hearings afford to involve the organization's leaders, who typically deliver the testimony. For membership organizations, hearings are an opportunity for a photo and an article in the newsletter demonstrating the importance and effectiveness of the Washington office. Schlozman and Tierney's survey of Washington lobbyists showed that 99 percent of their respondents indicated that their organization testifies before Congress.[10]

One assumes that the more important a group is perceived to be on the issue at hand, the more likely it is that it will be allowed to testify. Groups more sympathetic with the committee or subcommittee chair's position are probably also favored, but since the Democrats controlled Congress at all three points in time, there is some constancy on this point. Committee members from the minority party also influence the list of participants.

The findings in table 2-1 are striking. As a proportion of all groups participating, citizen groups increased from 23.5 percent in 1963 to 31.8

Table 2-1. Testimony of Interest Groups at Hearings, 1963, 1979, 1991

Percent of total number of interest groups testifying during that year

	Interest groups						
Year	Citizen groups	Corpo- rations	Trade associations	Professional associations	Labor unions	Other[a]	Total
1963	23.5	18.1	31.8	12.9	6.3	7.4	100
1979	26.2	22.0	28.9	11.8	4.4	6.7	100
1991	31.8	19.1	25.5	14.5	3.8	5.3	100

Note: In comparing the rate of change over time for citizen groups to the rate of change of all other interest groups, t, .004. (Total, 1963, N for hearings, 74; N for groups testifying, 1,373; 1979, N for hearings, 57; N for groups testifying, 947; 1991, N for hearings, 74; N for groups testifying, 922.)

a. Veterans, nonprofits, churches, and other groups.

percent in 1991. At all three points in time citizen groups are overrepresented in the legislative process, although the 1981 baseline population figure offers the only true comparison. If the proportion of citizen lobbies was around 7 percent, the comparable 1979 data indicate that they testified at a rate of close to four times their numbers in the interest group population. For 1963 the percentage of citizen groups in the population is unknown, but it's inconceivable that it was equivalent to the 23.5 percent of the testimony offered that year. This testimony largely reflected the participation of local, state, and national environmental groups on legislation in that area and a huge number of groups from all over the country that testified on behalf of the 1963 civil rights bill.

The lack of a firm population baseline for 1991 may raise some question about the trend line in the magnitude of overrepresentation. Since the proportion of testimony from citizen groups increased from 1979 to 1991, can we assume that citizen groups were overrepresented at an even greater rate by the end of this period? If during this time citizen groups grew as a proportion of the lobbying population, the magnitude of over-representation may not have increased.[11] Although there is no one baseline to use for 1991, strong evidence suggests that the proportion of citizen lobbies decreased during this decade. The legislative case histories for 1991 reveal that the number of groups started in the previous decade is small. This stands to reason: many of the citizen group "markets" had already matured by 1981. The environmental market, for example, was saturated by then by advocacy groups working on behalf of a wide variety of environmental issues. Between 1970 and 1980 environmental groups in the United States listed in the *Encyclopedia of Associations* grew from 221 to 380. In 1990, however, only 396 were listed.[12] In contrast, some business sectors experienced a boom in Washington representation. In health care, for example, around 100 health-related lobbies were operating in Washington in 1979. In 1991 there were more than 700.[13] By themselves, these additional 600 health groups in Washington surely exceeded the total number of all new citizen groups that opened up shop in Washington during the same time. Business developments in fields like telecommunications, computers, and biotechnology make it obvious that Washington representation expanded greatly for these industries as well.

It is fair to conclude that by 1991 citizen groups had fallen to less than the 7 percent of all Washington representation that was found in 1981. If Schlozman and Tierney's narrower gauge for organizations with Washington offices is used, a similar conclusion would be reached: citizen groups would be less than the 14 percent of offices in the 1981 population figures. By whatever standard used, the overrepresentation of citizen groups grew between the 1979–81 period and 1991. Even allowing for some imprecision in the data, the inescapable conclusion is that the overrepresentation is enormous: by the early 1990s, this relatively small proportion of organizations lobbying in Washington was offering roughly a third of all congressional testimony from interest groups. All the more impressive is that citizen groups increased their share of the hearings limelight at a time when the opportunities to testify were becoming a scarcer resource. The average number of groups to testify at a hearing in 1979 was 16.6; in 1991 it was 12.5.[14] And although the opportunity to testify was becoming scarcer, the overall number of interest groups in Washington was increasing.

These findings from the data lead to two questions. First, why have citizen groups been so successful in gaining a disproportionate share of these attractive opportunities to gain publicity for their policy stands? Second, how meaningful is this form of overrepresentation in the legislative process? Do these data on participation at hearings tell us anything more about the legislative process except that one set of groups seems unusually successful at gaining this chance to go on stage?

Citizen lobbies are unusually proficient at gaining slots at congressional hearings for a number of reasons. First, they have historically depended on an information strategy in their legislative lobbying and have relied heavily on mobilizing public opinion as a part of their effort to influence legislation. Citizen groups firmly believe that if they can get the "facts" out to the public, opinion will swing their way. Traditionally, business did not greatly rely on an outside strategy, though this position has changed over the years as some industry sectors have perceived themselves in more competitive situations with other sets of lobbies. Impressionistic evidence suggests that business is relying more heavily on public relations campaigns. The Health Insurance Association of America's Harry and Louise ads targeting the ambitious Clinton health care proposal are perhaps the best known example of a business or industry going public. Second, and relatedly, citizen groups have allocated their resources to emphasize research and the dissemination of information. Jobs and work assignments are designed to maximize publicity for their cause through low-cost outlets. Third, as will be shown in the chapters that follow, citizen groups were the primary initiators of many of the proposals that these committees were holding hearings on. It stands to reason that the groups pushing an issue on to the congressional agenda, and working with sympathetic legislators and their staffs to make that happen, would be given substantial opportunity to testify on its behalf. The breadth of each type of lobby's advocacy counts too. However, we do not know if the typical citizen group works on a wider range of issues than the typical business lobby.

The second and more difficult question is whether these groups' overrepresentation in the hearing process represents anything meaningful in terms of legislative policymaking. If it was business that was so significantly overrepresented in the committee hearings, it would surely be interpreted as just one more indication of the political system's bias in favor of corporate America. Citizen groups may seem less threatening to the integrity of the system, particularly because few combine their legislative activities with campaign donations. One might argue that viewing the amount of representation through the numbers of groups participating is misguided because how widely views are held in society should be the baseline, not the population of lobbies in Washington. This argument is logical and compelling since the values espoused by citizen groups, such as environmental protection, women's rights, and family values, tend to be shared by very large portions of the American population. It is certainly beneficial to the political system that such popular values are widely articulated on Capitol Hill. At the same time, there is no way to operationalize this standard since public opinion is hard to interpret in light of the real trade-offs among conflicting values that legislators must contend with when fashioning legislation.

Measuring congressional testimony is, of course, only the starting point in assessing the role of interest groups in the legislative process. If the tests of influence in the chapters to come reveal that these groups have little overall impact on the content or passage of legislation, a final assessment of the hearings data might be that they constitute symbolic participation: citizen groups are humored by legislators who allow them to testify but then largely ignore them while consulting and negotiating with traditional farm, labor, and business groups. With responsibility for almost one-third of all congressional testimony, what we can conclude about citizen groups at this point is that they are brilliant at getting their foot in the door.

Who Counts?

One way to test these initial findings is to determine not simply who participates but whose participation seems to count the most. Who are the most important actors in these legislative struggles? This question will be examined in several ways as this study progresses, but the purpose in this chapter is simply to determine who had the most visibility among the groups involved in each of the 205 issues before Congress. This will be done by looking at the press coverage of these issues by the three sources used throughout: the *New York Times*, the *Wall Street Journal*, and *Congressional Quarterly Weekly Report*.

The assumption is that the beat reporters for these publications have some sophisticated understanding of the issues they are covering—or at least of the politics surrounding the issue—and that their stories reflect reasonable conclusions about which groups deserve mention in their descriptions and analyses. When all the articles about the 1963 debate over the Domestic Cotton Price Equalization bill were examined, it was found that the reporters repeatedly cited the American Textile Manufacturers Association, the National Cotton Council, and the American Farm Bureau Federation, while there were only a few mentions of regional groups headquartered outside of Washington. Such judgments are taken to be a relatively accurate reflection of who are the most important spokesmen for the interests involved. Possibly, the regional groups were a little more important and the National Cotton Council a little less important, but it seems a good bet that experienced journalists for some of the nation's most respected publications can determine which groups are most involved on an issue.

Table 2-2. Press Coverage of Interest Groups

Percent of total number of interest groups mentioned in the press that year

| | Interest groups | | | | | | |
| | Citizen groups | Corpo-rations | Trade associations | Professional associations | Labor unions | Other[a] | Total |
Year							
1963	28.9	10.7	31.1	15.5	9.7	4.1	100.0
1979	26.9	17.2	26.5	11.6	15.5	2.3	100.0
1991	40.2	1.8	23.7	26.7	5.6	2.1	100.1

Note: In comparing the rate of change over time for citizen groups to the rate of change of all other interest groups, t, .16. (Totals: 1963, N for issues covered, 55; N for groups mentioned, 1,194; 1979, N for issues covered, 49; N for groups mentioned, 691; 1991, N for issues covered, 49; N for groups mentioned, 766.)

a. Veterans, nonprofits, churches, and other groups.

The data in table 2-2 reveal a pattern similar to that on congressional testimony. Although the percentage of corporations cited in 1991 decreases sharply, the cumulative rates for all sources of business representation—corporations, trade associations, and professional associations combined—drop about 5 percent between 1963 and 1991. Labor drops from 15.5 percent in 1979 to just 5.6 percent in 1991. Citizen groups are more than a quarter of all interest groups mentioned in press coverage of these issues in 1963 and 1979. By 1991 citizen group citations grow to roughly four out of every ten mentions of lobbying organizations.[15] For example, the 1991 Cable Television Consumer Protection Act was portrayed largely in the press as a fight between the primary trade group, the National Cable Television Association, and a single citizen's group, the Consumer Federation of America. A campaign advertising bill that same year was described repeatedly as a fight between the National Association of Broadcasters on the one side and Common Cause and the League of Women Voters on the other.

The press coverage of these issues is convincing evidence that citizen groups were central participants in these legislative conflicts. Their views and actions were given great prominence by reporters who saw them as major players representing one of the sides in battles over legislation. Although we do not yet know about the success of these groups in getting their legislation enacted, we do know that citizen lobbies were important and enduring participants in legislative policymaking.

Most significant, a pattern of enormous overrepresentation of citizen groups again occurs when they are compared against a population baseline. And again, these groups may proportionally represent public opinion—we do not have the appropriate data to know—but their participation in the legislative process is far in excess of their proportion in the interest group universe. Since citizen groups in Washington in 1991 are estimated to be decidedly less than 7 percent of total group representation and the proportion of all press citations to citizen group activity that year is 40 percent, the level of overrepresentation is enormous. If the actual percentage of citizen groups in 1991 was 4 percent, which is a generous estimate, the overrepresentation of press citations is on a magnitude of 10 to 1. If the measure of organizations with their own offices in Washington is the baseline, the overrepresentation is smaller but still substantial. Whichever standard is used, clearly these groups participate in legislative politics at a rate far greater than their numbers would suggest. Indeed, they are at the center of debate in Washington over public policy.

Roots

The ability of such a small proportion of groups to attract such a large proportion of these opportunities to gain attention begs an obvious question: what is it about these groups that leads to such a disproportionate share of the limelight? Before proceeding with more data analysis, it is useful to look at the historical roots of contemporary citizen groups. The origins of these groups may help us to understand how they have come to achieve their distinctive role in the policymaking process.

There is little doubt that the central underlying catalyst in the development of this sector was the social and political unrest of the 1960s.[16] All the seeds of the 1960s would not fully flower until years later (as the data above indicate), but this period is the foundation of citizen group advocacy today. Referring to the 1960s is, of course, shorthand for referring to two central political movements, the civil rights and antiwar movements, and the political and social rebellion that they signified. These two political movements were notable for many reasons, but particularly striking is how destabilizing they were. The American political system during the 1950s was exceptionally stable. Even during the depths of the Great Depression, political dissent outside the mainstream was rather modest.

The depth of anger of movement followers, their cynicism toward government, and the fury of their street protests shook American society. Movement leaders called into question the very legitimacy of American government. Although conservative critics charged that these movements represented the fringe of American society, less ideological observers came to believe that the political system was in serious trouble. When the Chicago police beat up antiwar demonstrators in Grant Park during the 1968 Democratic convention, it became widely apparent that there was a need to reform American politics so that the disaffected could participate in a less confrontational manner. The best-known effort was the Democrats' reforms aimed at bringing the left back into the party. For the development of citizen groups, however, the most important reform effort was initiated by the Ford Foundation. In 1970 it embarked on a program to fund public interest law firms because it saw a need "to advance necessary social change constructively."[17]

The Ford move was seminal. The foundation supported a cadre of sixteen public interest law firms whose avowed intention was to broaden representation before government and to open up the governmental process. The litigation model was inspired: change-oriented advocates would work within the system "constructively" but could push proposals designed to shake up the government. By 1975 Ford had made grants of $12 million to public interest law firms, and the prestige of the foundation legitimized these groups before the rest of the foundation world. Ford estimated that in 1970 it provided more than 90 percent of the funding of the public interest law movement. Within a few years more than thirty other foundations were making grants to public interest law groups, and Ford was funding only around half of these groups' budgets.[18]

What Ford did was to nurture an advocacy model that was sustainable. The Ford-supported groups, like the Environmental Defense Fund and the Natural Resources Defense Council, were able to use their Ford seed money to support themselves while they litigated important cases before the courts. In turn, their early victories in the courts and before administrative agencies gave them the credibility to attract individual donors whose financial support replaced that of Ford. These two groups have been a powerful legal arm of the environmental movement ever since, and they are widely respected in Washington for their advocacy work. Citizen group organizations have not, of course, been limited to the public interest law model, but this early emphasis on the law helped to define citizen groups as participants within the system rather than outside of it.

Another strong taproot of the citizen group movement was Ralph Nader and the many organizations founded under his auspices. Nader became a public figure in 1965 with the publication of *Unsafe at Any Speed*, an expose of the Chevrolet Corvair's safety problems. General Motors made an unwitting gift to the consumer movement by hiring a private investigator to look into Nader's background. When this response became public, and GM officials were forced to testify before Congress on why they had a private eye snooping around, Nader became an instant folk hero.[19] Nader initiated a number of serious book-length studies of policy problems and administrative agencies, like *The Nader Report on the Federal Trade Commission*, which exposed incompetence and favoritism in government. In 1970 he started Public Citizen, an umbrella organization designed to raise funds for a small empire of advocacy organizations.

In the same spirit of the Ford program, Nader viewed change through the lens of the legal system. He surrounded himself with young lawyers, nicknamed "Nader's Raiders," and together they took aim at laws and regulations they found objectionable. Nader added to his credibility with his ascetic life-style, living in a modest rooming house and demonstrating no interest in anything but his work. Donors knew their money would be well spent in his hands. For all of his outrage and bluster, though, Nader never let himself or his disciples move too far to the left. He proposed no grand economic reforms; he was no British socialist trying to find another industry to nationalize. Nader may have been the nation's most important critic of business, but superficially, at least, he was still a capitalist.

Over the years citizen groups flowered in a hundred different hues. Women's groups emerged strongly at the grass-roots level, and a handful of Washington-based groups led by the National Organization for Women began pressing the federal government for equal rights. Also fighting for equal rights were Hispanic organizations, disability rights groups, and in the past decade, gay and lesbian advocacy organizations. Conservative public interest law firms followed the liberal ones funded by Ford, and some of these focused on religious freedom issues. Also on the conservative side were new groups aimed at restoring traditional moral values and strengthening the American family.

One thing this diverse multitude of citizen groups has in common are leaders who were able to identify potential donors and develop an adequate funding base. This process was aided immeasurably by the emergence of direct mail as a major fundraising technique in the 1960s and 1970s. More broadly, though, citizen group entrepreneurs succeeded in tapping foundations, the government, and large donors in addition to the support provided to them by membership dues. They also proved adept at developing new sources of support when existing sources dried up.[20]

What they also have in common is the development of a successful organizational model that they were able to market to the public. Although there is certainly variation among the structure of these groups, the tactics they use, and the constituencies they try to organize, what they share is much more important. They embody the Ford Foundation's vision of change-oriented advocacy groups that would work soberly and responsibly within the system. Ford's justification for sponsoring public interest groups was that they were needed to broaden "representation of the underrepresented."[21] That's exactly what these groups communicate: that they are simply trying to broaden representation, not to restructure government and not to challenge traditional American values. They do not represent radicals but the suburbanites next door.

Movements must all go somewhere from the streets or they die—and die they often do. Born out of two protest movements, the liberal political organizations that emerged were pushed toward conventional channels of political participation by Ford, Nader, and other early leaders. Leftists would say that the liberals were co-opted by the system. Defenders would say that the liberals chose to be effective rather than engage in symbolic politics.

Institutional Change

Since the basic structure of our political system favors interest group politics, the evolution of protest movements into lobbying organizations may seem perfectly logical. But if the gravitation from protest to conventional lobbying was predictable, the endurance and popularity of citizen groups were not. The liberal groups that emerged in the early years faced an uncertain political environment. There was considerable conservative sentiment in the country that crystallized in the aftermath of the 1964 civil rights act and the Great Society legislation. The congressional elections of 1966, which resulted in a Republican gain of forty-seven seats in the House, were widely interpreted as a repudiation of Lyndon Johnson's Great Society. Shortly after the Ford Foundation started its public interest law program, Richard Nixon handed antiwar Democrat George McGovern one of the worst presidential election defeats in American history. Political currents were flowing in different directions during these crucial years, and there was nothing foreordained about what would happen to the new liberal citizen advocacy groups.

The survival of these early citizen groups and the development of new ones was aided, however, by changes in the structure and operation of American government. Although the American political system is conducive to pluralist politics, it became even more so during the late 1960s and 1970s. By the time Ronald Reagan came into office in 1981 and set out to "defund the left" by killing grant programs that supported these groups, it was too late.[22] American government had already institutionalized the participation of citizen groups in the political process.

The single most important structural change in government that helped to spur both the growth of citizen groups and their incorporation into the policymaking process was simply the growth of the federal government itself. From the early 1960s until the election of Ronald Reagan, the national government reshaped itself by dramatically expanding the welfare state and broadly extending itself into areas of "social" regulation. As new laws and programs were created, and new bureaucracies formed to carry out the tasks prescribed in those laws and programs, the opportunities for citizen groups swelled. In many cases citizen groups lobbied on behalf of the relevant legislation that helped them prosper, but in the early years the legislation sometimes came before the groups. When the food stamp program was first started in the early 1960s, interest groups were only marginal participants. In the wake of the program's development, however, two liberal advocacy groups, the Community Nutrition Institute and the Food Research and Action Center, were born. The Community Nutrition Institute established a financial footing by publishing a newsletter that people involved in the food stamp program at the state and local level found very useful. The organization also won training grants from the government to help educate community organizers about food stamps. The Food Research and Action Center got off the ground with government grants.[23]

More programs meant more constituencies. More constituencies meant more opportunities for entrepreneurs to organize advocacy groups. As Virginia Gray and David Lowery found in their study of interest groups on the state level, the formation of lobbies follows the growth of available resources and expanded government activity.[24] Thus, there is a "supply side" to interest group formation: not only do groups demand new programs but new programs demand new groups.

New programs and new bureaucracies created more points of access to government. Environmental groups were buoyant before the Environmental Protection Agency (EPA) was created in 1970, but this new agency presented endless new opportunities for these groups to participate in government. Before its budget was cut in the Reagan years, the EPA had substantial grant money to disperse to environmental lobbies. No matter that it was well endowed with a large dues-paying membership, the Sierra Club could easily gain a couple of hundred thousand dollars a year from the EPA to fund new activities.[25] New laws like the Clean Air Act Amendments (1970) meant extensive rulemaking, and the environmental groups had the scientific and legal expertise to participate effectively. When the Carter administration took over in 1977, it put two environmental lobbyists, Barbara Blum and David Hawkins, in top policymaking positions at the EPA.[26] They threw the door wide open for their former colleagues in the environmental movement. Four years later, when the conservative Reagan administration took over, liberal lobbies were banished from the EPA, but this move only helped these groups raise money from the public to fight the environmental infidels.

It is not merely that there were many new programs and bureaucracies that worked to the advantage of citizen groups, but that the policies to be administered were so complex. Under the Toxic Substances Control Act, the EPA is ostensibly responsible for screening 60,000 separate chemicals used in commercial applications. For a group like the Natural Resources Defense Council, with staff scientists as well as lawyers on board, the EPA became an easy target for litigation when it inevitably failed to carry out all that it was supposed to do.[27] The liberal citizen groups understood that corporations and trade associations were powerful not just because of their money or contacts but also because they possessed information that was valuable to those in government. As noted earlier, the leaders of these citizen groups consciously built their organizations so that they had substantial technical expertise and information capacities.

Access to government extended beyond administrative agencies to both the courts and Congress. Liberalization of the rules of standing in the federal courts was a major boon to public interest law firms. In the 1960s the courts broadened the standing to sue to include those without direct economic injury.[28] Congress also passed several laws providing for fees for public interest litigants who were successful in particular areas of the law. By the 1980s, a more conservative regime narrowed both the rules of standing and provisions for reimbursing public interest litigants, but by then the public interest law movement was firmly entrenched. A frustrated President Reagan denounced the liberal public interest law groups as "ideological ambulance chasers."[29]

Congress, always open to interest groups, became even more accommodating during the 1960s and 1970s. The party leadership weakened, reforms limited the power of committee chairmen, and both houses became increasingly decentralized. Most evident was the proliferation of subcommittees. In the 84th Congress (1955–56), there were 102 committee and subcommittees in the House. Ten years later there were 173. The numbers in the Senate were almost identical.[30] Although these trends would be at least partially reversed in later years, the decentralization of Congress offered all interest groups greater access to policymakers. In particular, the proliferation of subcommittees created more and more overlapping jurisdictions. A recent study found 110 separate committees and subcommittees claiming some jurisdiction over the EPA.[31] The more subcommittees, the easier it becomes for any interest group to find a sympathetic subcommittee chair who is willing to work with the group to push a particular policy alternative.

Citizen groups pressed for a lot, and in some cases fell short of their goals in opening up and restructuring government. During the Carter administration, consumer groups pushed for an Agency for Consumer Protection, a superregulatory agency that would have represented citizens in rulemaking proceedings in other regulatory agencies. Business not only believed that such an agency would institutionalize a strong consumer role in all regulatory deliberations, but that under the Democrats this agency would be highly responsive to Ralph Nader and his lieutenants. The proposal is credited by many with reinvigorating business lobbying in Washington. Trade groups and corporations realized that they had to be more aggressive——"proactive"——in fending off the consumer movement. There was also the start of a program at the Federal Trade Commission (FTC) to sponsor intervenor funding to balance representation in administrative rulemaking. Since consumers have much less incentive to organize and pay lobbyists to participate in complex and time-consuming regulatory proceedings than do business groups, Congress funded a program in 1975 to subsidize consumer representatives at the FTC. Consumer groups that wanted to participate could apply for funds that would offset their costs. This program was killed in the Reagan years.

Despite these defeats, citizen groups generally benefited from the structural changes in the governmental process. These changes were not accidental or haphazard but came about because government was under pressure to reform itself. The calls for reform came from many sectors, but citizen groups were instrumental in building the case for change in government. They pushed for an expansion of government services and regulations; they pushed the envelope in court suits asking for new interpretations of the legal code in areas such as standing; and they pushed Congress to reform itself and open up the system. To their credit, citizen groups played a major role in creating the opportunities they have so skillfully taken advantage of.

Conclusion

Our data on hearings and newspaper citations show that citizen groups have become prolific and enduring participants in legislative policy-making. Their success in getting their views before policymakers and the public is evidence of their acceptance as a normal part of interest group politics. If not part of the establishment, they are certainly part of issue networks, the communities of groups and policymakers who negotiate over the issues before government. They are so much a part of government today, it is easy to forget that these organizations were the direct outgrowth of angry, impassioned social movements that began in the 1960s. The groups of this period challenged and fought with a government that they saw in need of fundamental reform. The public interest law firms and Nader's consumer groups that followed chose a different path than movement politics. Outsiders at first, they pursued more conventional forms of participation and gradually gained respect as the legitimate representatives of broad, underrepresented constituencies. Women's groups, conservative groups, disability rights groups, and all other citizen lobbies followed the vision of constructive activism promoted by the Ford Foundation and these early groups.

Some social scientists see the fate of social movements in the hands of government. The powers that be permit a social movement challenging the system to achieve some small successes, but as soon as the intensity of public opinion wanes, the government, acting on behalf of society's most powerful members, simply shuts off the challenge to its authority. This is the message of Doug McAdam's sympathetic study of the civil rights movement.[32] After some successes in the early 1960s, the opportunities to participate were sharply restricted by the government. The state allowed participation but then took those opportunities away.

McAdam and other disciples of political opportunity theory would have a difficult time explaining the success of citizen groups in gaining a hold in the policymaking process. Government certainly didn't welcome the participation of these new challenging groups. Citizen groups generated conflict and uncertainty, and they relentlessly attacked established relationships and policymaking procedures. Although not all citizen group sectors fared equally well, their increasing prominence over the three decades of this study demonstrates that government wasn't very effective at shutting off whatever opportunities it initially granted. The real truth, of course, is that opportunities to participate weren't given to citizen groups—they demanded them. The increasing participation of citizen lobbies is a reflection of their continuing success in creating opportunities in the political system.

Citizen groups were certainly aided by structural changes that made it more difficult for government to restrict their participation. Government policymaking processes changed for several reasons, including the advocacy of citizen groups pushing for more participatory and more open structures of government. Consumer and environmental groups put business on the defensive, and part of the growth of business lobbying reflects a countermobilization to citizen group advocacy for expanded government regulation. Business developments stimulated the remainder of this growth, and the number of lobbies in some policy domains grew by the hundreds.

Yet if interest groups did well generally during this time, something different happened to citizen groups. Measured against a population baseline of all interest groups represented in Washington, citizen groups became increasingly overrepresented in terms of those permitted to testify and those whose views merit mention in the press. Congressional committee chairs and reporters must regard these groups as representative of important and broadly held views. But just what do these groups stand for that deserves such attention? It is to that subject that we turn.

CHAPTER THREE

The Rise of Postmaterialism

THE CONGRESSIONAL AGENDA changes continuously as new issues come to the fore, old ones decline, and others mutate into something a little different from what they were in the last session. Yet the agenda of Congress is a limited resource; it cannot encompass all the problems that people believe government should be addressing. Interest groups thus compete against one another to gain the attention of committees that might consent to work on relevant legislation. It is not only interest group advocacy that causes change in the congressional agenda. Public opinion, presidential priorities, and the policy preferences of the legislators themselves also shape what Congress takes up and what it leaves aside. Still, whenever Congress selects an issue, it is working on behalf of some interest group constituency. Over time certain constituencies receive more attention for their concerns and others receive less. In recent years Congress has devoted increasing attention to *postmaterial* concerns: issues that involve people's quality of life in ways unconnected with their financial pursuits.

The clash between material and postmaterial values animates much of politics today. The opposing forces have different visions of America. For corporations, trade associations, and professional associations, government's primary duty is to nurture individual industries and maintain a growing economy. For labor, government's job is improve workers' standard of living. For citizen groups, however, government should be doing more than helping people and corporations to make more money. They see government as having a primary responsibility for enhancing

34

equality, expanding rights, protecting the environment, supporting the traditional nuclear family, and policing corporations so that they are more socially responsible.

This chapter and the one that follows examine the rise of postmaterialism in American national politics. The mix of issues before Congress has changed over time, and as postmaterialist concerns show up more and more often on the congressional agenda, a critical question arises. Who is being served by this changing mix of issues before Congress, and who is being hurt?

The Affluent Society

In the industrial democracies, the traditional political division has been between workers on the one hand and owners, managers, and professionals on the other. The major political parties tend to be closely identified with workers or business, though issues such as ethnicity, race, religion, or region can complicate matters. Race, of course, influenced the development of American parties, but during the Great Depression the Democrats clearly became the party of workers and organized labor, while the Republicans became even more closely identified with the interests of business. But as the industrial revolution ran its course, the class dynamics underlying American politics weakened. Daniel Bell was one of the first to envision what postindustrial society would look like. "The major source of structural change," wrote Bell in 1973, "is the change in the character of knowledge."[1] Over time, service industries devoted to gathering and disseminating highly specialized knowledge came to be an increasingly large segment of the economy.

As the structure of the economy changed, a growing cadre of knowledge workers did not fit neatly into either party. They did not abandon the party system, but they began to look for political organizations that offered meaningful representation for their concerns.[2] Political scientist Ronald Inglehart argues that the critical variable in this changing political landscape is the relative affluence of those living in postindustrial societies. In his pioneering 1977 book, *The Silent Revolution*, Inglehart contends that growing up under conditions of affluence has led to an increased sense of economic security in Western democracies. The high standard of living, the high levels of education, and prosperous, expanding economies caused younger west Europeans to place a higher value on quality-of-life issues. Less concerned about finding or holding a job, these younger cohorts showed greater support for postmaterial priorities than older workers whose life experiences were different.[3] They look beyond their own financial self-interest and place aesthetics, morality, rights, and other nonmaterial political objectives above the pursuit of economic gain or enhanced physical security.

Postmaterial values are, in essence, nonmaterial concerns. Unfortunately, "post" is a misleading prefix in at least two ways. First, groups have pursued postmaterial policies long before this current period of economic security. The abolitionists, for example, placed freedom, human dignity, and a code of morality ahead of the economic prosperity that slavery brought to the South. Nativism, temperance, the teaching of evolution, and women's suffrage were divisive issues that incorporated postmaterial values. From the very founding of our country, quality-of-life concerns have been part of the mix of issues debated by citizens and policymakers. The theory of postmaterialism does not argue that such concerns are new to the age of affluence but only that the age of affluence stimulated a trend toward increasing popular support for making quality-of-life policies a priority. Since the approach utilized cannot go back much further than the earliest of our three sessions of Congress, no direct comparison can be made with previous periods in American history. I hope other researchers will be able to use different tools to assess the level of postmaterialism in previous eras.

Second, "post" suggests that younger cohorts have put material concerns behind them, when in fact, only some of them, according to their survey responses, place postmaterial values ahead of material values. Moreover, individual value priorities may change over time, and sustained economic decline would likely induce a rise in material preferences. Despite the imprecision, the material and postmaterial labels have gained currency in political science and remain widely used, providing a useful vocabulary for distinguishing fundamental political orientations.

Inglehart's initial work was built on surveys of different West European countries in the early 1970s, though his most recent work extends his research to forty countries around the globe.[4] The first surveys simply gave respondents a list of four items and asked which two "seem most desirable to you." The four statements listed were "maintaining order in the nation," "giving the people more say in important political decisions," "fighting rising prices," and "protecting freedom of speech." The items on maintaining order and fighting rising prices tapped material sentiments, while the statements on giving people more say and protecting freedom of speech were designed to elicit postmaterial concerns.[5] Although some variations existed from country to country, a basic pattern emerged: the younger cohorts had higher percentages of postmaterialists. In his 1977 work, all countries had considerably more materialists than postmaterialists, but more recent surveys show that the gap between materialists and postmaterialists has narrowed considerably, and in some countries there are actually more postmaterialists.[6]

Over the years much debate about Inglehart's work has occurred, especially regarding how accurately value change can be measured through the type of survey research he has used.[7] A central criticism made is that respondents can rank values without having to contemplate trade-offs. If one assumes that government can pursue postmaterial policies without damaging the economy, there is little dilemma in having to make the choice about national priorities. In the real world, stringent air quality standards might put some workers out of jobs as economically marginal plants find themselves unable to absorb the costs of the necessary pollution control equipment. The survey respondent is free to ignore such a possibility. As Everett Ladd has shown, when Americans are asked if the rate of business growth must be slowed in order to protect the environment, or if we must relax environmental protections to achieve new job growth, or if we can achieve both environmental protection and economic growth at the same time, a majority responds that both can be achieved at the same time.[8]

Since the research in my analysis is not based on surveys of attitudes, resolving this debate about the validity of Inglehart's approach can be left to others. The data for this study come from what went on in Congress. There are no hypotheticals, no politics without trade-offs. Even so, Inglehart's work remains an important guide because it provides a theoretical foundation for understanding the broad-scale societal change that citizen groups have sought. And what they have sought is a Congress less concerned about the needs of business and more concerned about how to protect the earth and preserve our souls.

The Search for Personal Growth

Inglehart's argument about the impact of affluence on political change is grounded not in economics or political science but in social psychology. He draws on the work of Abraham Maslow, a psychologist who searched for the wellsprings of human motivation. Inglehart uses Maslow's hierarchy of needs, which rank-orders human drives to satisfy our wants and desires.[9] People first try to meet their most basic needs, such as food, shelter, and physical safety. After that, they may seek love, a sense of belonging, and self-esteem. In Inglehart's mind, this threshold between basic needs and more personal, psychological gratification is crucial. Once basic material needs are met (economic and physical security), people begin to try to satisfy other concerns. Thus affluence—a level of economic resources that enables individuals to feel comfortable in turning their attention to politics—is the threshold that leads from exclusively material pursuits to a life that combines earning a living with making the world a better place.

Maslow's scholarship is not primarily, or even secondarily, concerned with politics. Rather, his focus is on personal growth. As people move up the hierarchy of needs, they can go beyond the search for love and community to pursue "self-actualization." The healthiest individuals—the self-actualizers—find ways to fulfill their "potentials, capacities, and talents." Self-actualizers are motivated to seek creative outlets for their talents and to become "fully human" and "everything that the person *can* become."[10]

Maslow concludes that few achieve self-actualization because it demands a relatively high level of personal psychological unity and integration. Still, physical and economic security certainly offer people the luxury of searching for meaning in their lives. But how does this search for growth and self-actualization lead to postmaterial politics, or politics of any type for that matter? As one of Inglehart's critics notes, "The theory of motivation proposed by Maslow is a theory of *individual* thought and behavior."[11] When people move up the hierarchy of needs, taking on activities to give their lives more meaning and trying to make themselves "fully human," how might it be that one of the consequences is the expansion of *collective* political action?

From Self-Actualization to Washington Lobbying

The logical connection between the search for self-actualization and interest group politics is the assumption that the quest for personal growth motivates some individuals to devote time or money to making their community, their nation, or the world a better place to live. Politics is only one of many paths individuals may choose to follow as they look for ways to make their lives fuller, more meaningful, and more satisfying. Politics is a central pursuit, however, because people have such a strong desire for bonds of community. Community life is enriching and offers opportunities for friendship, learning, and accomplishment.

As increasing affluence liberated many Americans from a preoccupation with material concerns, political entrepreneurs saw the chance to offer people the opportunity to link the core values of their life to political activity. As Hugh Heclo points out, it would be a mistake to view the citizen lobbies that grew out of the social movements of the 1960s as "conventional meat-and-potatoes interest groups." Rather, the central attraction of these organizations was "one of 'meaning': what people thought they were to make of themselves, individually and as a society. In an era of secular modernity, the raw materials of social life— identities, solidarities, and meanings—could not be considered as givens; they were constructions to be labored over and achieved by people increasingly aware of themselves as the creators and contenders for power."[12]

The low rate of voting in the United States often leads to the misconception that Americans are a relatively inactive and apathetic people. Discouraging as it might be, Americans' lack of enthusiasm for voting is a misleading indicator of their overall involvement in community and political affairs. Americans are very generous in volunteering time to charities, community organizations, churches, schools, and other civic-minded groups.[13] Such organizations do many different things, only some of which may involve trying to influence public policy. In terms of organizations that are avowedly and exclusively political, participation is much lower. Even when it is relatively easy to participate in neighborhood political organizations, where people can work most directly on their most immediate "community," participation is modest.[14]

Although "community" can be defined in the geographical terms of neighborhood or city, there are broader contexts to community.[15] People feel connected to those whom they have never met but who share some common interest or background characteristic. In politics we identify with those who hold similar views on an issue or set of problems. Thus, we might join an organization to support our interests as environmentalists, African Americans, Christian conservatives, or feminists. Even though there may not be much of an interpersonal tie when activity is limited to sending a check to a national lobbying organization in Washington, such participation in politics is still part of the search for community. As Robert Bellah and his colleagues write, "The sense of being part of a living national community colors the meaning of life."[16]

For some people, participation through contributions to a national organization is enough to satisfy their need for political involvement and their need to try to improve the quality of life for their community. This kind of "checkbook participation" is extensive in America and plays no small part in the success of citizen lobbies in Washington.[17] At the same time, many of those who contribute money to national organizations are active in other ways in their community or participate at the local level in an organization working on the same problem as their national group. Of those belonging to women's rights group, a third have attended a meeting of their organization. Of those belonging to a group working on a specific political issue (like gun control or taxpayer rights), the figure for attending a meeting is only 20 percent. For those who belong to a civic group promoting good government (like the League of Women Voters), the figure is an impressive 60 percent. A major study of participation concludes that "the evidence is mixed as to whether Americans are a nation of gregarious organizational activists or have retreated to the privacy and relative inactivity of checkbook participation."[18]

Citizen groups have been blessed by this confluence of a changing work force and the quest for community. Those who are more educated are more likely to possess the skills necessary to navigate the political system. As people learn more and more about the political world, those whose values have relevant political manifestations begin to search for outlets for their interests. In the United States, as in Europe, the rise in those holding postmaterial values has been significant. Between 1972 and 1992, the percentage of postmaterialists in the U.S. population doubled from 9 percent to 18 percent. Those whose values mix postmaterial and material sentiments rose from 55 percent to 65 percent, while materialists dropped from 35 to 16 percent.[19] This substantial and increasing pool of those possessing both postmaterial values and some understanding of how the political world works formed a base for political change.

The Changing Mix of Issues

Although postmaterialist politics makes sense in theory, it may be insignificant in practice. The underlying conditions are certainly favorable to the rise of citizen groups advocating postmaterialist politics. But demographic change, growth in postmaterialist attitudes, and the rise of citizen groups do not demonstrate that Congress reacted in any way whatsoever. Since the conventional view of interest group lobbying is that business dominates American politics and its power is enduring, one would not expect that rising postmaterial concerns catalyzed a significant congressional response.[20] Most postmaterial policies are hostile to business, and corporations and trade groups would certainly push postmaterial challenges aside if they could.

The immediate task at hand is to determine if, in fact, there was any significant turn toward postmaterialism in the policies considered by Congress. To make such an assessment, I analyzed the content of the legislation in the 205 hearings. Since this was not a sample of hearings, but virtually the universe of hearings on all significant domestic social and domestic economic issues, these data should be highly reliable. Congressional hearings seem ideally suited for measuring changes in the congressional agenda.[21] By definition, a hearing means the problem is on the agenda, the issue is of at least modest significance, and there is some public record of what went on. There are many more potential topics crowding a committee's prospective calendar than can be taken up in any one session. When a hearing is held it means that some committee members and interest groups have succeeded in gaining recognition for their issue priorities over those of other legislators and interest groups. If the issue is new, hearings also signify that proponents have succeeded in having their problems defined as political issues.

The examination of hearings does not, of course, reveal which problems failed to reach the agenda and who succeeded in keeping those problems in legislative purgatory. Studying what didn't take place in Congress is exceptionally difficult. The underlying reason why certain problems are never taken up may have to do with long-standing societal values, ideological predispositions, and political socialization that legitimizes some approaches to public policy while delegitimizing others.[22] It's a bit like analyzing the voice of the dog that did not bark. Despite this shortcoming, hearings are a valuable indicator of changing priorities among issues that do reach the agenda of Congress. Over time, changes can be quite sharp, and differences should be clearly evident. In the late 1960s, for example, Congress held only a handful of hearings on health care. In 1992 it held 180.[23]

To proceed with the analysis, Inglehart's concepts of material and postmaterial concerns had to be operationally defined so that the bills before committees could be classified. There is no obvious way of doing this since Inglehart's research is based on values and attitudes on the part of the public while the case studies assembled for this study focus on congressional hearings and interest group advocacy. Bills before Congress do not come neatly labeled as material or postmaterial. When the House Committee on Science, Space, and Technology held hearings on surface transportation issues in 1991, environmental groups like the Sierra Club and Greenpeace pushed postmaterial policies designed to reduce air pollution through mass transit. For business groups working on the legislation, like the American Trucking Association and the American Road and Transportation Builders Association, the policies had direct material implications. In short, policymaking on this one bill was driven by both material and postmaterial concerns.

In contrast to legislation, the interests of lobbying groups may seem relatively easy to categorize. It's safe to assume that the American Medical Association, Exxon, and the National Association of Realtors are primarily concerned with the economic well-being of their members or shareholders. On a particular bill, however, the American Medical Association may work with consumer groups and against other health industry lobbies. For this reason alone classifying the goals of citizen groups can be problematic. We do know from survey research that people who belong to these groups possess attitudes that are disproportionately postmaterial in orientation.[24] Yet any group's membership is going to incorporate a variety of views. More seriously for purposes of this analysis is that some citizen groups pursue both material and postmaterial objectives. When a civil rights group works for a job training program, it is trying to improve the economic well-being of its members. When the same organization works on voting rights, it is pursuing empowerment for its members rather than any material good.[25]

To avoid these entangling complications and to keep the analysis within the boundaries of its data, my focus is on what actually happened in Congress. The bills before the congressional committees were evaluated on the basis on whether advocates were pushing material or postmaterial interests or both. For interest groups, we again ask only what were they advocating. Although the underlying values within any organization's membership fuel the work of their lobbyists, there is no way to empirically link such attitudes to the data about the policymaking in each of our 205 legislative case histories.

In some cases, only material interests were being advocated.

Following the logic of Inglehart's theory, material interests involve economic or physical security. This category would include pensions, social security, taxation, crime, agricultural subsidies, job training, trade restrictions and subsidies, economic regulation, and medical care. Material interests on such bills typically reflected the demands of organized labor, farmers, or business.

It is much more common for a bill to be fought only around material concerns than it is for legislation to be debated solely along postmaterial lines. When quality-of-life concerns were at issue, it was usually the case that they were raised in the context of legislation that pitted material concerns against postmaterial concerns (as with the surface transportation bill). Postmaterial advocates aim at improving the quality of life of Americans in ways other than improving their economic standard of living. In the cases documented, groups pursuing postmaterial interests were usually working in policy areas such as the environment, social equality and discrimination, abortion, various individual rights, consumer protection, education, family values, and government reform.

It's important to emphasize that judgments about which interests were being pursued were not made in a political vacuum. If there was a bill before Congress promoting some business enterprise that had potentially adverse consequences for the environment, but no interest group was advocating the environmental side, the legislation was defined as including only material concerns. I did not impose my own judgment on what I think should have been debated. For this reason there had to be evidence that at least one interest group was actively advocating a material or postmaterial position for the legislation to be coded as incorporating that point of view.

Before turning to the data analysis, a few more distinctions need to be made. When examining a group's material interests in a legislative issue, some judgment had to be exercised to distinguish whether the material reward being sought was truly significant for members. At first glance, consumer protection policies may seem to fall into the material category. If legislation is aimed at ensuring better products or services, doesn't that improve the economic well-being of consumers? Most consumer activism in Washington, however, is really directed at making corporations act more responsibly rather than improving the standard of living of group members. Donors to Public Citizen, the Ralph Nader fundraising arm, have little idea of what product or price improvements might come their way in exchange for their contributions. They do know, however, that Nader will fight for regulatory standards designed to restrict the freedom of corporations to market their products as they see fit. Where consumerism is ideological in nature and aimed at corporate responsibility, the advocacy is classified as postmaterial. Where the advocacy is truly designed to bring about a direct and significant financial gain to a group's constituency, the advocacy is coded as material.

Advocacy for postmaterial interests also includes social welfare issues on which the proponents are public interest groups whose donors will not benefit from the lobbies' endeavors. Public interest groups like the Children's Foundation are supported primarily by foundations and large individual contributors. The donors derive no economic gains from the lobbying and simply want to improve the lives of others.[26] In interest group politics those who advocate policies establishing some material benefit are usually the same constituencies who derive that benefit. When this is not the case, and groups push for benefits that will reward those who cannot adequately represent themselves in public policymaking, it's appropriate to make a distinction and include such efforts in the postmaterial category. These advocates' benefit is ideological, and it is they who worked to put the issue on the agenda. (As it turns out, these kinds of issues, where public interest groups push for benefits for a disadvantaged constituency, were a tiny proportion of the three sets of congressional hearings.)

Politics is messy and doesn't always offer the analyst a set of perfectly demarcated distinctions and definitions. The categories used in this analysis are not as self-evident or as clearly differentiated as might be ideal. Yet at the heart of this study is a fundamental distinction. For some political issues the only concern is how to divvy up the economic pie. Other issues involve a conflict between those who want more of the economic pie and those who say that economic growth is not everything and there are more important things in this world than improving wages, profits, and benefits.

Surging Postmaterialism

It is not surprising that over almost thirty years the mix of issues before Congress would show some change. A lot happened in America during this era. What is surprising, however, is just how dramatic the change is. The legislation in the case studies was divided into two categories. The first contains bills in which only material interests were advocated by any

Table 3-1. Materialism versus Postmaterialism in Congress, 1963, 1979, 1991

Issues	1963	1979	1991
Material	64.4	45.5	28.8
Postmaterial	35.6	54.5	71.2
N	73	55	73

Note: Four hearings were excluded because the content of the legislation fell into neither category. X^2 significant at .001 level.

of the groups involved. The second category is composed of legislation in which at least some of the groups were advocating a quality-of-life position. In most cases the postmaterial interests were opposed by lobbies pushing material concerns. This second category also includes those bills where only postmaterial positions were being advocated by all the groups actively participating in the legislative policymaking.

In 1963 the typical issue was exclusively material in nature (table 3-1). Examples of such legislation include the Hours of Work bill, Manpower Retraining, the Domestic Cotton Price Equalization Act, the Marketing of Imported Articles bill, and the Feed Grain Act. When the Senate Agriculture Committee considered the Feed Grain Act, it did not have to contend with consumer groups wanting to know why grain farmers would continue to receive price supports. Nor were there any environmental groups complicating policymaking by asking about pesticides used on the feed grains. This important agricultural bill sailed through the committee with ease and was signed into law only two weeks later.

Only about a third of the issues in 1963 could be classified as having a postmaterial side, the most notable of which was the 1964 Civil Rights Act. There was some important environmental legislation as well. All in all, though, the 1963 session of Congress was largely a year devoted to bills pushed by farm, labor, and business lobbies that were generally considered in the absence of citizen group critics. By 1991, 71 percent of all hearings were on proposals that had a postmaterial side. The largest group involved environmental matters like the Water Pollution Prevention and Control Act and the Wetlands Conservation bill. Although the Bush administration was decidedly unsupportive of environmental legislation, the Democrats in Congress and environmental groups pushed hard on a number of important bills.

Although many environmental bills were to be expected, less anticipated was a considerable amount of business legislation in which a central part of the debate was a quality-of-life concern, such as the fight over the North American Free Trade Agreement (NAFTA) and the AT&T Consent Decree's Manufacturing Restriction bill. For the House committee considering NAFTA in 1991, the ostensible issue was whether the trade agreement would be subject to amendments when submitted to Congress. Environmentalists, however, were interested in turning a trade bill into an environmental bill that forced the Mexican government to reduce the pollution that was a by-product of the increased manufacturing near the border with the United States. "The connection between trade and the environment is gaining a long-overdue recognition," said a lobbyist working the issue for the Natural Resources Defense Council.[27] The AT&T bill involved a proposal that would have allowed the regional Bell phone companies to manufacture telephone equipment, thus overturning a restriction imposed as part of the original consent decree that broke up AT&T. The Consumer Federation of America jumped into the fray to fight a change in the consent decree even though relaxation of the restriction would have had no practical impact for residential consumers on the choice, availability, or price of telephones. Rather, it was concerned about the Baby Bells gaining more concentrated power, both in political and market terms. The ACLU fought the proposal too, worrying that the Baby Bells would gain new advantages that might somehow be dangerous in the marketplace of ideas. Gene Kimmelman, the legislative director of the Consumer Federation of America, became a leading spokesman for the coalition of citizen groups and business trade groups that fought the proposal. The bill passed the Senate but died in the House.

The percentage of hearings devoted to issues with a postmaterial side is so high that one wonders how much higher it can go. In examining the small number of issues that didn't evoke postmaterial advocacy, it's clear that many of them just don't raise the kinds of concerns that motivate citizen groups. When a veterans' compensation bill came before the Congress in 1991, no citizen groups participated to argue for or against a standard of living adjustment for disabled vets or became involved in a dispute over those exposed to Agent Orange. Veterans are hardly a weak or underrepresented constituency and need little help in getting Congress to pay attention to them. And if benefits are too generous, who is going to fund the lobby to fight against disabled vets? There were some business-related bills that might have evoked a postmaterialist response, but none was forthcoming. More telling, though, than the few bills that could have drawn citizen group advocacy but didn't was legislation such as the fight between the phone companies in which citizen groups threw themselves vigorously into a struggle that really wasn't of much interest to consumers. The exceptional rate of participation by citizen groups and their coverage of so much of what's on the congressional agenda indicate the representation of citizen interests extends far beyond the visible and controversial issues that attract their contributors. Indeed, there is little in Congress that seems to escape the attention of these groups.

A Test of Significance

The pattern of rising postmaterialism is so striking that some may wonder if the incidence of quality-of-life concerns has somehow been exaggerated. If this measure is misleading or the relationship is spurious, then the substantive implications of table 3-1 would have to be reconsidered. The first step toward validating the findings of this measurement is to ask if the rise of postmaterialism applies to all issues equally. As already noted, legislation supported by business was increasingly coupled with postmaterial concerns, so it is clear that this trend was not confined only to nonbusiness bills. Still, this initial measure did not control for the importance of the legislation before Congress. It may be that on the most important bills before committees, postmaterialism has been less of a factor over time than it has on bills of less consequence. The core of the legislative agenda for all three points in time could be the same type of business, farm, and labor bills that are most critical to the nation's economic well-being. The new issues that came on to the agenda could be disproportionately less significant and more postmaterialist in orientation than these enduring, basic, material issues.

Another reason to question this initial finding is that the news hole increased between 1963 and 1991. Over time the sheer quantity of coverage of legislative issues in the *New York Times*, the *Wall Street Journal*, and *Congressional Quarterly Weekly Report* increased. As these publications added pages and sections over the years, they may have expanded their reporting to pick up more secondary issues before Congress. If so, this development would be reflected in these data. These secondary issues could be where most of the growth in postmaterialism occurred.

To see if the trend line held up when the less significant legislation was

Table 3-2. Materialism versus Postmaterialism in Congress, Higher-Salience Issues

Issues	1963	1979	1991
Material	63.8	42.9	27.3
Postmaterial	36.2	57.1	72.7
N	47	42	44

X^2 significant at .01 level.

excluded, only those hearings where press coverage was sufficiently broad to allow a full narrative case study to be constructed were included in this computation. It is not a problematic assumption to consider bills with extensive press coverage as more important than those with more modest coverage; this is a common strategy in political history research.[28] The results in table 3-2 turn out to be virtually identical to those in table 3-1. The more important issues are coupled with postmaterialist advocacy at virtually the same rate as the less important issues.

Finally, it is conceivable that while Congress paid ample attention to postmaterial issues in the hearings held by its committees, the legislation that was passed tells another story. What eventually worked its way into law could disproportionately favor the bills that were exclusively material in orientation. This doesn't turn out to be the case either, as there is no consistent pattern over the three sessions of Congress in the comparative rate of passage of material or postmaterial legislation.[29]

The rise of postmaterialism in Congress cannot be explained away as being largely associated with minor issues or issues that never make it into law. In almost all policy areas, on issues of varying importance, quality-of-life concerns have become pervasive in the debate over domestic social and domestic economic legislation.

Whose Quality of Life?

"Postmaterialism" is an abstraction, a concept that political scientists find useful to describe evolving trends in advanced industrialized democracies. Yet it has no meaning in the real world of politics. No lobbyist ever asks to speak to a legislator about his "postmaterial concerns." No representative or senator would care about how the issues were defined for the purposes of coding the data for tables 3-1 and 3-2.

Those outside of academe may wonder why this jargon is necessary. Since the lobbying groups discussed in this study are clearly to the political left or political right of center, why not just talk about liberals and conservatives rather than "postmaterialists"? Political scientists, while accepting the need for theories and their accompanying vocabulary, may still wonder, why this particular theory? Why try to adapt a theory on comparative politics and attitude formation to a study that is about neither?

The use of theories is easy to defend. Theories help scholars to organize data and analysis. Theories give us tools to understand broad, complex social processes, including political change. They are helpful for framing the questions to be investigated, and using theories facilitates normal science by providing continuities in research. And continuities in research further cumulative analysis and a deeper understanding of the problems scholars study.

But, again, why this theory? Why not something that provides continuities with previous research on liberals and conservatives in national politics? The most direct answer is that what makes the theory of postmaterialism so valuable is that it challenges our common notions of liberal and conservative. As I demonstrate more clearly below and in the following chapters, postmaterialism of the left and right is not conterminous with conventional definitions of liberal and conservative. It is not just that these citizen groups largely avoid material concerns but that they pursue issues representing value orientations that are vitally different from traditional ideologies of the left and right. When conservative citizen groups pursue policies requiring a strong, active national government, or when liberal citizen groups turn away from issues of economic equality for working Americans to focus on preserving wildlife, it constitutes something more than just a slight variation from the central thrust of postwar conservatism or liberalism.

In this vein, the theory of postmaterialism is useful in studying interest group politics because it offers a way of trying to link value change by the public with policymaking in Washington. Although the link can only be made indirectly here because of the limitations with the data, the research is a step toward trying to understand interest groups as agents of social change. Precisely because of its emphasis on attitudes and value change, the theory of postmaterialism effectively captures the dynamics of citizen group politics. Traditional interest group scholarship is built around business lobbies, and the subfield's dominant theory for the past three decades explains how trade and professional associations get around the collective action problem.[30] New theories that acknowledge the central role that citizen groups play in the modern polity are needed. As Russell Dalton notes, "We see these new [noneconomic] interests not as supplanting the traditional economic interests of Western democracies but as adding a new political dimension that competes with and potentially contradicts established lines of political division."[31]

The theory has its shortcomings of course. Exactly when a society becomes affluent enough to ignite rising postmaterialist attitudes is entirely unclear. Along the same lines, since there is some level of post-material politics present in nonaffluent societies, what are the other factors missing from this theory that explain postmaterialist attitudes and political movements?

Whatever its drawbacks, the theory of postmaterialism offers a useful way of understanding the clash of values in politics today. Although interest group members, lobbyists, and policymakers may have no idea what the term "postmaterialism" means, those who are politically engaged do think about the relevant underlying problems. Many in the business world worry that environmental protection standards have become too stringent and are damaging the economy. Traditional trade union liberals worry that both business and the environmental movement gain ground at the expense of working-class Americans. In a different language—the language of everyday politics—people do argue about whether society is too oriented toward postmaterialism or not oriented enough.

One way of examining the relevance of postmaterialist theory is to more closely examine how liberal citizen groups pushing quality-of-life issues have fared in comparison to more traditional advocates on the left. Has the success of these newer (postmaterial) liberal lobbies come at the expense of traditional liberal groups who press for greater economic equality and for the interests of the working class? Do the advocates of these two different types of liberalism coexist peacefully, or are they antagonists?

Two approaches will be used. The first is to examine the content of legislation to see if these two forms of contemporary liberalism directly confront each other in the legislative process. If so, decisions must be made about trade-offs. If not, legislators can vote on bills without having to consciously choose between these competing interests. This part of the analysis will use environmental legislation because it is in this area that these two wings of liberalism seem most likely to clash. Second, analysis will turn to material issues where there are no competing postmaterial objectives. Are liberals still divided? To answer this question, legislation promoting economic equality will be used. These are the bills that most clearly involve traditional liberal interest groups. Do these bills offer *all* liberals some common ground around core issues of economic justice and equality?

Trees versus People

Environmentalists have long been charged with being "elitists." The indictment is straightforward: middle-class suburbanites who enjoy hiking and summer vacations in the national parks write checks to the Sierra Club and the Wilderness Society so that these groups can fight for policies that protect the great outdoors. Such policies can have the effect of putting blue-collar workers into the unemployment lines as development slows or the costs of regulation rise. In this view, the environmentalists are the ultimate postmaterialists whose affluence blinds them to the difficulty working people have in making ends meet. William Tucker, a trenchant critic of environmentalists, puts it this way: "Having made it to the top, they become far more concerned with *preventing others from climbing the ladder behind them*, than in making it up a few more rungs themselves."[32] Remarkably, this criticism comes from the right, the left, and the center of the political spectrum. Conservatives believe that the environmental lobbies are naive about the need for continuing economic expansion and that their advocacy hurts workers and business alike. The center worries about a Democratic party espousing the views of these groups and turning off voters who are concerned about jobs. Some on the left see environmental groups as too mainstream, too hesitant to address the underlying issues of corporate irresponsibility and greed that cause ecological decline. From this perspective, environmentalists are seen as decadent yuppies who are concerned about animals and forests rather than economic change.[33]

The charges of elitism are especially credible when saving an endangered species is pitted against the economic development of some area. When the Fish and Wildlife Service determined that logging of forests in the Northwest had put the survival of the spotted owl into doubt, controversy erupted because placing the bird's remaining habitat off limits meant eliminating the jobs of thousands of blue-collar workers. (A popular bumper sticker that angry truckers and loggers living in the area put on their vehicles read, "I like spotted owls . . . fried.") These fights place environmental lobbyists in the uncomfortable position of advocating policies that harm people but help animals. Nevertheless, they pursue them, believing that the long-term need to maintain the rich and diverse ecology of the United States outweighs the short-term pain of those put out of work.

This criticism of elitism has waned in recent years. The strong economic growth of the 1990s has much to do with this change, though a serious economic downturn would surely revive this line of attack on environmentalism. Budget pressures on the federal government have also constrained expansion of wilderness and national park areas, reducing the number of potential cases where jobs and environmental protection are set against each other in emotionally charged political conflicts. New mechanisms for negotiating conflicts between local environmental groups and business have gained popularity. Over the years at least some business leaders have begun to learn how to live with environmentalists and to understand that compromise rather than resistance might be the best course of action. Another reason why environmental groups have been able to survive these attacks of being elitist is that they succeeded in distancing themselves from the environmental intellectuals whose work is so antagonistic toward capitalism. Prominent environmental thinkers like Amory Lovins (*Soft Energy Paths*), E. F. Schumacher (*Small is Beautiful*), and Paul Ehrlich (*The Population Bomb*) advocated a world based on self-sufficiency and warned of environmental catastrophes.[34] Yet their antigrowth perspective never came to define the large, mainstream environmental groups. Few came to believe that the Audubon Society wanted to stop economic development—it just wanted to save birds. And no one thought the National Wildlife Federation wanted us all to grow our own pesticide-free vegetables in the backyard. As a whole the environmental groups did an effective job in positioning themselves as mainstream organizations. They made a credible argument that they were interested in *balancing* growth and jobs and that they were not interested in replacing capitalism with a more human-scale economic system.

How groups are perceived by their supporters does not mean that the critics' charges are unjust. Regardless of their success in marketing themselves, the organizations could still be elitist in terms of the issues they choose to work on. Even if it is not their avowed philosophy, their agenda could work to advance the interests of the affluent at the expense of the economic development that blue-collar workers depend on. The legislative case studies in which environmental questions are central are revealing on this point. To begin with, over time more stability than change prevails in the kinds of environmental issues that come before Congress. The biggest change is that in 1963 more bills concerning preservation of particular areas, like the Fire Island National Seashore (which passed) and the Oregon Dunes National Seashore (which failed), appeared. It's possible that today more government-mandated preservation comes at the administrative level rather than in Congress. At the same time, a number of controversial and far-reaching legislative proposals were made. In 1963 committees held hearings on the National Wilderness Preservation Act, the Water Pollution Control Act Amendments, the Clean Air Act, pesticide controls, and an urban transportation bill. All were passed into law in that Congress, except for the water pollution bill, which was passed and signed into law in 1965. All were fought vigorously by business, and the urban transportation bill was fought by labor as well.

In 1979 hearings were held on a wide range of environmental bills, but only the bills on Alaska lands, aviation noise, an excess profits tax on energy companies, and domestic energy resources involved disputes in which jobs and business expansion were central. In 1991 there was more legislation of this type, and the bills on wetlands conservation, NAFTA, surface transportation, biological diversity, federal lands, motor vehicle fuel efficiency, grazing fees, pesticides, and a national energy policy were all opposed by business interests warning of economic harm. On two of the issues, NAFTA and motor vehicle fuel efficiency, labor also fought the environmentalists. (Despite concessions on environmental protection, some environmental groups fought with labor against NAFTA.)

In looking at environmental legislation in this historical perspective, there does not seem to be any increasing tendency of environmental groups to back policies damaging to blue-collar workers. More important, relatively few bills really threaten labor or the overall levels of employment. One of the exceptions is the Motor Vehicle Fuel Efficiency Act, which was fought by the United Auto Workers because it favored small cars, a market in which foreign manufacturers compete more effectively. Most bills backed by environmental groups directly affecting employment would be more accurately described as involving job shifting or job creation. Debate over the 1963 and 1979 urban transportation bills centered on how much would be spent on roads and how much would be spent on mass transit. Spending on either creates jobs, but not for the same workers. The cumulative impact of environmental laws has been to create a whole new industry employing people who work at cleaning the environment. For example, another of the 1991 environmental bills, the Resource Conservation and Recovery Act Amendments, had support from business rather than opposition. That support came from the solid-waste industry, an industry that owes its life to environmental regulation.

On this first count of the indictment, that environmental groups are antagonistic toward the interests of blue-collar workers, the verdict is only "slightly guilty." On some issues overall levels of blue-collar employment are threatened by environmentalists, but this dilemma is not a general pattern. On all the environmental issues that came before Congress in these three separate years, organized labor was a combatant in only a small number of cases. Had working men and women been more broadly threatened, unions would have been extensively involved in lobbying Congress on these issues.[35]

A second count of the indictment, that environmentalists hurt workers indirectly by working for business regulation, is more difficult to adjudicate. The environmental bills listed above did, for the most part, aim to restrict what industries can do, raise their costs of doing business, or both. Industry, environmental groups, and academics have different conclusions on the impact of the environmental laws on economic expansion. If it weren't for environmental laws protecting parks, wilderness, and federal lands, there certainly would be more logging, more mining, and more real estate development. How much of this is truly lost economic activity and how much of the available investment funds have been channeled productively into other industries is not known. More generally, measurements of the impact of environmental protection on the economy are derived from complex econometric models, and competing models show contradictory results. In the end, whether people should justly regard environmental groups as elitist in regard to business expansion is not likely to be settled by any set of facts. Inevitably, it comes down to a question of values—postmaterial values versus material values. As noted earlier, those who support environmental groups with their dues and contributions surely believe that these organizations work not so much against economic interests as for an appropriate balance between growing the economy and protecting the earth. When the economy is strong, it's a compelling argument.

When the economy is weak, the charges of environmental elitism have more bite.

Economic Equality

The data indicate that environmentalists and labor are direct antagonists relatively infrequently. It seems more likely that the greatest damage that the liberal postmaterialist groups do to labor and other traditional liberal groups is to detract attention from the material issues these lobbies pursue. A first step is to see if, in fact, the issues most ardently backed by the traditional liberal wing of the Democratic party have become a smaller portion of the legislative agenda. To determine the answer I analyzed all the hearings on bills promoting economic equality over the three sessions of Congress. This category included issues designed to increase wages, benefits, or pensions, expand job training, improve working conditions, and provide income maintenance or basic health coverage. Such legislative proposals are designed to use the power of government to narrow the gap—if only a little—in incomes, benefits, job security, and opportunities to climb the economic ladder.

Over time, economic equality issues become only a slightly smaller proportion of the legislative agenda. In 1963 they constituted 13.5 percent of all domestic social and domestic economic issues that came before congressional committees. By 1991 the figure had dropped to 9.5 percent. In statistical terms, this drop is insignificant. In substantive terms, however, there was a real decline. For those concerned about economic inequality, the content and fate of this legislation paints a grim picture.

Of the ten bills aimed at ameliorating economic inequality that came before congressional committees in 1963, eight dealt with workers' pay, working conditions, or job training. The other two bills were Medicare and a workers' pension matter. In 1979 only one of the seven issues concerned wages, working conditions, or job training (a narrow bill benefiting nurses). The other issues dealt with welfare or pensions, and the two pension bills were oriented more toward white-collar than unionized workers. Finally, in 1991, one of the seven issues revisited a job training program (Amendments to the Job Training and Partnership Act) and another two dealt with working conditions. The other four covered a variety of issues.[36] In sum, between 1963 and 1979 legislation moved increasingly away from the issues of wages and job training affecting blue-collar workers and moved further toward issues of welfare and pension reform—issues that focus on the poor and the middle class.

A related concern, of course, is which legislation passed. Although what gets on the congressional agenda is critically important, what ultimately passes may be the truest test of real change. After controlling for legislative success, a pattern emerges in line with the findings above. In 1963 six of ten bills designed to reduce economic inequality passed; in 1979 four of seven, and in 1991 two of seven. Over time Congress has come to consider less legislation designed to reduce economic inequality, consider fewer bills designed to raise wages or improve job skills when it does take up such legislation, and pass a smaller proportion of all these economic inequality bills reaching the agenda stage.

These changes may have taken place even if no new set of liberal citizen groups pushing postmaterialist causes had arisen. It seems likely, however, that some "crowding out" is taking place: as these new liberal organizations draw attention and resources to their causes, there is less energy available for the traditional economic equality issues. It may, however, be the case that even though the liberal postmaterialist groups draw attention away from the issues important to labor and poverty groups, the lobbyists and activists for the postmaterial groups are still *liberals,* and they will work with the old left on issues on which they find common ground. For example, environmental groups, stung by the criticism that they are elitist, might look for issues on which there is a confluence of interests with labor. A bill promoting both energy conservation and fuel assistance for the poor could attract such a coalition.

This possibility of new left–old left coalitions was explored by examining the interest group coalitions that emerged in support of the economic equality legislation just discussed. This legislation shows a clear pattern of coalition formation and, again, for those concerned about economic equality, the results of this analysis are discouraging. In 1963 legislation in this area was typically pushed by broad-based coalitions of liberal advocacy organizations. The Equal Pay Act, a gender equity bill, was pushed by the AFL-CIO, the American Civil Liberties Union, the National Federation of Business and Professional Women's Clubs, the United Auto Workers, the National Council of Churches, the National Consumers League, the American Association of University Women, and the Retail Clerks Union. A bill on migratory labor brought together unions, churches, the National Farmers Union, and the National Consumers League. Medicare was pushed by a coalition that included labor, senior citizen groups, the

Americans for Democratic Action, the National Association of Social Workers, and the National Catholic Welfare Conference.

Even though there were far more interest groups by 1991, coalitions backing economic equality legislation were far narrower. Only two issues, affordable health care and the Family and Medical Leave Act, generated broad supporting coalitions. What is also striking is how many of the groups that fought alongside labor in 1963 failed to show up in the 1991 cases or clearly fell to minor status. The Americans for Democratic Action used to be a respected advocate of traditional liberal causes. When did it become irrelevant? The mainstream churches seem to play a less prominent role in 1991, a serious blow to the left because of the moral authority that came with their advocacy. Some new poverty groups have emerged over the years, such as Bread for the World (1975) and the Center for Budget and Policy Priorities (1981), but the coalitions working for economic equality have narrowed nevertheless.[37]

Citizen groups organized around postmaterial policies have never been a strong ally of traditional liberal groups, but what little common ground there was seems to have declined over time. Washington lobbies operate with scarce resources and must set priorities among all the issues they would like to be active on. They are usually consumed with issues that are at the heart of their policy concerns. Lobbies might participate in a peripheral way on secondary issues by signing on as a member of an ad hoc coalition—but doing little more than lending their name to the groups who are really doing the work on the matter.

Liberal citizen groups have concentrated on issues that appeal to their middle-class supporters. Civil rights groups and women's groups do direct some of their advocacy on issues facing the poor, and a handful of citizen groups do concentrate on poverty issues. For the most part, though, the agenda of citizen groups has focused largely on issues unconnected to the problems of the poor, the disadvantaged, or even the working class. The data collected indicate unequivocally that as the new left grew and grew, the old left was left increasingly isolated.

Elitism and the Right

Although the liberal citizen groups are not directly antagonistic toward the interests of the poor and working-class Democrats, their issue orientation has certainly left them open to the charge of elitism. The liberal citizen groups assume that the economy can grow at an adequate rate despite extensive regulation of manufacturing and strict controls on development. But what of the citizen groups on the right? These groups, especially the Christian Coalition, are no stranger to controversy over the issues they choose to pursue. Elitism, however, is not one of the charges usually hurled against conservative citizen groups. The analogous question to that asked of liberal citizen groups is this one: do conservative citizen groups pursue policy solutions that work to the disadvantage of blue-collar workers and those of modest means?

In economic status, the liberal postmaterialist groups and the conservative postmaterialist groups stand in stark contrast. A survey of four major environmental lobbies found that half of the members had two or more years of graduate level education (compared with 7 percent of the population).[38] In comparison, a survey of identifiers with different religions showed that of those who described themselves as evangelicals, just 7 percent had any postgraduate education. Only 21 percent of evangelicals had family incomes of $40,000 or more, whereas the same was true of 32 percent of Catholics and 36 percent of those who belong to mainline Protestant denominations.[39] These are not figures for actual members of politically conservative citizen groups, but clearly the constituency represented by the Christian Coalition and similar groups is at the lower end of the economic range of American conservatives.

Conservative citizen groups market themselves largely around the politics of abortion and other related family value issues such as prayer in public schools, vouchers for private schools, home schooling, pornography, and moral decay exhibited in the movies and on television. Since lobbying on these issues does not directly support the aspirations of those whose conservatism is grounded in free-market economics, the Republican Party also finds a real division between what their citizen group constituencies want and what their traditional interest group base wants. The real problem for the business groups who form the traditional core of the Republican Party is not that the Christian right is hostile toward business and the issues it cares most passionately about, such as taxes and regulation. Indeed, the Christian Coalition has professed support for the pro-business goals of the Republican Party.[40] Rather, it is the belief that these groups' inflexible position on abortion damages the chances of GOP presidential nominees. However, business has benefited from the activism of Christian conservatives in congressional campaigns, which has been vitally important to the GOP.[41]

Although citizen groups are positioned at different economic poles of the two parties, they have played a similar role as insurgents. Both sets of postmaterialists have engaged in a fight for the soul of their party. Both have had some success in redefining the parties. The postmaterialist groups of the left have made the Democrats more publicly identified as the party of women's rights, civil rights, and environmentalism. The Christian right has made the Republican Party increasingly identified with opposition to abortion and support of the traditional nuclear family. One of the key differences, however, is that the liberal citizen groups have pushed the Democrats to become more a party of middle- and upper-class suburban professionals, while the postmaterialist groups of the right have tried to pull the Republican Party away from its moorings among middle- and upper-class suburban professionals and businesspersons.[42] It is the citizen groups of the right, and not of the left, who are more attuned to the interests of those on the lower rungs of the economic ladder.

Conclusion

The changing face of American liberalism has important implications for who is represented in the legislative process. It's clear from the data presented here that the issues supported by liberal postmaterialist groups have gained an enormous share of the congressional agenda. The value change evidenced in attitudinal surveys is manifested as well in legislation before Congress. There is no appropriate baseline like the population figures for interest groups used in chapter 2 to judge whether the interests of the liberal citizen groups are, in fact, overrepresented in the policymaking that commences with congressional hearings. Nevertheless, the conclusion seems inescapable that the interests of the liberal postmaterialists in the population are exceptionally well represented in the congressional agenda.

While liberal postmaterialism has soared, traditional liberalism has stumbled. Government has become less committed to improving wages and benefits to those people lowest on the economic ladder and has demonstrated little interest in providing the kind of training that will enable the economically marginal to become more productive members of the labor force. These findings are depressing for those who believe that the working poor and the low skilled are deserving of more government assistance. These data are also further evidence of the decline of organized labor as a political force.

It's likely that advocacy on behalf of the poor and the working class would have faded even if new liberal citizen groups had never arisen. The success of conservative Republicans in elections since 1980 may have been enough to cause the traditional liberals' decline. It seems plausible, however, that advocacy aimed at promoting economic equality has been adversely affected by the rise of environmentalism, consumerism, and other liberal, postmaterial causes. Well-educated liberal activists have found these organizations attractive at the local and national levels, and their generous support has enabled these lobbies to become major players in Washington politics. In short, it may be that Ralph Nader liberalism helped to crowd out Hubert Humphrey liberalism.

CHAPTER FOUR

The Power of Citizen Groups

THOUSANDS OF INTEREST groups compete for space on the congressional agenda. In alliances and by themselves, they try to convince legislators to take up their cause. Since groups vary so much in their available resources, the perceived importance of their issues, and the degree to which they face active opposition from other lobbies, it's very difficult to predict how and why some groups succeed in gaining a spot on a congressional committee calendar while others fail.

The dramatic rise in the proportion of postmaterial issues on the congressional agenda certainly suggests that the citizen groups that back these policies have been successful in persuading Congress to consider their proposals. Yet no direct evidence of citizen groups initiating the postmaterial issues has yet been offered. If citizen groups were significant in influencing the congressional agenda, we should be able to find some historical data to support this contention. Were citizen groups, in fact, responsible for pushing these postmaterial issues onto the agenda of the U.S. Congress?

The rise of postmaterialism also implies that business has lost some of its preeminence in the congressional process. There is good reason to be skeptical of any claim that business's political prowess has diminished. Business influence can be felt in ways that extend far beyond the bills that Congress considers and acts on. Still, citizen groups have challenged business and have created an increasingly competitive and complex legislative environment for corporations and trade groups. How has business fared when confronted with citizen groups that are more interested in increasing regulation than in growing the economy?

Agenda Builders

Since public opinion moved toward increased support for postmaterialist concerns, it may seem unremarkable that Congress took up such issues. If the voters back home voice increasing support for parks, wilderness, clean air, and endangered species, why wouldn't legislators rush to accommodate their constituents with relevant environmental programs and policies? There's a simple and a not-so-simple answer why Congress might not be responsive to public opinion. The simple answer is that members of Congress may find substantial opposition to such legislation. Everyone is for clean air in the abstract, but the corporations that must comply with new standards are going to try to kill or at least water down legislation that hurts their bottom line. Since public opinion is often contradictory—people want jobs and a clean environment—Congress's optimum response may be symbolic legislation that ostensibly cleans up pollution while doing little to force real changes in manufacturing practices.

The not-so-simple reason is that the interplay of public opinion, interest group advocacy, political party behavior, and legislative action is exceedingly complex. All these factors can't be sorted out here. What we do know is that given all the potential roadblocks in the legislative process, and the competition that exists among interest groups and among legislators to get their proposals on to the agenda, powerful forces are necessary to push bills forward. Legislation just doesn't happen. As Ronald Inglehart warns, "We cannot take it for granted that if increasing numbers of people hold given values, their political system will automatically adopt policies which reflect those values. It depends partly on how politically skilled those people are. And it depends at least equally on the political institutions of the given country."[1]

The degree to which people holding some value are "politically skilled" is largely reflected in their ability to join together into some vehicle for promoting their mutual interests. In practical terms, this means people must join together in an interest group or political party. Scholars have no precise model of how interest groups influence the congressional agenda and disagree on just how important lobbies are in moving issues onto the agenda. Nevertheless, agenda building is a major component of interest group advocacy. Although lobbying on front-burner concerns—bills currently being debated in Congress or regulations pending before an agency—is the number one priority for interest groups, they also think strategically about their back-burner objectives and how to get government to pay attention.

Agenda building by interest groups entails several different tactics. At its most basic level, it is a process of educating policymakers, journalists, and the public about a problem they may be unaware of, or at the very least, don't consider a vital priority. Periodically, for example, business lobbies will try to educate policymakers about a broad challenge facing corporate America. Before legislation has a chance of passage, Washington needs to be convinced that capital formation or global competitiveness is a serious issue needing government action. It may take an extended "softening up" period while studies are issued, journalists are spun, forums are held, and committee staffers lobbied, before the congressional leadership is ready to push the issue forward.[2]

Interest groups are also highly active in issue framing or problem definition.[3] That is, they work on issues that are already on the table but try to get policymakers and others to understand the problem in a way that is different from the prevailing conception. Agriculture subsidies were long sold to the American people as a way of preserving the family farm. The Environmental Working Group saw the issue differently. The citizen lobby published a 1995 report, "City Slickers," that documented $1.2 million in agriculture subsidy checks being mailed to addresses within the zip code boundaries of Beverly Hills 90210. It made irresistible copy and a gusher of publicity ensued.[4] If the problem at hand is redefined as subsidies for rich absentee landowners rather than protecting the family farm, the legislative outcome is likely to be altered.

Sometimes the politics of problem definition revolves around a word or a label associated with a policy. Antiabortion forces had great success in getting the media and the public to view the issue of late-term abortions as a problem of "partial birth" abortions. If people focus on the gruesome specifics of how a late-term pregnancy is terminated rather than on the medical reasons why such abortions may be necessary, then the issue will play out differently in the political process.[5]

Interest groups must also be prepared to take advantage of events that may trigger awareness of a problem. A classic example is the collapse of Consolidated Coal's No. 9 mine in West Virginia in 1968. All seventy-eight miners trapped in the cave-in died before they could be rescued. The tragedy along with subsequent wildcat strikes and a march on the state capitol created an opportunity for the United Mine Workers to push mine safety legislation in Congress. Even though he was not favorably disposed toward the legislation, President Richard Nixon signed the bill that Congress sent him.[6]

The reason to believe that citizen groups are responsible for the rise of postmaterial issues on the congressional agenda is that the matters that show up in the case studies are, of course, the issues that these groups were advocating. As will be discussed more fully in chapter 6, these organizations have significant resources at their disposal. Research has shown that when sectors of society become increasingly mobilized, a significant impact can be made on the congressional agenda.[7]

At the same time, there is reason to be doubtful that citizen groups caused such a political sea change. To begin with, the government's agenda may change because it is government that decides among competing interests which issues *it* wants to take up. In tracking the evolution of health issues in the late 1970s, political scientist John Kingdon found in his interviews with health policy specialists in 1977 that only 3 percent regarded health maintenance organizations as a major issue. In 1979, the figure rose to 63 percent. Kingdon did not attribute the change to interest group politics but to the choice of top policymakers at the Department of Health, Education, and Welfare who decided to push HMOs as "a major policy initiative of their administration."[8]

Another reason why the rising proportion of postmaterial issues might overstate the influence of citizen groups is that their lobbying could be a rearguard action. Conceivably, the agenda remains firmly in business's hands and while citizen groups are involved, their efforts are largely directed at trying to trim the worst excesses from bills designed to help some particular industry. If all citizen groups are doing is raising an environmental or consumer objection while a subsidy or regulatory relief bill is being debated, their power would seem rather modest.

How any set of interest groups fares over time is the product of many factors, and each issue has its own unique context.[9] Although the case studies listed in appendix B do not offer a complete history of each issue, and some of the subtleties of agenda building are not captured by this approach, there is sufficient information in the set of higher-salience issues to gauge which groups were pushing each piece of legislation forward. By the time a bill reaches the hearing stage, it is being supported by a coalition of groups and legislators. After identifying the goals embodied in the legislation, the next stage in my analysis was to couple those objectives with the appropriate set of lobbies. Thus, the data are

Post Hoc Ergo Proctor Hoc

Table 4-1. Initiating Side

Percent of congressional agenda, high-salience issues

Initiator of legislation	1963	1979	1991
Material side	55.3	38.1	36.4
Postmaterial side	31.9	31.0	45.5
Mixed, unclear, government	12.8	31.0	18.2
N	47	42	44

X^2 significant at .10.

coded as to which side, "material" or "postmaterial," was advocating the legislation. A residual category includes bills initiated by government alone.[10] Whatever bill was before a committee, some advocates wanted it passed. Whose issues were these?

Table 4-1 shows that over time, the postmaterial side became the most frequent initiating side in the legislative process. By 1991 it was the lobbies and legislators backing bills on the environment, consumer protection, good government, and various rights issues who were having the most success driving legislation forward. In reading the case studies, it appears that only on a small minority of issues was the postmaterial side responding to an initiative from corporations, trade groups, or professional associations. One such instance was the 1979 Aviation Safety and Noise Abatement Act, which proposed exempting two- and three-engine planes from noise control requirements and was pushed by the Air Transport Association. The National Wildlife Federation and Ralph Nader's Congress Watch joined the National League of Cities, the U.S. Conference of Mayors, and the Airport Operators Council in opposing the bill. Much more often, however, the material side was responding to postmaterial initiative. The Federal Lands and Families Protection Act, proposed in 1991, is a case in point. It was backed by the Audubon Society and the Sierra Club, who wanted to preserve old growth forests in the Northwest, but timber industry groups fought the act. Overall, the statistical relationship is not strong enough to be conclusive, but it seems clear that the postmaterial issues on the congressional agenda are closely linked to the advocacy of citizen groups.[11]

A Step Back in Time

Despite these findings, the question about agenda building has not been fully answered because the groups supporting a bill in one session of Congress may not have been the set of groups that influenced Congress to pay attention to the issue in the first place. And if the real source of power is the ability to get people to pay attention, this is a significant distinction. As noted, it can take years from the time a group first starts working to get its issue onto the agenda to a point at which Congress actually starts working on legislation. For strategic reasons, citizen groups may want to take the initiative on problems that had earlier been raised by their adversaries. The citizen groups may have been trying to stop a bill in previous sessions of Congress but realize that in *this* session of Congress some action on the issue is likely. Consequently, they go to a sympathetic committee chair and get him or her to frame hearings in such a way that some of the quality-of-life concerns take center stage.[12] When the Bush White House proposed energy legislation, its bill was primarily focused on promoting greater supplies of energy by expanding oil drilling and easing regulations on utilities and the nuclear power industry. The alternatives proposed in Congress and backed by environmentalists were full of energy conservation policies. Debate in Congress focused on these bills and not on the Bush initiative.

A second, similar reason why we may not want to assume that the groups pushing bills in any one session of Congress are the true interest group initiators, is that interest groups can be very opportunistic in terms of attaching their long-standing policy priorities to new problems that emerge. Family planning groups were generally unsuccessful in getting advertisements for condoms on television until the AIDS crisis hit. In this view, argued by John Kingdon, the congressional agenda is influenced by a good deal of happenstance. Different groups and policymakers work separately on various issues and then, because of some circumstance (an election, a dramatic event, a change in the national mood), some of these issues come together, and a new legislative proposal emerges. When these windows of opportunity open, it may not be the interest groups that have worked longest and hardest on developing a policy solution that are favored.[13]

To see if the origins of issues revealed something different than the immediate source of interest group advocacy in a particular session of Congress, we traced the legislative history of the forty-four high-salience bills from 1991. By using congressional hearings, committee reports, and *Congressional Quarterly Weekly Report*, we tracked the forerunners of the 1991 legislation until they disappeared.[14] We also made a concerted effort to find information about the initial force pushing the issue forward. Whatever the bill's original form, who was backing it?

Table 4-2. Issue Origins, 1991 Bills

Percent of congressional agenda, high-salience issues

Initiator of legislation	1991 coding	Earlier histories
Material side	36.4	40.9
Postmaterial side	45.5	43.2
Mixed, unclear, government	18.2	15.9
(N, 44)		

The coding of data again distinguishes which side was playing offense, that is, advocating the legislation: those who were promoting some material interest or those who were supporting a quality-of-life issue. In table 4-2 the results from 1991 are again shown, allowing comparison of the 1991 bills and their earlier history. The statistics are close to identical. Business-backed bills in 1991 were almost all business-backed bills in their earlier versions, and citizen group bills were almost all citizen group-backed bills in their original form.[15] This second test leads to the same conclusion reached in the first: the rise in postmaterialism on the congressional agenda is linked to citizen group advocacy.

Old-Fashioned Lobbying

The legislative histories of the 1991 bills are an unusual data base and allow the analyst to look broadly at the roots of an entire domestic agenda in a single session of Congress. How did the forty-four issues get on to the agenda?

At first glance the agenda-building process seems mundane. Some bills involve reauthorizations of existing programs, with interest groups vying for new advantages to be appended to the statute. Other bills represent new initiatives backed by extensive interest group advocacy. Sometimes this support goes far back into history. The Insurance Competitive Pricing Act, long pushed by consumer groups wanting the antitrust exemptions for the insurance industry lifted, had been kicking around in Congress for more than a decade before hearings were held once again on the issue in 1991. Still other bills reflected administration priorities and commitments articulated in the last election.

To put this first impression to a more rigorous test, I tried to determine if any kind of outside event catalyzed serious consideration of these issues at some point in their legislative history. The larger purpose of this line of inquiry was to see if issues on the legislative agenda were primarily the consequence of traditional lobbying, involving coalition building among legislators, interest groups, and administration officials, or if such lobbying activities were typically coupled with some external event that created opportunities for proposals languishing in the nether-world of the legislative process. "Event" was defined rather generously to denote any report, scandal, disaster, election campaign issue, court ruling, or other such external stimuli that might enhance the chances that a proposal would be taken up by a congressional committee. Of the forty-four highly visible issues in 1991, only thirteen (29.5 percent) had an identifiable external stimulus at some point in their legislative history. None was quite as dramatic as the Consolidated Coal Mine cave-in, though a few involved highly charged events. The Savings and Loan crisis of the 1980s led to the introduction of legislation aimed at strengthening the Federal Deposit Insurance Corporation. The proposed Civil Rights Act of 1991 was an effort to overturn six Supreme Court decisions in the area of employment discrimination.

Most of the legislation receiving a committee hearing in 1991 had origins devoid of any notable event. Instead, those hearings were the culmination of work by interest groups and their legislative allies. This, in turn, raises the question of who was more important in getting the legislation moving forward: policymakers spearheading the effort to gain hearings and then passage, or the interest groups who were lobbying Congress for help. The advocacy of interest groups and their key legislative allies become quickly intertwined once a proposal gains even the slightest momentum. Furthermore, legislators are not passive beings waiting for interest groups to approach them with ideas for legislation. The legislators and their extensive staffs are entrepreneurial, looking for policy gaps, areas where they can make their mark, show their effectiveness, and produce results that will help the legislators win reelection.[16] In some cases it appeared that the legislator was the more important partner in the alliance with an interest group. In pushing the Child Labor Amendments to the Fair Labor Standards Act, Senator Howard Metzenbaum (D-Ohio) became the central protagonist. The Children's Defense Fund worked on the issue, too, but over time Metzenbaum made the larger contribution in trying to fashion legislation to punish employers who violate the Fair Standards Act. (The business lobbies opposed to the legislation prevailed.)

More often than not, however, the interest groups show up in the histories as making the first important steps toward gaining recognition for a problem. Typical is the Bureau of Land Management Reauthorization, which became a vehicle for a plan to raise grazing fees for ranchers using federal lands. The Natural Resources Defense Council and the Sierra Club were the initiating political force behind the proposal, caring little about upsetting the Western legislators from both parties who were dead set against a rise in fees. The same is true of proposed amendments to the Immigration and Nationality Act, which was designed to protect artists and performers from foreign countries working in the United States. The Judiciary subcommittee handling the legislation acknowledged that it wasn't aware of the problems faced by foreign performers until approached by some arts groups.

The farther back legislation can be traced, the more apparent the role of interest groups in pushing the legislation forward. As public opinion tides waxed and waned, administrations changed, and new committee chairs replaced retiring ones, interest groups stayed the course. When the Brady bill on handguns came up in 1991 as part of a crime bill, it seemed as if it had been kicking around Congress forever (but, of course, only since the assassination attempt on President Reagan and the maiming of James Brady in 1981). There were liberal legislators willing to work for the bill and against the National Rifle Association, but it was Sarah Brady and her organization that kept the flame alive, both in mobilizing public opinion and in buttonholing legislators.

The findings in this study apply to all types of interest groups. There is nothing distinctive about the role of citizen groups in agenda building. They attempt to get proposals on the congressional agenda with the same kind of old-fashioned lobbying that all groups use. They identify existing studies; they conduct and publicize new research; they cultivate the press, trying to stimulate coverage; they begin the slow process in Congress by working with staffers, attempting to convince them that their boss can profit from taking up a particular issue; and they lobby other interest groups to join them in a coalition. In general, the historical case studies indicate that citizen groups succeeded through rather undramatic, traditional lobbying and not because of outside events that created opportunities for them to get their issues considered. Mother was right: hard work pays off.

Empowering Ideas

Important and visible legislation moves forward not only because of the advocacy of interest groups and policymakers but also because there is support to be found among the public. Another way of looking at the work of interest groups in agenda building is to examine their role in popularizing the core ideas that are at the foundation of public support for the general goals they pursue. Agenda building is a long-term process, and interest groups understand that part of their task is to educate the public about why a particular direction in public policy is desirable. Not all groups have the resources to work on issues beyond what's already on the congressional agenda, and not all place the same emphasis on agenda building even if they have the resources. For citizen groups, however, long-term agenda building and the mobilization of public opinion have always been at the heart of their work.

Almost all of the postmaterialist issues these groups work on embody one of five core values: equality and rights, environmentalism, consumer protection, good government, and family values. It is not possible to offer a detailed history of how each of these values has been incorporated into political movements, advocacy campaigns, and congressional enactments. Even so, a modest review should offer important clues on the role of citizen groups in shaping the agenda of Congress. This overview asks only a single, simple question: for each of these values, who was responsible for converting the intellectual into the political? That is, who mobilized those individuals who were sympathetic toward one of these values?

For modern citizen groups working in the area of equality and rights, the roots of their endeavors are easy to distinguish. All advocacy for equality and rights builds upon the civil rights movement. Beginning with the *Brown* decision and the Montgomery bus boycott, and then gathering steam with demonstrations in the South and the March on Washington, the early civil rights movement put the idea of equality squarely in the center of the debate over domestic social policy. The Republican Party was generally unsupportive, and the Democratic Party was split between Northern sympathizers and Southern antagonists. The groups working for the equality of blacks, the NAACP, the Southern Christian Leadership Conference, CORE, SNCC, and countless grassroots groups, were the driving force in the struggle for civil rights. When Lyndon Johnson swung the power of the presidency in support of civil rights legislation, the most important work with public opinion had already been accomplished by the civil rights groups.

Following the efforts of blacks to achieve civil rights, Hispanic farm workers led by Cesar Chavez began marching too, and fought farmers with a boycott of table grapes. The women's movement gathered strength in the 1970s and emerged as a major force in American politics. Gays and lesbians organized to fight against discrimination. The groups that followed the example of the black civil rights organizations had their own intellectual roots to be sure. The origins of feminism, for example, are rich and complex and extend beyond the issues of discrimination raised in the civil rights movement. Nevertheless, the civil rights groups provided a model of advocacy: determined, moral, aggressive, passionate, and effective. History is a persuasive teacher, and the tactics of successful social movements are copied by newly emergent movements.[17] As these later movements fought for both material and nonmaterial policies that would promote equality, they were following the example of these earlier organizations that used everything from demonstrations to lawsuits to gain rights for their followers.

The environmental movement has very deep roots going back to the development of conservation as an important value before the turn of the century. The impetus for the modern environmental movement is often credited to Rachel Carson's *Silent Spring*, which opened Americans' eyes to the destructive impact of pesticides when it was published first in the *New Yorker* and then as a book in 1962.[18] Carson's work certainly spurred environmentalism forward, but ongoing environmental advocacy was already in place when the book was published. The 1963 agenda studied reveals an ambitious set of environmental proposals. The Sierra Club, the National Wildlife Federation, the Wilderness Society, the Izaak Walton League, and the Audubon Society were active Washington lobbies before her work was published.

By exploiting the attention given to *Silent Spring*, these groups were able to expand their memberships and take on a broader legislative agenda. (This was a case of an outside event creating opportunities, though it was the long-term lobbying that finally paid off.) The old-line groups were also aided by the emergence of new environmental lobbies. As noted in chapter 2, a legal arm of the movement developed with the support of the Ford Foundation, which channeled funds to the Environmental Defense Fund, the Natural Resources Defense Council, the Sierra Club Legal Defense Fund, and other groups. Business, of course, fought most of the environmental groups' initiatives, and its opposition explains Congress's initial hesitancy in acting on environmental legislation. However, as these organizations grew, and it became increasingly evident that they spoke for a large segment of the population, the government began to respond. Twenty-nine significant pieces of regulatory legislation in environmental policy were enacted in the 1970s.[19] As Walter Rosenbaum, an expert on environmental policy put it, "Environmental organizations have proven to be extremely adept at arousing public concern on environmental matters and turning it into political advantage."[20]

Although the environmental movement was pushed forward by a number of large organizations, leadership of the consumer movement was more concentrated in the hands of Ralph Nader and his empire of advocacy organizations. Raising funds through Public Citizen and other vehicles, he established lobbies like the Health Research Group, the Aviation Consumer Action Project, Congress Watch, the Corporate Accountability Research Group, the Public Interest Research Group, and the Public Citizen Litigation Group. Other groups, notably Consumers Union and the Consumer Federation of America, were important too, but Nader defined the movement. At the core of his philosophy was a certainty that if corporations were left to marketplace pressures, they could not be trusted to act in a responsible manner. His solution was the traditional liberal approach of more government regulation.

With its business constituency, the Republican Party was unsurprisingly hostile toward Nader and the consumer movement. Although initially cautious, the Democrats enthusiastically embraced consumerism when they regained the White House in 1976. Nader visited presidential candidate Jimmy Carter at his home in Plains, Georgia, during the campaign and was rewarded for this tacit endorsement with the appointment of many public interest activists to high-level policymaking positions in the administration. Nader's star began to wane with the defeat of the proposed Agency for Consumer Protection in Congress in 1978. Public opinion has always been harder to gauge in the area of consumer protection, and Nader's influence declined as legislators came to believe that the public was more preoccupied with the faltering economy than with corporate responsibility. Consumerism has hardly disappeared, however, and the consumer movement has had remarkable success, especially in the early 1970s, with the establishment of the Consumer Product Safety Commission and the revitalization of the Federal Trade Commission.

Of the five policy areas emphasized by citizen groups, governmental reform has had the least success. It is probably not coincidental that this is also the area in which the citizen group population in Washington is the smallest. Most significant are Common Cause and the American

Civil Liberties Union. These two groups and a handful of others have fought secrecy in government, worked for campaign finance reform, and pushed for new lobbying laws. They have enjoyed only a small number of striking successes, such as the Freedom of Information Act and the Federal Election Campaign Act. Given the public disdain of politicians and the cynicism over campaign finance, one might expect that a basic overhaul of the Federal Election Campaign Act could make its way through Congress. Neither political party wants to upset the current system, and the weakness of citizen group advocacy on campaign finance is all too obvious.

Finally, the only policy domain to receive any sustained attention from conservative citizen groups is in "family values." Conservative citizen lobbies have worked on issues such as abortion, school prayer, home schooling, and the moral quality of television programs. Conservatives in America have a much broader agenda, especially in the areas of taxation and regulation, but business lobbies rather than citizen groups lead the fight on such policies. The formation of conservative citizen groups generally lagged behind the liberal ones, but in the 1970s a new set of groups arose to fight a government that they believed was unconcerned about the decline of the traditional nuclear family. These organizations certainly played an important role in the defeat of the Equal Rights Amendment and in curbing at least some access to abortion. The early groups were represented by organizations such as Phyllis Schlafly's Eagle Forum and the National Right to Life Committee. In 1979 the Reverend Jerry Falwell founded the Moral Majority, whose avowed purpose was to bring Christian values into the political process. The organization never developed a coherent or effective political strategy and it folded in the late 1980s.

The Reverend Pat Robertson's Christian Coalition followed in the Moral Majority's footsteps, and it has developed into an imposing grass-roots organization. The group has been highly active in Republican Party politics, and cadres of volunteers have worked in the congressional campaigns of conservative, family-values-oriented Republicans.[21] The Republicans were, in fact, quick to embrace the Christian right after the Moral Majority was formed, and despite the ensuing controversy about the separation of church and state, the GOP has maintained a highly visible and friendly relationship with the Christian Coalition. Indeed, of all the major citizen groups in these five areas, the Christian Coalition is the most closely intertwined with a political party. So far, however, the

Christian right has failed in its most important objective, a reversal of the Supreme Court's basic abortion rights policy.

The range of issues covered by these organizations is striking. These five core values touch upon much of what American citizens care most passionately about in terms of public policy. There is little doubt that it has been the citizen groups who have effectively mobilized political support around them. This is not to diminish the contribution of intellectuals, such as Betty Friedan or Rachel Carson, or the importance of other institutions, such as the church in the civil rights movement. The general pattern is one of citizen groups forming, gaining public support, and Congress and the political parties responding tentatively at first. Consistently, it was the citizen groups pushing to be heard, pushing to get on the agenda. Consistently it was the citizen groups who were the first to organize around these issues and the first to expend resources to try to gain the attention of policymakers. Only in the case of the Christian right and family values did one of the parties respond quickly and enthusiastically to the entreaties of a set of citizen lobbies. Eventual success has been uneven, with the groups advocating civil rights, environmentalism, and consumer protection being more successful than those working on behalf of good government or family values. Still, the scope of what groups in all of these five areas have done to alter the congressional agenda is most impressive.

Who Won?

The success of citizen groups at the early stages of the legislative process leads logically to the question of who eventually won. Are citizen groups effective at raising issues but weak at getting them enacted into law? If so, their powers at agenda building may be a misleading indicator of their influence.

There is no agreed-upon way to measure interest group wins and losses in the final outcomes of legislation, and any approach is likely to be a blunt instrument. Even if the method lacks precision, though, meaningful trends may still be deduced. The coding of the data was straightforward: which side came closest to getting what it wanted? As straightforward as this measurement is, some serious reservations come to mind. First, this approach may seem to miss the subtlety of a process that is built around compromise. If one set of groups wants policy A, its opponents want policy B, and the ultimate legislation (policy C) gives both sides something of what they wanted, can we really determine a winner or loser? The answer is yes. Even though compromise is part and parcel of the legislative process, compromise does not mean that each side gets an equal division of the spoils. The case histories assembled for the high-salience issues usually left little doubt as to which side in the dispute came out ahead. For example, in conflicts in which one side pushed for a bill and it failed to win passage, the legislative opponents were called the winners. A conscious effort was made to look for information on the subissues that developed and to determine how those issues were resolved. Did the side that ostensibly lost the war actually win the most important battles? If so, they weren't the real loser. The coding was aided by the culture of congressional journalism: when reporters tell the story, they like to identify winners and losers. It adds drama and human interest and even poignancy as losers try to explain what happened and where they go next. Consequently, if the "score" wasn't easily discernible from the context of the passage or defeat of the legislation, I relied on press accounts to come up with the answer.

A second concern with this method is that when faced with a sticky issue, Congress can opt to do something and nothing at the same time. As already noted, legislators can pass a bill that makes it appear that they have dealt with a problem, even though the content was gutted and the law enacted was largely symbolic. Yet it's unlikely that such actions would escape the attention of the experienced beat reporters for *Congressional Quarterly Weekly Report*, the *New York Times*, and the *Wall Street Journal*. In reading through the case histories it seemed that there was little in the way of symbolic legislation where only a minimum of substance was left in. Finally, although the analysis focuses on high-salience issues only, there is still variation in terms of the intensity of the interest groups' efforts for or against the legislation. In other words, some losses are worse than others.

For each of the three years, separate ratios were calculated for all business-related groups and for citizen groups by dividing each set of groups' wins by their losses. The business category includes corporations, trade groups, and professional associations.[22] Unsurprisingly, over time business continues to be the most frequent winner, with win-loss ratios of 3.8 (1963), 1.9 (1979), and 1.8 (1991). By comparison the citizen groups' ratios were 1.0 (1963), .9 (1979), and 1.4 (1991). From an earlier period of losing only infrequently, it is evident that business faced a much more hostile environment as citizen groups grew in number and became more active in the legislative process. By 1991 business held only a modest advantage over citizen groups in its win to loss ratio.

Although the data on agenda building and the ratios on victories indicate that business has lost some of its influence, it's important to recognize that these measures do not tap all the dimensions of business power. As mentioned in chapter 1, Charles Lindblom argues that business has a "privileged position" in the political system because elected officials need a prospering economy to maximize their chances of reelection.[23] This guarantees them a special degree of access to policymakers who want to do what they can to help businesses grow, generate profits, create jobs, and increase wages. More broadly, we are socialized to accept a market economy as the embodiment of freedom and, as a result, some egalitarian policy alternatives are never considered. What is kept off the agenda——which has not been measured——has long been held to be a critical component of business power.[24]

Business also has an edge because it is the wealthiest sector of the interest group community, and it can use that money in many different ways to create advantages for itself. The campaign finance laws are written in such a way as to stack the deck in favor of business.[25] Business's financial strength also works to its favor in the use of litigation, an interest group tactic that requires substantial financial resources. There is no measurement of regulatory lobbying or direct interaction with the White House, arenas where business might do better than in Congress. In the end, though, the legislative agenda is critical to any set of interest groups' aspirations, and the data in this study demonstrate that business may not be as strong in Congress as it once was.

A Self-Inflicted Wound?

Given the advantages that business has within the political system, it may seem surprising that its influence in Congress has apparently waned. With business lobbying expanding during the time of this study, and the economy weak in both 1979 and 1991, one might have guessed that despite any broad value change among the American people, business would have fared better than the data indicate. One possibility is that business didn't do as well as it might have precisely because so many new corporations and trade associations opened up offices in

Washington. The conventional wisdom is that interest group politics is no longer a system of subgovernments with a single, strong trade association dominating the interest group side of the policymaking process in each issue area. Today, there are issue networks with large numbers of interest groups involved in most policy areas, and it's possible that the influence of individual lobbies has been reduced by the increased competition among them.[26]

This logic is illustrated by the Bush administration's 1991 legislation proposing a restructuring of the banking industry. The bill had a number of different goals, including reforming the FDIC and replenishing the funds that had been depleted by the collapse of so many savings and loan institutions. The most controversial part of the legislation was a provision for interstate bank branching. The bill set off a lobbying frenzy because of the stakes involved and the implications for all sectors of the banking industry. The insurance industry was affected by the proposed legislation as well. Favoring the bill were the Consumers Bankers Association, which represents large retail banks; the Financial Services Council, which represents large banks and diversified financial services companies; the National Association of Realtors, the National Association of Manufacturers, and a number of insurance trade groups. Fighting the legislation were the Independent Bankers Association of America, which represents small- and medium-sized banks; the Association of Bank Holding Companies, the Securities Industry Association, the National Federation of Independent Business, the Consumer Federation of America, the American Association of Retired Persons (AARP), the National League of Cities, and the Conference of State Bank Supervisors. The most prominent trade group in the industry, the American Bankers Association, also lined up against the bill, but its leadership was compromised by splits within its ranks. Conflict erupted on several dimensions, most conspicuously large retail banks versus smaller lending institutions. The insurance industry also fought against the smaller banks. Consumers and seniors were against the legislation because they feared consolidation in the industry, a likely outcome of the legislation if enacted into law. Bigger and fewer banks would mean less competition and higher banking fees for customers. The securities industry didn't want the big banks to gain a greater market share either, fearing that they would encroach on the investment industry even more severely.

The divisions among all the interested parties could not be overcome, and only a scaled-down version of the legislation passed. The bill signed by President Bush included the reforms and repairs of the FDIC system but no interstate banking provision. It also included a Truth-in-Savings component, which required banks to give customers simple and intelligible information about interest rates. The small- and medium-sized banks were the big winners, and consumer groups could claim victory too.

If this kind of legislative free-for-all is typical of contemporary business lobbying, then a distinct structural explanation exists for what happened to business over time. A revised interpretation of the data reported earlier would stress that the change in the congressional agenda was due not only to increased citizen group advocacy but also to growing divisions among business lobbies. If the expansion of business lobbying and the growth of issue networks brought more competition among different parts of an industry, or more competition among industries as they try to encroach on others' markets, Congress would surely be less interested in taking up business legislation. And if it did take up legislation that catalyzed significant fighting within or among industries, the conflict might reduce chances for passage or, as in the case of the banking bill, result in much more narrowly drawn final legislation.

The legislative case histories for the high-salience issues contain enough information to judge whether conflict among interest groups was present, and if so, what the lines of cleavage were. If the collapse of iron triangles and subgovernments led to more business conflict, it should be detectable in comparing the aggregate data over time. Three different measures were used. First, was there any sign of *intraindustry* conflict? For each of the bills, did one part of any industry engage in lobbying against another part of the same industry? Second, was there *interindustry* conflict? That is, were different industries fighting one another? Both intraindustry and interindustry conflict could be found on the same issue, as with the 1991 bank restructuring legislation, although this was not usually the case. Third, did the legislation deal with more than one industry? The more industries involved in any one bill, the more conflict is likely.

Table 4-3 offers the results of these tests for all those cases in the higher-salience group where there was some identifiable business lobbying. This amounts to 72 percent of the high-salience case histories for 1963, 60 percent for 1979, and 82 percent for 1991. The data on intraindustry conflict do not reveal any statistically significant trend toward increased legislative battles among segments of the same industry. Although many industries have expanded and their markets grown more complex, individual industries do not seem much more likely to be

Table 4-3. Congressional Agenda and Intra- and Interindustry Conflict and Number of Industries Affected

Presence or absence of conflict or number of industries affected	1963	1979	1991
Percent of legislation causing conflict within one industry[a]			
Conflict	20.6	36.0	27.8
No conflict	79.4	64.0	72.2
N	34	25	36
Percent of legislation causing conflict among two or more industries[a]			
Conflict	26.5	32.0	30.6
No conflict	73.5	68.0	69.4
N	34	25	36
Percent of legislation affecting one or more industries[a]			
Single industry	52.9	48.0	50.0
More than one industry	47.1	52.0	50.0
N	34	25	36

a. X^2 not significant.

politically disunited in 1991 than in 1963. The test for interindustry conflict shows similar results. Over time there is only a small and statistically insignificant increase in conflict among industries.[27] Apparently issue network politics has not brought an increasing number of industries with conflicting goals into the legislative process on the same individual issues. This finding is reinforced by the results for the count of industries involved on each issue. The proportion of bills affecting a single industry has not significantly changed since 1963.

Although these data show that it is relatively unusual for business to be fighting business, when such conflicts do occur, they might enhance the leverage of citizen groups that choose to coalesce with one side or the other. There were ten instances where there was an intra- or interindustry conflict *and* where citizen groups lined up with one set of business partners against the other set of business combatants. Of the ten cases, the business side that coalesced with citizen groups won nine times. Ten cases is too limited a number to allow any firm generalizations, but it seems to suggest that business groups fighting other business groups would be wise to try to find areas of common interests with citizen groups actively involved in the same policy area.

These tests don't tap all the evidence that might be useful in evaluating changes in business lobbying. The legislation with which business is involved has certainly become more complex over time, though it is not clear what all the ramifications of this development are in a policymaking environment with increasing numbers of interest groups. More trade groups seem involved on issues, possibly signifying a lesser role for central trade groups like the American Medical Association or the American Bankers Association.[28] Nevertheless, the legislative case histories show that business is not increasingly at war with itself. Industries seem no less unified than in the 1960s, and industries are not fighting one another at a much greater rate either. The issues may be different, and there are certainly more business groups around, but the pattern is more one of stability than change.

Iron Triangles

The iron triangle model, revered for so many years by political scientists, held that tightly controlled, autonomous communities of key administrators, committee chairs, and lobbyists from the dominant trade groups formulated policy in a consensual manner.[29] Contemporary issue networks, by contrast, are typically described as being characterized by high degrees of conflict.[30] If these two models accurately portray their respective eras, some trend toward increasing intraindustry or interindustry conflict should have been evident in the data.

One possible explanation of these findings is that the expectation surrounding 1963 is flawed. No rigorous research documenting a pervasive pattern of iron triangles was ever published. The research on individual policy areas was certainly suggestive, but political scientists of the 1950s and 1960s were too prone to generalize about the policymaking system from a set of highly interpretive case studies.[31] As testimony to its enduring popularity, the iron triangle and subgovernment model was still accepted by many political scientists well into the 1980s even though little new research supported the model.[32] Since the 1963 data offer an opportunity to examine a domestic legislative agenda in its entirety along with the level of conflict surrounding each issue, the iron triangle thesis can be tested for a session of Congress when these closed communities were said to control policymaking. (The earlier figures on single industry versus multiple industry issues do not indicate whether iron triangles were present since Congress can focus on a single industry without any

Table 4-4. Conflict among Interest Groups over Legislation

Percent of legislation causing conflict

Year	1963	1979	1991
Conflict	76.6	71.4	84.1
No conflict	23.4	28.6	15.9
N	47	42	44

X^2 not significant.

involvement of a closed policymaking community.) Rather than restricting the analysis to business-related conflict, a further test measured interest group conflict of any type. Besides the intraindustry and interindustry conflict, divisions could exist between business and labor, citizen groups and business, citizen groups and labor, and from other assorted combinations. Whatever lobbies were involved, was there any significant division of interest groups into two or more sides on the legislation?

The results in table 4-4 are revealing. All three years exhibit very high levels of interest group conflict. In 1963, when iron triangles were still regarded as paradigmatic, it turns out that there was interest group conflict on fully three-quarters of all domestic social and domestic economic issues before Congress. In reading through the legislative case histories, one is struck by just how conflictual the policymaking environment was back then. There is nothing that suggests quiet, consensual policymaking between interest groups and congressional committees. When the 1963 Congress took up its most important financial services bill, the pattern was not all that different from what was observed on the 1991 Bush administration bill. The legislation to increase the regulation of the securities industry uncorked a furious lobbying battle among stock exchanges, trade groups, professional associations, insurance groups, and individual brokerage houses. The Revenue Act of 1963 also sparked a huge amount of lobbying, and differing groups coalesced along at least fourteen different policy dimensions. The farm legislation that year is also instructive. There were six separate agriculture-related bills among the high-salience issues in 1963. The average number of interest groups actively lobbying on the six bills was thirteen, hardly a small tidy number that could have driven an iron triangle forward. All six issues were characterized by interest group conflict. Consistently on commodity legislation, the American Farm Bureau Federation, the most prominent farm trade group, lobbied against commodity groups and the subsidies they wanted from Congress. Groups of this era did not go along to get along. On the Area Redevelopment Act Amendments, which provided funds for community development, the AFL-CIO, the National Farmers Union, and the National Housing Conference strongly supported the bill because it would benefit working-class Americans. The NAACP, however, generated considerable conflict when it demanded an amendment that would have prohibited any business that discriminated against blacks from participating in the program. Such a provision made passage more difficult because of the opposition of Southern Democrats.

It's possible that iron triangles were more prevalent among the less salient issues in the complete 1963 set of hearings. Even if this was true, these less visible issues were considerably less important, and any model of policymaking that describes the process that these minor bills went through should not be regarded as typical of the way legislation was fashioned. Iron triangles never existed in significant numbers, if they existed at all.

Again, Citizen Groups

Perhaps the enduring high level of conflict among interest groups should come as no surprise. In *Federalist 10* James Madison warned that "faction" is "sown in the nature of man."[33] He understood that open political conflict between groups was the price of freedom. Yet political scientists have not always perceived interest group politics and legislative lobbying in the same light. Generations of scholars have viewed the political system as highly static, resistant to change, and protective of the privilege of big business.

The findings that intraindustry and interindustry conflict remained constant over time may seem to support the belief that the political system is fundamentally conservative and works to the advantage of industry leaders who have established a privileged position in the governmental process.[34] The data on agenda building, however, suggest that congressional policymaking is highly dynamic and insurgent citizen groups were highly effective in bringing their issues to the fore. Was their success a bloodless coup? That is, were they able to get their issues before congressional committees because many of those issues didn't engender much conflict with business?

The legislative case histories are coded according to whether each of the high-salience issues incorporated a struggle between material and

Table 4-5. Material versus Postmaterial Conflict

Type of conflict	1963	1979	1991
Material-postmaterial conflict	23.4	31.0	54.5
No material-postmaterial conflict	76.6	69.0	45.5
N	47	42	44

X^2 significant at .01 level.

postmaterial interests. Table 4-5 reveals a strong pattern of increasing material-postmaterial conflict. In only a relatively few cases are the material-side combatants labor unions. Typically, they are corporations, trade groups, and professional associations. This finding is supported by Kay Schlozman and John Tierney's survey, which demonstrated that business lobbies are much more likely to cite citizen groups as their primary antagonists rather than labor unions.[35] The results indicate that increasingly over time citizen groups are not only able to put their issues on the agenda but are able to get Congress to consider policies that are obnoxious to business and energetically fought by corporations and trade groups.

The level of conflict between citizen groups and business increased because as the number of citizen groups grew, and their resources expanded, they showed no hesitation in taking on entrenched business lobbies representing important sectors of the American economy. The citizen groups were not strategic politicians, carefully looking for uncontroversial issues they could prevail on and leaving the tougher issues for another day. When Congress took up the Pesticide Safety Improvement Act in 1991, it was undertaking a familiar task. As *Congressional Quarterly* noted a few years later, "For the better part of two decades, lawmakers had wrestled in vain over proposals to substantially rewrite pesticide regulations."[36] The Natural Resources Defense Council led the charge for new legislation and did not let up because of its failure to get Congress to act. The legislation backed by the NRDC and its legislative allies was bitterly opposed by the National Agricultural Chemicals Association, the Professional Lawn Care Association, the American Farm Bureau Federation, and 180 chemical companies and trade groups that formed the Coalition for Sensible Pesticide Policy. The NRDC failed again in 1991, but the group kept at it, and in 1996 a pesticide bill backed by environmentalists passed the Republican-controlled 104th Congress and was signed into law.

Legislative conflict also grew because despite the many years business and citizen groups have butted heads, they have not developed the
kind of working relationship in which they usually try to reason together
to find a middle ground. Although coalitions do sometimes develop
between citizen groups and one set of business groups so that they can
fight another set of business groups, all concerned seem more comfortable in the role of adversary rather than ally. Each side has also been
emboldened by its allies in the White House, and this support has meant
that the side with a sympathetic president in office has not always been
eager to strike a compromise and take half a loaf. As discussed earlier,
liberal citizen groups received exceptional support from the Carter
White House. On the environment, consumer protection, women's
issues, and civil rights, the Carter White House was as good a friend as
interest groups get. Having this administration support surely influenced the liberal citizen groups' strategy in the 1979 legislative session.
In 1991 business groups were enjoying the eleventh year of unyielding
support from a Republican president.

Most fundamentally, though, the reason why roughly half of all the
domestic legislation in the contemporary Congress is characterized by
conflict between business and citizen groups is that their goals are so
antagonistic. When auto manufacturers squared off against environmental groups over the fuel efficiency standards in 1991, they had to
fight a proposal that would have gone a long way toward putting them
out of the large car business. Environmental groups seemed to want to
dictate what kinds of cars the companies could manufacture. When environmental groups considered the National Energy Security Act of 1991,
the provision to allow oil drilling in the National Arctic Wildlife Refuge
was absolutely unacceptable to them. There was no room for compromise. (That part of the bill was eventually removed before final passage.)
If oil executives believe that environmental groups don't want them to
drill anywhere new, they're surely not far from the truth.

Although two parts of an industry may be bitterly opposed on legislation affecting the regulation of their markets, they still have a common
frame of reference. Both sides still have the same basic goals: to expand
market share, gain subsidies, and be freed from onerous regulations. The
divide between business and citizen groups is a different vision of
America. One side believes that ongoing economic expansion is necessary; the other believes that it is time for noneconomic goals to take
precedence.

Finally, to evaluate what happened in Congress when these opposing visions clashed, the win-loss ratios discussed earlier were recomputed for such direct confrontations only. Expressed as ratios of business wins divided by citizen groups' wins (business losses), the scores are 3.0 (1963), 1.0 (1979), and 1.6 (1991). (This means that on direct confrontations in 1963, for example, business won three times for every time citizen groups won.) Given all the resources at its disposal, the results for business in 1979 and 1991 are not terribly impressive. Although this score is not a definitive test of business power and the number of cases is small, there is little doubt that citizen groups have proved to be formidable competitors of business lobbies in the legislative process.[37] Citizen groups have not only been effective in pushing an agenda bitterly opposed by business, they have also proved they can hold their own when issues come up for a vote. Indeed, they win a fair share of the time.

Conclusion

Space on the congressional agenda is a precious commodity. The sharp turn toward postmaterialism documented in chapter 3 did not just happen because America reached some threshold of affluence or because public opinion grew more supportive. Those may be necessary conditions, but they are not sufficient ones. Citizen groups were the primary political force that pushed these quality-of-life concerns on to the agenda of Congress. Although their legislative allies became crucial partners, it was the citizen groups that first organized around these issues and that first advocated the policies that later became specific legislative proposals before the committees of Congress.

Because citizen groups are a small proportion of all interest groups, their achievement is all the more remarkable. At the same time, what they did was not particularly dramatic or innovative. They engaged in traditional forms of lobbying, doing what other interest groups do to try and influence Congress. They skillfully built public support through a variety of tactics and were willing to expend a large share of their resources on agenda building. They were persistent and did not hesitate to take up issues that would be difficult to get through Congress.

Citizen groups have proved to be a particular nemesis for business lobbies. Over time the proportion of issues pitting material versus postmaterial concerns has risen considerably to just over half of all the legislation in 1991. Despite business's fervent opposition to most of the post-material proposals, they have not been able to keep them off the agenda. Nor have they been able to easily defeat the citizen groups in recent years: when they go head to head, business has found them tough competitors. Business surely remains, however, as the most powerful interest group sector and may be doing considerably better in other venues than the House or the Senate. But the data strongly indicate that they have lost influence in Congress. Business has not declined because of more conflict between and among industries. Rather, the conflict is with citizen groups—liberal citizen groups who don't share the view that the solution to most of our problems is more prosperity.

CHAPTER FIVE

Liberals
Ascendant

THE TURN TOWARD postmaterialism in the congressional agenda between 1963 and 1991 proceeded in an almost exclusively liberal direction. The quality-of-life issues brought before Congress primarily involved environmentalism, consumer protection, good government, and social equality, while postmaterialist concerns of the right received relatively little attention by House and Senate committees. This trend in Congress may seem surprising, since conservative citizen groups and the Republican Party were drawn closely together between 1979 and 1991. Moreover, the Reagan and Bush administrations successfully pushed public policy in a conservative direction in several areas, especially taxes and government spending. In the elections during this period voters seemed content with these administrations' philosophy of a smaller, less activist, federal government.

This study is not well suited for tracing the impact of elections or public opinion on legislative policymaking, but it can say something about why the liberal advocacy organizations were so successful in working with their legislative allies during what appeared to be a rather inauspicious time. In this chapter and the two that follow, the focus turns to the resources possessed by the liberal organizations and the strategic decisions they make in allocating them. The argument is not only that the liberal groups have developed strong organizational capabilities but that the conservative citizen lobbies are considerably weaker organizations.

In comparison to the liberal citizen lobbies, conservative groups are less efficient in their fundraising practices, invest their resources less effectively, and have proved less stable over time.

I also take up an alternative (but not mutually exclusive) explanation for the liberals' success. Possibly, the real key to the rise of liberal postmaterialism was the control of Congress by the Democrats during the years studied. Lobbies don't enact legislation and, as emphasized earlier, the liberal citizen groups have worked as partners with sympathetic legislators to get their issues considered and acted on. If the Republicans controlled Congress, wouldn't one expect to find that the conservative groups were placing their issues on the agenda and getting their legislation passed? The Republican-led 104th Congress, with its revolutionary zeal and sharply ideological and partisan outlook, offers the opportunity to test this thesis.

Liberals Everywhere

One of the greatest testaments to the success of liberal citizen groups is that they have been a major stimulus to the growth of citizen groups on the right. The citizen advocacy of the "old right"—the conservative groups of the 1950s and 1960s—was largely oriented toward the fight against communism. Groups like the American Security Council and the Christian Anti-Communism Crusade tried to educate the public and policymakers about the insidious threat of communism, both from abroad and from within the United States. Beginning in the 1970s, however, newly established conservative citizen groups began to focus on social issues.[1] Liberals—especially feminists—became enemy number one for the new right. In the eyes of conservative activists, social engineering prompted by liberal advocacy groups was undermining the traditional nuclear family. New right historian Alan Crawford captures the world view of social conservatives in the 1970s: "Divorce rates are soaring, venereal disease has reached 'epidemic' proportions, teen-age pregnancies (despite great emphasis on sex education and the availability of contraceptives) are increasing, abortions in some cities have outstripped live births, homosexuality is on the rise, more and more women are having children out of wedlock. Drug abuse and teen-age alcoholism are reaching into the high schools, where violence and crime increase—and test scores plummet."[2]

More than anything else, abortion galvanized conservatives, and new groups arose to fight the policy established by the Supreme Court's 1973 *Roe* v. *Wade* decision. The National Right to Life Committee led the struggle on the national level, but many other prolife organizations emerged at the grass roots. Other causes attracted conservative rank and file as well, including the Equal Rights Amendment, the content of school textbooks, and prayer in school. Citizens on the right mobilized on a broad scale, and many new lobbies and political action committees were organized.

The legislative case histories contain information that allows for direct comparison of advocacy by liberal and conservative citizen groups. All interest groups mentioned in press accounts were recorded, and from a variety of sources it was relatively simple to classify each citizen lobby on whether it stood closer to the left or the right on the ideological spectrum. These data were used rather than the most comprehensive list of interest group participants—those who testified before the committees—so that the most peripheral participants would be filtered out. Thus, the resulting data set is composed of the groups that have gone beyond testifying to more extensive participation in the legislative process.[3] Participation in legislative lobbying was recorded for exclusively material issues and for issues with a postmaterial side, and only the high-salience set of bills was used.

Since it is clear from earlier chapters that the liberal groups had enormous success in getting their issues on to the congressional agenda, these data will facilitate judgments about whether groups on the right managed to counterattack and if they were able to dilute the initiatives of the liberals. Did the conservative citizen groups pick up the gauntlet thrown down by the liberal lobbies?

Apparently not. The comparative figures on citizen group participation in the legislative process in table 5-1 reveal a stunning contrast. Starting from a relatively high base in 1963, the liberal citizen groups were found to be actively participating in roughly two-thirds of all domestic social and domestic economic issues in 1979 and 1991. Although this might have been expected, given their record on agenda building, the breadth of the liberals' lobbying endeavors is impressive. The conservative groups were negligible participants in 1963, lobbying on only three of the high-salience issues in that Congress (6.4 percent). Despite the mobilization on the right during the 1970s and 1980s, conservative citizen groups did not significantly expand their involvement in the legislative process. In 1991 they were active on only two issues (4.5 percent).

Table 5-1. Percent of Liberal and Conservative Groups Lobbying on High-Salience Issues

Groups active	1963	1979	1991
Liberal[a]	46.8	69.0	65.9
Conservative[b]	6.4	11.9	4.5
N	47	42	44

a. X^2 significant at .06.
b. X^2 not significant.

It's unclear what percentage of issues conservative groups should be lobbying on given their resources and the number of right-leaning organizations in the population of citizen groups. Political scientist Ronald Shaiko reviewed a sample of 155 "public interest groups" contained in the 1986 edition of *Public Interest Profiles*, a directory published by the Foundation for Public Affairs. He classified 26.5 percent of these groups as conservative. The classification scheme in *Public Interest Profiles* does not match that used in this study, so this figure offers only the crudest of guidelines.[4] Still, Shaiko's figures appear to reflect a growth in the proportion of conservative groups since my earlier survey of 83 public interest groups in 1972–73, which found that only 8 (9.6 percent) of the advocacy groups were conservative.[5]

Although comparisons against a firm baseline are not possible, what is known is that a lot of conservative groups were active in either 1979 or 1991 or both. A listing for these years would include the Alliance for America, American Center for Law and Justice, American Coalition for Traditional Values, American Conservative Union, American Family Association, American Life League, Center for Individual Rights, Center for Law and Religious Freedom, Christian Coalition, Christian Legal Society, Christian Voice, Concerned Women for America, Eagle Forum, Family Research Council, Free Congress Foundation, National Association of Evangelicals, National Rifle Association, National Right to Life Committee, National Taxpayers Union, Washington Legal Foundation, and Young Americans for Freedom. There were plenty of conservative citizen groups raising money to fight for conservative principles. Not many of them, however, seemed to regard lobbying on Capitol Hill as part of their job.

The two issues in which conservative citizen groups were involved in 1991 were a proposed crime bill that included handgun restrictions and a reauthorization of the National Institutes of Health that would have reversed the ban on fetal tissue research. The handgun control section of the crime bill, popularly known as the Brady bill, drew the ire of the National Rifle Association. The NRA vigorously attacked the legislation, and the group certainly played a major role in keeping the crime bill from passing. The NIH reauthorization, usually a routine piece of legislation, became controversial because prolife groups believe that biomedical research using fetal tissue contributes to a permissive attitude toward abortion. The National Right to Life Committee and the Family Research Council tried to kill the bill because it would have overturned an administrative ruling banning such research. The two groups certainly deserve significant credit for President George Bush's veto of the legislation.

The level of conservative citizen advocacy is so low that one cannot help but wonder if somehow the research failed to detect these groups' activities. Is it possible that the conservative groups were more involved behind the scenes and covered their tracks so effectively that the journalists for *Congressional Quarterly*, the *New York Times*, and the *Wall Street Journal* failed to detect it? This idea seems far-fetched. Of all types of interest groups, citizen lobbies are the most likely to try to draw maximum publicity to their cause. These are ideological groups who believe that they are representing the public interest. They want to bring issues out into the open because they believe that if their followers are aware of the issues, they will bring pressure to bear on legislators. Moreover, it seems unlikely that a measuring technique that is so sensitive to liberal lobbying would not detect the advocacy of similar organizations on the other side of the ideological spectrum. Finally, is it possible that excluding think tanks might have thrown off the calculations since some of the conservative think tanks reject the passive model of "universities without students" in favor of a more openly ideological and aggressive stance? The think tanks could provide the shoe leather for the conservative movement on Capitol Hill. However, recoding the data to include think tanks does not make a difference. The 1991 figure for conservative participation rises only to 9.1 percent (four issues) with think tanks included.

There are two more likely explanations for these results. First, perhaps the issues on the congressional agenda during these years tended to be of little interest to the conservative citizen groups. Second, the lack of legislative lobbying may reflect a deliberate strategic decision on the part of conservative groups to focus on other ways of trying to influence public policy.

A look at the content of the legislative agenda for the three years shows that a high proportion of the hearings did not deal with issues closely matching the interests of the conservative citizen lobbies. The greatest concentration of conservative groups in 1979 and 1991 focused on family values. The liberal Democrats controlling the Congress in those years had little interest in holding hearings on bills that would lead to floor votes on school prayer, abortion, educational vouchers, or any of the other hot-button issues backed by conservative citizen groups.

Since a great deal of legislation is initiated by business groups and their allies in Congress, wouldn't citizen groups on the right work on behalf of these conservatively oriented bills? Although a few of the conservative citizen groups are avowed proponents of deregulation, lower taxes, and other free enterprise policies, it is understandable that as a whole the conservative citizen groups do not devote much in the way of resources to lobbying on business legislation. It's fair to assume that these groups believe that corporations, trade, and professional groups can adequately represent the business point of view and that their own resources would be better spent on important issues that business is not interested in.

Legislation backed by liberal citizen groups did not stimulate any significant countervailing advocacy by conservative citizen lobbies. In 1991 not a single piece of environmental legislation was challenged by a conservative citizen group. The same is true of all consumer legislation. Who but business is going to bankroll lobbying to fight against environmentalism and consumer protection? One would not expect rank-and-file conservatives to get hopping mad about an expansion of national parks, an effort to restrict the use of pesticides, or regulation of cable television. They may even support some of these endeavors. In short, it's difficult for conservative leaders to identify broad constituencies who will financially support advocacy against environmentalists or consumer activists.

Surely more surprising is that conservative citizen groups left their guns in their holsters on a range of 1991 social issues too. They were not to be found on a major educational reform bill. Neither an affirmative action bill nor legislation to prohibit state-sanctioned sports gambling attracted their attention. It is difficult to understand why the conservative lobbies ignored these social issues. While conservatives were quiescent, liberal groups were everywhere. Since 60 percent of the bills backed by the liberal postmaterialists and their legislative allies passed in 1991, the work by these citizen groups was amply rewarded.[6]

Although it was certainly true that Democratic committee chairs made it difficult for the conservative groups to get their issues framed the way they wanted, these organizations had ample opportunity to lobby on legislation in their areas of interest. Even when the other side has the votes, there is value for citizen groups to emphasize consciousness raising by developing counterproposals, holding press conferences, asking friendly legislators to introduce amendments, releasing studies, and doing anything else in Washington that can gain publicity for the cause. The conservative groups had a great number of allies in Congress, and their failure to work alongside of them in an effort to stall, weaken, or even defeat the liberal social legislation is surprising, to say the least.

The raison d'etre of the conservative groups is to fight the liberals. Their direct mail and other fundraising pleas say give us money so we can fight Ted Kennedy, the National Organization for Women, and the American Civil Liberties Union. Until the Republicans swept the 1994 elections, Congress was always portrayed as the enemy, and conservative groups promised their donors that they would carry the voice of the people into the legislative process. Yet when liberal citizen groups were enjoying enormous success in their legislative lobbying, conservative citizen groups stood on the sidelines and watched.

Strategic Choice

The general content of the legislative agenda is not a convincing explanation for the tiny amount of lobbying by conservative citizen groups. Their lobbying posture may instead be the result of strategic choice. The leaders of conservative citizen groups could believe that there are more effective ways to influence the political process than direct legislative lobbying. Instead of concentrating on the slow, methodical, and often fruitless discussions and negotiations with legislators, staffers, and other lobbies, some groups may focus on changing the membership of Congress.

Large Revenues, Little Money

After the reform of the campaign finance laws in 1974, political action committees proliferated. Leaders on the ideological left and right formed "nonconnected" political action committees (PACs)—independent organizations without ties to Capitol Hill lobbies. Although they are a different set of organizations from the ones that are the subject of this study, ideological PACs draw on the same donors and have the same policy goals as the citizen groups that ostensibly lobby policymakers. Unfortunately, there is no conclusive evidence as to how effective ideological PACs have been in influencing election outcomes or public policy decisions. Ideological PACs—and PACs of all types—remain controversial because of the widespread allegations that campaign donations buy influence. For the purposes of this analysis, the concern with ideological PACs is a matter of effective use of resources: for the rank-and-file conservative with $50 or $100 to donate each year, what is a better investment: a conservative political action committee or a conservative lobbying organization?

Conservative PACs have been highly successful at raising money. As Thomas Gais demonstrates, however, the most prominent conservative PACs have expended relatively little of their funds on either donations to candidates or independent campaign expenditures. Among all nonconnected PACs (left and right), only 47 percent donate more than 20 percent of the money they raise for political purposes. Most of their money, and in many cases almost all of their money, goes to cover fundraising costs (usually direct mail). The largest conservative PACs have been exceptionally inefficient in their ratio of funds raised to funds contributed. Gais documents this pattern with his careful examination of some of the best known of these organizations. In the 1980 election, the three largest PACs of any kind were all conservative organizations. All together, the National Conservative Political Action Committee (NCPAC), Jesse Helms's National Congressional Club, and the Fund for a Conservative Majority raised an imposing $18.6 million. Over time, however, their debts from fundraising costs grew, and NCPAC and the Fund for a Conservative Majority went out of business. The Congressional Club struggled to stay alive, donating a mere 3.3 percent of all the money it raised in 1992 to candidates for office. It did not do appreciably better in 1994 or 1996.[7] These were not exceptions, and other conservative PACs like the Committee for the Survival of a Free Congress, the Life Amendment Political Action Committee, and the National Security PAC also declined because of a crushing debt load.[8]

Conservative PACs compete for the same dollars with conservative citizen lobbies by drawing on the same well-worn mailing lists to seek members and donors. Indeed, some of the conservative PACs' mailing lists used for prospecting are the memberships of conservative citizen groups (and vice versa). Direct mail typically has a return rate of only 1 or 2 percent, and mailings that prospect for new members usually lose money. New members added to the house list may eventually repay the costs of the prospecting with additional donations over time, but direct mail is always a risky proposition.[9]

More than any single individual, businessman Richard Viguerie has been responsible for building conservative organizations through direct mail. Yet for those on the right Viguerie has been a mixed blessing. New organizations have sprung up out of nowhere, born out of the emotion-laden, anger-inducing appeals that Viguerie has mailed to hundreds of thousands at a time. But groups he is responsible for developing have sometimes found themselves with little money left to hire lobbyists. In one of the worst cases of Viguerie fundraising, his direct mail created a conservative seniors group, the Seniors Coalition, whose purpose was to demonstrate to Congress that not all senior citizens' views are represented by the liberal behemoth, the American Association of Retired Persons (AARP). He mailed so many times that the group's director complained, "After a year or two, we had an enormous amount of debt because we mailed so much, and the cost was unbelievable. It wasn't [Viguerie's] debt, it was ours."[10] Viguerie then proceeded to help set up a second conservative seniors group, the United Seniors Association, which prospected for new members with the Seniors Coalition's mailing list (which Viguerie had an ownership interest in). This, of course, ensured that even more of the money raised would be consumed by fundraising costs. Viguerie wasn't through, however. He created a third seniors group, 60/Plus, that searched for members among the exact same constituency as the other two groups. In 1994, 60/Plus raised a respectable $1.3 million, but after the expense of the direct mail that year, it could employ only two staff members.[11] Not surprisingly, none of the three groups has become an important player in social security or medicare policymaking. Viguerie is, in a sense, a one-man tragedy of the commons. He gets paid first, so if the group he is working for (or created himself) is left with little money to try to influence the political process, it does not affect him materially.

Many liberal citizen groups also use direct mail and pay a high premium for the money raised from this source as well. Anyone who belongs to one environmental group is frequently solicited by others. What is different about the liberal organizations is that compared with conservative groups, fewer of the liberal groups are little more than direct mail drops. There are no figures that systematically compare the fundraising costs of liberal and conservative citizen groups, but impressionistic evidence suggests that the conservatives have done more damage to themselves by overfishing the same fundraising waters. Whatever the fundraising costs are for liberal groups, the data in table 5-1 show that these organizations have created a sufficient financial base to hire enough lobbyists to be a presence on Capitol Hill. Whatever the comparative virtue of the liberals' strategy of focusing on traditional lobbying, they have developed the resources to carry it out.

Foot Soldiers

One precious organizational resource that a few conservative groups have in abundance is volunteers. Modern campaigns easily degenerate into media contests, and money for television commercials is, of course, what makes PAC donations so critically important. Despite this preoccupation with media advertising, volunteers who are willing to stuff envelopes, make phone calls, and walk the precincts are still an invaluable resource to a campaign. For years labor unions have provided volunteers who have been the backbone of many Democratic congressional campaign organizations. Labor has been the exception and not the rule, though, as few interest groups have chosen to get involved in the electoral process beyond their campaign donations. Most corporate, trade, and professional lobbies want to maintain at least a veneer of bipartisanship. Citizen groups, ideological by definition, have no need to pretend that they value each political party equally.

In 1994 a major effort was undertaken by the Christian Coalition, Concerned Women for America, and Focus on the Family to instill a Christian point of view into the off-year elections. The widespread mobilization of volunteers by the groups and their other efforts to inform and persuade voters to back family-oriented Republicans is widely credited with helping the GOP to sweep the House and Senate elections that year. The Christian Coalition claimed to have distributed 33 million voter guides nationwide and estimated that 75,000 of its followers volunteered in campaigns.[12] In Oklahoma alone, the Christian Coalition distributed more than a half-million voter guides, all of which were supportive of Republican candidates. An affiliate of Focus on the Family placed voter guide inserts in two of the state's major newspapers. Volunteers from churches and Christian right organizations were plentiful and played a significant role in turning the state's 5-3 Democratic majority in its congressional delegation into a 7-1 Republican advantage.[13] It was a Republican year, and the party would have done well without the Christian right's volunteers, but in many close races the winning candidate was aided by conservative citizen groups.

The 1996 elections were not as bountiful, and President Clinton's easy reelection was a sobering indication of the limits of the Christian right's strength in the electoral arena. Even more disturbing to the Christian right was Republican candidate Robert Dole's lukewarm embrace of the movement and his failure to emphasize their social issues during the campaign. Dole was so fearful of being associated with the Christian Coalition that he turned down their request to appear at their national conference during the campaign. Only after mounting criticism from the Christian right for his awkward rebuke of the organization did Dole make a brief and unscheduled appearance before the Christian Coalition to introduce his running mate, Jack Kemp, who was to address the gathering.[14]

Liberal citizen groups have not involved themselves in the electoral process in any comparable way. Although citizen group activists are commonly involved in party politics too, this cross-fertilization tends to take place on an individual rather than organizational level.[15] Environmentalists have made some efforts to publicize the voting records of incumbents who have shown little support for environmental protection. There are also a few key liberal PACs that have gained respect on the left for their campaign efforts. EMILY's List, a feminist PAC, has had a great deal of success in "bundling" campaign donations. Contributors write checks directly to candidates endorsed by the PAC but send their checks to EMILY's List, which then forwards them. Contributors (who also make a minimum $100 donation to pay EMILY's List's overhead) know that 100 percent of their bundled checks will help the campaigns rather than be wasted on PAC fundraising costs. In the 1994 campaign, the organization claims to have channeled $8.2 million in bundled contributions to prochoice women candidates.[16] Nevertheless, the conservative citizen groups have made the greatest effort to get their sympathizers elected to the House and the Senate.

Lobbying the Public

Leaders of conservative citizen groups would likely explain the disparity in table 5-1 as a reflection of their efforts to influence public policy at the grass roots rather than in Washington. They would emphasize that the way to move Congress is to mobilize constituents so that legislators are getting phone calls, letters, faxes, and e-mails telling them what the people back home want done. This is a credible argument: legislators care a lot more about what voters think than what lobbyists think.[17] Consequently, a number of conservative groups devote their available resources to educating people at the grass roots and mobilizing support for their policies through campaigns to prompt letters and phone calls to members of Congress.

The Christian Coalition is the most prominent case in point. In the first six months of 1996 alone, it spent $5.9 million on political advocacy. The money was primarily spent on phone banks, legislative alerts sent to members and activists, and a cable television show. Little was spent on direct lobbying of members of Congress and their staffs, as the organization employs only three full-time lobbyists in its small Washington office. Senator Rick Santorum (R-Pa.), an ardent conservative idealogue who supports much of what the group advocates, told *Congressional Quarterly*, "I'm not even sure I know the Christian Coalition's lobbyists."[18] By way of contrast, the Americans United for Separation of Church and State, a 50,000-member group that fights the Christian Coalition on many issues, has twenty-two people in its Washington office.[19]

Campaigns designed to mobilize the grass roots can draw on two basic strategies. One approach is public relations through paid newspaper, magazine, television, and radio advertising. One of the most ambitious public relations campaigns by an interest group illustrates the problematic nature of this strategy. When President Clinton introduced his far-reaching plan to reform the nation's health care system in September of 1993, the Health Insurance Association of America (HIAA) swung into action. The trade group represents small- and medium-sized insurance companies—companies that believed they would be hurt by the Clinton plan. The HIAA spent $14 million on a TV advertising campaign based on a series of commercials starring the same fictional couple, Harry and Louise. In the commercials Harry and Louise dissected the plan and expressed their anxiety over what they saw as its misconceived goals and ill-advised reforms. The ads became quite controversial and were popularly credited with being one of the important reasons why the Clinton plan failed to pass Congress. Even so, a survey by Darrell West, Diane Heith, and Chris Goodwin determined that the Harry and Louise ads had no impact on public opinion. The ads probably influenced policymakers and emboldened legislative opponents of the plan, but the fact remains that an expenditure of $14 million on a clever and engaging set of commercials failed to move public opinion.[20]

Owing to the high costs of advertising and public relations campaigns designed to influence the public at large, most interest groups are restricted to far more limited efforts. When advertising is undertaken, it is more often directed at media like the *Washington Post* or CNN, so that it might at least be seen by policymakers. Yet limited advertising campaigns are an even more dubious investment than nationwide efforts and are used much more by corporations and trade groups than citizen lobbies.[21]

The second approach is directed at a group's membership or mailing list of followers. Typically a group mails a legislative alert to its members or contacts its organizational activists through phone calls or faxes. These appeals request—implore—that the recipients call or send a letter, telegram, fax, or e-mail to their legislators in Washington, asking them to vote for or against some piece of legislation. This strategy, though generally less expensive than the first, still entails significant costs as resources must be committed for the staff involved and for the mailings, phone calls, or faxes to members.

Mobilizing the membership to do their civic duty by writing their members of Congress is a very common interest group tactic.[22] Americans are more than willing to cooperate with their interest groups: during the 1993–94 session of Congress, 158 million pieces of mail were sent to congressional offices.[23] Not all of it is prompted by interest groups, of course, but groups with large memberships are capable of generating considerable mail. One of the reasons such campaigns consume significant resources is that if a group undertakes a letter-writing campaign, it needs to make sure the campaign is successful. If groups on the other side are doing the same thing, it is imperative that one's own side produces enough letters to Congress so that it doesn't appear to be the weaker combatant. This, in turn, produces opportunities for consultants—Washington's hired hands—which drive up the costs.

For many years political scientists were skeptical about how effective "manufactured" letters were in influencing legislators. The most obviously stimulated communications, like identically worded postcards, or coupons cut from a newspaper and simply inserted into an envelope, probably do get discounted by congressional offices. Still, lobbyists believe that letters from group members are vital. When political scientist Kenneth Goldstein told a lobbyist of this traditional view by scholars, he responded sarcastically, "Sure, we spend tens of millions of dollars on all this because it does not work."[24]

Interest group leaders, lobbyists, and political scientists can disagree about the relative value of letter writing because it is exceptionally difficult to measure its impact. There is little question that a substantial number of communications pressing a legislator to vote this way or that furthers an interest group's cause. Valuable as letters might be, a number of problems are connected with relying on communications from the grass roots. To begin with, the reason lobbyists encourage their organizations to spend the great sums required to generate numerous letters to Capitol Hill is not because they think the letters will work by themselves. Rather, the lobbyists assume that letters give their own efforts legitimacy, believing that congressional offices will be more responsive if staffers and legislators know that some constituents back home are closely following what's going on. The conservative groups stand apart from most other interest groups by not combining outside-the-beltway and inside-the-beltway tactics of advocacy.[25]

A second problem in relying on grass-roots pressure is that letter writing usually comes relatively late in the process. Legislators hammer out policy in committee mark-ups and in the negotiating that precedes mark-ups. Although substantial public relations campaigns might help in getting problems on the agenda, letter writing is not usually the best investment when Congress isn't even working on an issue. Too often letter writing campaigns commence when both sides are fully mobilized and legislators are hearing from competing interests. If a close vote is anticipated, and communications are concentrated on the fence sitters, the most effectively mobilized side might gain an advantage. This, however, is the very end of the legislative process.

Although it is difficult for an interest group to move national opinion on any specific issue, a cumulative effect may occur from all the efforts conservative groups have made in the past two decades. Public opinion is generally more stable than many would guess, but it has certainly turned more conservative in certain areas.[26] Conservative citizen groups deserve some of the credit for growing public pressure to balance the budget and shrink government. That is no small achievement. There is no conclusive evidence that these groups' campaigns helped to cause these shifts, but it's reasonable to think that all the ads, all the direct mail, all the sound bites on the news and talk shows, all the research reports issued by activist think tanks, and all the story leads given to journalists have had some impact.

Finally, another reason at least some of the conservative citizen groups have not made day-in, day-out Capitol Hill lobbying a priority, is that their leaders have focused on developing and nurturing ties with the Republican congressional leadership, and, indeed, on becoming part of the leadership of the national party.[27] Among the most visible and important leaders of conservative citizen groups who have followed this strategy over the years are Gary Bauer, Terry Dolan, Jerry Falwell, Grover Norquist, Howard Phillips, Ralph Reed, Phyllis Schlafly, and Paul Weyrich. They have all regarded themselves more as Republican strategists than as legislative lobbyists. It's certainly of great value to be close to congressional leaders as they have a disproportionate influence on what gets through Congress.[28] Yet the highly respected leaders of liberal citizen groups have not emphasized becoming political allies of Democratic congressional party leaders. Even though their party controlled Congress during these years, the liberal group leaders did not become especially important players in the national party and did not depend on good relations with the Democratic congressional leadership for favorable action on their legislation. Nationally recognized leaders like Marian Wright Edelman, Eleanor Smeal, and Ralph Nader never became part of the leadership of the Democratic Party. Respected heads of liberal citizen groups like Bob Greenstein, Michael Jacobson, Fred Wertheimer, and Sidney Wolfe were all comfortable in the role of a traditional legislative lobbyist.

Interest groups are like any other type of organization: the degree to which they achieve their goals depends on how well they deploy their assets. Although much that is important is out of the control of interest groups—the national mood, who controls the White House or Congress, the wealth of their members and followers—the decisions made by leaders on how to invest scarce resources are critical to the success of their organizations. How much to invest in fundraising and determining what the acceptable ratio is between revenue (money raised) and earnings (income left after fundraising costs) is a business decision. The selection of issues to emphasize and the tactics and strategies to use ultimately determine whether money is wisely invested. Choosing the level of resources to devote to long-term agenda building and that which goes to immediate issue concerns is, as in the business world, a critical dilemma pitting the need for short-term "profits" against a long-term need to "grow the business."

Most of the data collected for this study pertain to the congressional agenda and the participation of interest groups on domestic issues of

national concern rather than on the internal decisionmaking of citizen lobbies. The conclusions reached about resource allocation must be inferred
from table 5-1 and from other sources. What is abundantly clear, however,
is that conservative citizen groups and liberal citizen groups have significantly different strategic orientations. Based on several different measurements of the congressional agenda and of their participation in the legislative process, there is no question that the liberal lobbies are getting a
substantial return on investment. The conservative groups' strategy of trying to influence Congress by influencing public opinion and mobilizing
members and activists is harder to evaluate. It is difficult to rigorously
measure the impact of these tactics, both because of the modest size of
most such efforts and the inherent methodological difficulties of distinguishing the distinct influence of any one group's campaign. Few would
doubt at least some significant cumulative impact from the efforts of conservative groups to persuade Americans that the country needs smaller
government and more Christian family values incorporated into policy
decisions. At the same time, the failure of conservatives to invest in Capitol
Hill lobbying that could be coordinated with their grass-roots efforts represents a strategic misallocation of resources.

Turning Point?

The leaders of conservative citizen groups would certainly point to the
Democrats' control of Congress during the three sessions analyzed in
this study as an underlying reason why their organizations chose to
focus on mobilizing the grass roots rather than lobbying legislators. This
reasoning still doesn't explain why the conservative groups weren't
working with Republican legislators to fight the liberals' agenda. Nor
does it explain why the conservative groups wouldn't be actively
engaged in working with their Republican allies to fashion alternatives
to the Democrats' initiatives that might enhance the leverage of conservative legislators when bargaining commenced. And it doesn't explain
why they made so little effort to gain publicity from Capitol Hill tactics
that are relatively cheap when they were paying "retail" for publicity
through their grass-roots efforts. Still, for whatever reasons the conservative citizen groups chose to largely abandon direct advocacy on Capitol
Hill during the Democrats' reign, in 1995 these organizations finally had
the opportunity to put *their* issues on the congressional agenda.

The GOP's surprising gain of 52 House seats in the 1994 election offered Newt Gingrich more than the Speaker's gavel. During the fall campaign more than 300 Republican candidates came to Washington to unveil the Contract with America on the steps of the Capitol. The contract had ten principal planks that the Republican candidates pledged to vote for if their party won a majority.[29] When the election results were in, the GOP controlled both houses of Congress for the first time since 1953. Although relatively little debate took place in the fall campaign over the contract or the majoritarian model of democracy it represented, Gingrich seized the moment and immediately declared that the election had been a referendum on the policy proposals embodied in the contract.

As Gingrich planned the GOP's legislative blitzkrieg for the first 100 days, he had a delicate problem in terms of what to do with the Christian Coalition. The Contract with America placed little emphasis on social issues and ignored abortion. Just as Gingrich was claiming that the American public had endorsed the Contract with America, so was Ralph Reed claiming that the public had swung behind the Christian Coalition's social issues and that his group had made the critical difference in delivering the House to the GOP. In a brilliant tactical move two weeks after the election, Gingrich said he would put a constitutional amendment to permit prayer in school at the top of his agenda. The amendment had been an issue since the early 1960s, when the Supreme Court ruled that prayer in school constituted state support of religion and was therefore unconstitutional. The proposed amendment has never come close to becoming part of the Constitution, but it remains dear to the heart of many Christian conservatives who regard the Supreme Court's decision as an affront to their faith and to the nation's rich religious heritage.

It's likely that Reed saw the offer as a sucker punch, and he quickly retreated. A major push on a school prayer amendment would be divisive, and even if Congress ever passes it, its chances of winning the endorsement of three-quarters of the states are slim. For Gingrich's purposes, he would have been able to repay his debt to the Christian Coalition regardless of what eventually happened to the proposal. Reed killed the prayer amendment in the 104th Congress when he told the press, "I want to make it perfectly clear that this is not our top priority." Somewhat surprisingly, instead of offering tactical reasons for this move, he downplayed the importance of the amendment, remarking "I, for one, don't think we'll turn the country around by having public acts of piety."[30]

Reed's real concern was that he wanted to participate in the development of the Republican program. He soon disclosed that the Christian Coalition would spend $1 million on phone banks, ads, and direct mail to support the Contract with America.[31] He also declared that the $500 per child tax credit in the contract was the group's number one priority. Thus Reed made sure that he was viewed by the Republican leadership as a team player. It made perfect sense to him to move the Christian Coalition in a more secular direction: the group would have more influence if it operated in a partnership with the Republican Party rather than being isolated on a small number of social issues that the leadership agreed to take on each session. Yet the constituent in the pew may have found this strategy puzzling. As the *Wall Street Journal* noted dryly after Reed's financial commitment on behalf of the Contract with America became public, "Capital-gains tax cuts, after all, were hardly the top priority for conservative Christian activists when they provided crucial support to GOP campaigns last fall."[32]

Family Matters

What Reed had also accomplished with his willingness to be a good soldier for the Republican Party was a strengthening of his position as the spokesman for all the conservative citizen groups oriented toward social policy. Until he resigned in September 1997 to start a political consulting firm, he was often the only one that the press sought out for comment on what conservative social activists wanted in terms of policy or what strategy the groups were planning. No liberal citizen group leader has ever achieved such a role as spokesman for left-leaning citizen groups. Even at his peak of influence, Ralph Nader was never perceived as the leader of the diverse set of liberal citizen lobbies that populate Washington. Other leaders of conservative citizen groups, like Gary Bauer, James Dobson, Phyllis Schlafly, and the Reverend Louis Sheldon, were marginalized by Reed's preeminence.

Reed, of course, could not completely ignore the social agenda, and after the Contract with America had been disposed of in the House by its 100-day deadline, he held a press conference to introduce the Contract with the American Family, the Christian Coalition's own agenda for the 104th Congress.[33] Copying the format of the Contract with America, the Contract with the American Family was composed of ten planks, including legislation allowing taxpayer money to be used for private schools, restrictions on abortion, elimination of the National Endowment for the

Table 5-2. Contract with the American Family

Issue	Outcome
Constitutional amendment to permit prayer at public events.	Not taken up by Congress.
Abolish the Department of Education and transfer funding and power to local school boards.	Bill attracted 120 cosponsors but never marked up. (GOP actually increased Dept. of Education funding for fiscal 1997 by 22 percent.)
School choice plan to allow parents to use taxpayer money for private school education for their children.	Did not make it to the floor.
Tax relief: $500-a-child tax credit; elimination of marriage penalty in the tax code; and homemaker individual retirement accounts.	Child tax credit passed Congress but was a part of a bill vetoed by Clinton; no abolition of marriage penalty; homemaker IRAs passed as part of minimum wage law.
Eliminate federal funding for the National Endowment for the Arts, National Endowment for the Humanities, Corporation for Public Broadcasting, and Legal Services Corporation.	Spending cut for these agencies for fiscal 1996. Congress stabilized funding for NEA and NEH in fiscal 1997 and increased fiscal 1997 funding for Legal Services.
Prohibit late-term abortions.	Passed Congress but vetoed by president. Veto overridden in House but not in Senate.
Restrict pornography on the Internet.	Passed and signed into law. (The Supreme Court later struck the law down.)
Criminals must pay restitution to victims for serious crimes before they can be released from prison.	Passed and signed into law.
Increased incentives for individuals to donate to charity.	Not seriously considered.
Parental rights bill to allow parents to sue government agencies that interfere with their rights as parents.	Approved by Senate Judiciary Committee but not marked up in the House.

Sources: David Hosansky, "Christian Right's Electoral Clout Bore Limited Fruit in 104th," *Congressional Quarterly Weekly Report*, November 2, 1996, pp. 3160–162; and various other issues of *Congressional Quarterly Weekly Report*.

Arts, enactment of a parental bill of rights, and other policies designed to strengthen families (table 5-2).

Ideally, an evaluation of the Christian Coalition's success with its agenda in the 104th Congress (and the environmentalists' performance discussed below) would follow the same methodology used for analyzing Congress in 1963, 1979, and 1991. Unfortunately, when the 104th Congress emerged as an interesting counterpoint to the years of Democratic control, it was not possible to add it to the study's original research design. Still, there is enough information available for a more modest effort to assess the rough contours of interest group performance in the 104th Congress. More specifically, in addressing comparable questions about citizen groups and the three previous sessions of Congress, it is important to ask, to what degree did the Christian Coalition and its allies influence the congressional agenda? And to what degree was it successful in getting its legislation through?

The Christian Coalition certainly deserves credit for gaining attention for its set of postmaterial concerns. It wasn't just the Christian Coalition or the Contract with the American Family: the conservative lobbies' impact on the congressional agenda came before the Contract with the American Family was announced. Of the issues in the contract, advocacy by conservative citizen groups has long been associated with school prayer, reducing the federal role in education, school choice, late-term abortions, and parental rights. A switch to Republican control should have yielded more serious consideration of these issues than when the Democrats were in charge, which turned out to be the case.

It's not clear what the Christian Coalition's strategy was for this agenda, because after Reed's press conference the Contract with the American Family disappeared from the political horizon. The Christian Coalition did much more on behalf of the Contract with America than it did on behalf of the Contract with the American Family. If its strategy was to have the leadership move the agenda through Congress, it doesn't seem to have done a good job of getting these leaders on board. Speaker Gingrich did attend the press conference and pledged hearings, mark-ups, and scheduled votes on the Contract's bills. Shortly after Reed's press conference, however, House Majority Leader Dick Armey played the bad cop to Gingrich's good cop. "The Contract with America was written and signed by House Republicans. This contract was not. We're not doing a second contract," said Armey.[34]

That the Christian Coalition's contract lived (and died) with the House leadership comes as no surprise. Since it had not developed a strong lobbying capacity outside of its relationship with the leadership, it's understandable that the group's formal agenda stalled after Armey's hostile comments. Although hearings were held on most of its issues, and four of the ten proposals passed Congress, the Christian Coalition's legislative success was much less formidable than meets the eye. The four items that passed Congress were the $500 child tax credit, the ban on late-term abortions, restrictions on pornography over the Internet, and victim restitution. The child tax credit was the heart of the Contract with America and would have passed Congress regardless of the Christian Coalition's efforts. The Internet pornography bill had broad support and was helped by *not* being identified as a bill of the religious right, though the group warrants some modest recognition for its passage. There is an omnibus crime bill in just about every Congress, but the Christian Coalition can claim some of the credit on a victim restitution component in this Congress's version. Only on late-term abortions do the Christian Coalition and other prolife groups deserve major credit for helping to get a bill through.[35] Though vetoed by President Clinton, it reemerged as a highly charged issue in the 105th Congress and was passed and vetoed a second time. There were, of course, issues besides those in the Contract that the Christian Coalition worked on. For example, the group gave strong backing to the legislation that gave states the right to ban same-sex marriages.

Other conservative citizen groups working independently of the Christian Coalition didn't fare much better in Congress. The National Rifle Association made a concerted push for a repeal of the ban on assault weapons. The House passed the repeal, but Senator Dole backed away from the bill as he judged it a political liability in the upcoming presidential race. Antitax groups worked on the tax provisions of the Contract with America, but it's not clear that their efforts were extensive enough to have been an influence on public opinion or Congress.

Over the course of the 104th Congress, the GOP became less and less interested in the Christian right's issues. Public opinion polls showed that the congressional Republicans were blamed by voters for the shutdown of the government during the budget standoff. Many GOP legislators running for reelection outside the South quietly distanced themselves from the Christian Coalition's agenda, and as mentioned above, presidential nominee Dole disassociated himself from the group. Election polling in 1996 showed that a main reason for the gender gap that hurt Republicans was that women tended to believe the Democrats were much better on education.[36] The Christian Coalition's ambitious proposals to reduce the role of the government in education, and to facilitate enrollment in private schools, is at odds with what's good politics for the GOP.

It is, of course, unfair to judge the conservative citizen groups on the basis of a single Congress. This study has tracked the liberals' success from 1963 to 1991, a period of close to thirty years. The impact of the liberal lobbies represents the cumulative effect of continuing advocacy by a large set of organizations following a highly focused strategy and using their resources effectively. History may demonstrate that the 104th was the beginning of an increasingly effective mobilization of social conservatives.

In this vein, however, what must be distressing for social conservatives is that the conservative citizen groups developed so little momentum after the initial flush of victory in the 1994 elections. When the 105th Congress opened in 1997, there was no Christian Coalition agenda, and there was a decided coolness between Reed and the Republican leadership as he sensed their lack of interest in working with the organization. In a March 1997 speech, a frustrated Reed finally lashed out at Gingrich, accusing the Republican leadership "of timidity, of retreat and of muddle-headed moderation."[37]

"Muddled," however, might be a good description of the Christian Coalition's efforts to develop a coherent legislative strategy in the wake of its disappointments in the 104th Congress. In January 1997 the Christian Coalition suddenly lurched to the left, announcing that it would seek federal funding for programs that would enable it to work in the inner city with blacks and Hispanics.[38] That initiative made limited progress at best, and a few months later Reed announced a major legislative push backed by $2 million in spending on the group's new major initiative for the 105th Congress. The issue the group chose, ironically, was a constitutional amendment to permit prayer in school.[39] Why Reed had changed his mind after dismissing the importance of the amendment at the beginning of the 104th Congress, when Gingrich was at the height of his power and had offered to make it the party's priority, is unclear. The new prayer amendment initiative was met with a collective yawn by Congress. Reed's replacements, former Reagan administration Secretary of the Interior Donald Hodel and former Representative Randy Tate (R.-Wash.), shifted the organization's priorities again when they took over its leadership in the summer of 1997. They backed away from the prayer amendment and instead chose as their priorities government action to stem religious persecution around the globe, an end to the "marriage penalty" in the tax code, and tax-free educational savings accounts.[40] They also terminated Reed's inner-city outreach project.

With the appointment of Hodel as president and Tate as executive director, an opportunity arose for an internal reassessment of the group's strategic deployment of its assets. Its 1996 gross income was $27 million, and after deducting fundraising costs and overhead, substantial resources were available to pursue ambitious political goals.[41] With clearer strategic thinking about how to select priority issues, the Christian Coalition could yet turn out to be a highly effective force on Capitol Hill. With control of many state Republican organizations firmly in the hands of conservative Christian activists, the Christian Coalition and other conservative citizen lobbies are going to continue to be an important force in GOP party politics.[42]

At the same time, the organization faces some serious challenges. Reed's outburst at Gingrich indicated a growing tension between the Christian right and the congressional Republicans over the GOP's failure to deliver the legislative goods. Unless Hodel and Tate are exceptionally skilled, they may find it difficult to establish the entree that Reed had with the highest echelon of the Republican Party. Leaders of other conservative citizen groups, like Gary Bauer of the Family Research Council and James Dobson of Focus on the Family, who chafed at Reed's informal anointment as leader of the social conservative lobbies, have not been so willing to fall in behind Hodel and Tate's leadership. When Reed announced that the school prayer amendment was the group's priority for the 105th Congress, a number of other Christian right organizations came out against the move or rejected the form of the amendment backed by the Christian Coalition.[43] This embarrassing fissure on the Christian right was a signal to the Christian Coalition that the other groups were now willing to challenge it. When Gary Bauer began to test the waters for a possible run for the Republican presidential nomination in 2000, it was another warning sign that the Christian Coalition was being challenged for leadership on the right. Although this may be bad news for the Christian Coalition, it could very well be good news for Christian conservatives. The movement would be strengthened by the emergence of more citizen lobbies that are strong, aggressive, and prominent. If these groups would devote more resources to the Christian right's agenda on Capitol Hill, the GOP might be persuaded to work a little harder for these organizations' goals.

Green Power

The question of how the Republican takeover of Congress affected the opportunities available to citizen groups of the right is just as pertinent for citizen groups of the left. When their allies lost control of the House and Senate, was the influence of the liberal groups seriously diminished? Research has shown that the access of citizen groups to the executive branch can be dramatically affected by a partisan switch in control of the White House. Mark Peterson and Jack Walker found, "When Reagan replaced Carter in the White House, there was a virtual revolution in the access enjoyed by interest groups in Washington."[44] The executive branch is controlled by a single party, of course, whereas the minority party in Congress still exerts influence over the legislative process and still offers interest groups considerable access. Conservative groups were helped by the change in power, but there was no "virtual revolution" in access to Congress. What, then, was the impact on the liberal lobbies?

Traditional, material-oriented liberal groups were under siege during the 104th Congress. The controversial welfare reform bill was a cata-strophic defeat for groups on the left that fought the legislation. Not only were they defeated by Republicans wanting to scale down the welfare state by pushing people off aid to families with dependent children (AFDC) and into the work force, but they were abandoned by President Clinton, who signed the bill. Labor did win an important victory with the passage of the minimum wage increase, but the overall emphasis on budget cutting and shrinking government made it a terrible Congress for traditional, economic equality liberals.

In an evaluation of the liberal postmaterialist lobbies, the same approach should be taken as was used in examining the Christian right groups. Analysis will similarly be limited to one sector—in this case, environmental lobbies. Environmental groups are the largest and most prominent set of liberal citizen groups, just as the Christian right groups are the most visible and successful set of conservative citizen lobbies. Specifically, the groups' influence on agenda setting and the groups' suc-cess in getting their policies through Congress will be analyzed.

Not surprisingly, when the Republicans seized control the environ-mental groups immediately lost their influence over the agenda. GOP leaders and committee chairs were eager to work with their business allies to rewrite environmental statutes that various industries found onerous and unreasonable. The Contract with America reached out to business in a number of areas, but the most far-reaching plank was the Job Creation and Wage Enhancement Act. Among its many provisions, it required that agencies use cost-benefit analysis to justify any significant regulatory actions in the area of the environment, health, and safety.[45] This radical proposal would have made it especially difficult for agency administrators to justify regulations to protect the environment since many of the benefits are aesthetic rather than economic. By itself the legislation promised to be a devastating setback to years of progress that environmental groups and liberal legislators had made in creating parks, preserving wilderness, and curbing pollution.

Beyond the Job Creation and Wage Enhancement Act, major revisions of the Clean Water Act, the Endangered Species Act, and the Superfund program, were also proposed. The environmentalists were further rocked when newspaper stories appeared revealing that corporate lawyers and lobbyists were rewriting the provisions of laws they didn't like and then giving their drafts to Republican committee staffers who were sticking them verbatim into proposed legislation. When the Senate Judiciary Committee took up its own measure to institute cost-benefit analysis, it turned the job over to attorneys from Hunton and Williams, a law firm with a large practice representing business clients with environmental problems. When Democratic staffers were briefed on the content of the legislation, it was Hunton and Williams lawyers who explained the bill's provisions to them.[46] After Senator Slade Gorton (R-Wash.) undertook the job of overhauling the Endangered Species Act, the *New York Times* reported that he turned the job over to "lawyers who represent timber, mining, ranching and utility interests that have been most critical of the law."[47] During oversight hearings by the House Resources Committee, lobbyist and former Representative John Rhodes (R-Ariz.) sat on the dais with Republican members of the committee. Rhodes was representing a client with an interest in the question before the committee.[48]

Republican legislators responded to the criticism of their close relationship with business lobbyists by noting that their consultation with them was no different than the Democrats' consultation with environmental lobbyists when they were writing legislation. Ironically, the Republicans' delegation of legislative drafting to corporate lobbyists probably worked to the advantage of environmentalists. The adverse publicity not only helped to arouse public support for environmental protection but was a spur to organizing efforts and fundraising by the environmental lobbies. The outcry from environmentalists over the regulatory changes in the Job Creation and Wage Enhancement Act passed by the House caused Senator Dole to distance himself from the bill written by the Hunton and Williams lawyers. He never brought it up for a vote. The House passed a rewrite of the Clean Water Act, but after environmentalists labeled it the "Dirty Water Bill," Dole ran from it as well, and the bill died without a vote in the Senate. When the rewrite of the Endangered Species Act was ready to come to the floor of the House, moderate Republicans sensed a looming public relations disaster, and their rebellion quashed the bill before any vote could be taken. A proposed rewrite of the Superfund law was easily beaten back by environmentalists. After ten months of bad publicity and legislative defeats, Speaker Gingrich threw in the towel on reforming the nation's environmental laws.[49] Toward the end of the 104th Congress, the Republicans actually worked to pass some *pro*-environmental legislation.

A look back at the 104th Congress shows that the Republicans and their allied business groups overplayed their hand. As was the case with other strategic blunders by the Republican leadership in the 104th, a policy mandate was read into the election results where none existed. As table 5-3 illustrates, the environmental lobbies, congressional Democrats, and, occasionally, moderate Republicans, consistently defeated the efforts to weaken environmental protection statutes. Of the twelve bills highlighted by *Congressional Quarterly* as the most significant issues involving environmental policy in 1995–96, the pro-environmental side was the loser on only one and the winner on ten.[50]

If the Republican-business proposals had been more moderate in their approach, they might have gotten half a loaf on some of these issues during the first six or twelve months of the 104th Congress. In the end, though, these legislative outcomes are not principally the consequences of faulty Republican strategy but instead reflect the power of environmentalism. Simply put, the environmental lobbies were successful because the public is strongly supportive of efforts to preserve the environment. At a time when the economy was buoyant, the GOP's bills designed to boost business turned out to be a tough sell. Environmental lobbies, aided by the press, had great success in framing the proposals as efforts to destroy apple pie and motherhood statutes like the Endangered Species Act and the Clean Water Act. Try as they did to frame the issues as "reforms," the Republican legislators and business lobbyists were never able to convince anyone but themselves that they were reformers.

Table 5-3. Environmental Issues in the 104th Congress

Issue	Winning side
Regulatory reform. House passes bill to mandate cost-benefit analysis and other reforms designed to limit environmental challenges. Senate fails to act.	Environmentalists
Clean water rewrite. House passes bill designed to weaken the Clean Water Act. Senate fails to act.	Environmentalists
1995 Rescissions Bill. Contains timber salvage provision that may lead to overharvesting of old-growth forests. Signed into law.	Timber companies
EPA appropriations. House first deletes and then passes restrictions on EPA's authority to enforce pollution control policies. Dropped from final bill.	Environmentalists
Endangered Species Act. House Resources Committee passes overhaul but bill fails to get to the floor.	Environmentalists
Rewrite of Superfund law. House Commerce subcommittee approves a bill that would weaken Superfund. Not brought up for vote in either house.	Environmentalists
Cattle grazing. Bill to overturn Clinton administration rules on grazing on public lands passes Senate but fails in House.	Environmentalists
Omnibus appropriations. Senate bill contains numerous environmental riders opposed by environmental groups. "Republicans are forced to retreat on almost all."	Environmentalists
Pesticides. Bipartisan rewrite of pesticide law supported by major environmental lobbies.	Environmentalists.
Safe drinking water. Overhaul is a compromise and while environmentalists don't endorse the bill "they laud many of its provisions." Signed into law.	No clear winner
Fisheries management. Bill that is passed and signed into law is designed to protect U.S. fisheries.	Environmentalists
Omnibus parks and lands. Bipartisan bill protects and preserves more than 100 different areas. Signed into law.	Environmentalists

Source: The descriptions of bills and quotations are taken from "The 104th and the Environment," *Congressional Quarterly Weekly Report*, October 12, 1996, p. 2919. Judgments as to the winning side are the author's based on articles in *Congressional Quarterly*.

Earlier, it was asked what difference it made when partisan control of Congress changes. For the formal agenda—the bills that committees take up—change makes a very big difference. It comes as no surprise that more probusiness legislation came onto the agenda and that the introduction of legislation favorable to the environment was sharply reduced. The Christian right also had much more success in getting hearings on its issues in the 104th than in the previous Congresses. The partisan change had much less impact on the legislative outcomes in the two areas studied. Despite the unusual nature of the 104th Congress, analysis of the effectiveness of liberal and conservative citizen groups reveals more continuity than change. Indeed, the findings for the 104th seem very much in line with the previous evaluations of the 1963, 1979, and 1991 sessions of Congress. The environmental lobbies continued to do well in the legislative process in 1995–96, though groups pushing for rights of women and minorities probably fared worse than usual. The Christian Coalition was certainly more visible on Capitol Hill than conservative citizen groups had been in the past, but the organization proved much less adept at legislative lobbying than at electoral politics. Few would have guessed at the outset of the 104th Congress that the biggest winners in that Congress would be the environmental lobbies, and the biggest loser would be the Christian Coalition.

Structural Explanation

Some might see this comparison of the Christian right and liberal environmental groups as evidence not so much of the failure of conservative citizen groups to capitalize on a great opportunity but as a cautionary tale about contemporary government. Isn't the real story that it has become harder to get anything at all done by the national government? Business lobbies were also disappointed by the 104th Congress and, unlike the Christian right, they have substantial support in both parties. It may very well be that the only reason the environmentalists did comparatively well is that it's much easier to defend existing statutes than to go on the offensive to try to get new ones enacted.

The basis of this argument is that American government has become increasingly fragmented over the years. Rising partisanship by legislators, Americans' increasing tendency to put one party in control of the White House and another in charge of one or both houses of Congress, and the growing numbers of interest groups active in Washington are all blamed for making policymaking much more difficult than in earlier times. Since this study has documented the growing success of liberal groups advocating quality-of-life concerns, the charge that interest groups have made policymaking more difficult merits close analysis. Different types of interest groups may be affecting the legislative process in different ways.

There are a number of reasons why the growth of interest group politics is seen as a cause of a decreasing capacity by Congress to address significant public policy problems. Some believe that the increasing number of lobbies has overloaded Congress with an avalanche of demands.[51] Others believe that Congress has the capacity to meet such demands, but the growth of groups has created a crossfire of powerful organizations with contradictory policy preferences. Legislators may find that the least risky alternative is to do nothing. Still others say the growth of groups is not the problem. Rather the decline of our political parties has left a vacuum that powerful lobbies are only too happy to fill. Whatever the path of causation, agreement is substantial that interest group politics is making it ever more challenging for the political system to solve the nation's problems.[52] As Washington journalist Kevin Phillips argues, "Washington is malfunctioning" because of "the enormous buildup and entrenchment of the largest interest group concentration the world has ever seen."[53]

Thus, there may be something to the idea that today it is easier for interest groups to play defense than offense. Intuitively, it makes sense that in an era of greater conflict or weaker institutional capacity, lobbies would have an easier time blocking legislation than convincing Congress to pass new laws. The legislative process is full of opportunity for delay and obstruction. Political scientists have not conducted research with the offense and defense dichotomy in mind, but by trading the sports metaphor for one having to do with traffic jams, we find a relevant literature on legislative gridlock. Among other things, this research on gridlock has tried to determine if it is becoming more difficult to get important legislation passed. The best known of these studies, David Mayhew's *Divided We Govern*, found that divided control of government between Democrats and Republicans did not result in less important legislation being passed compared with periods when one party controlled both the White House and Congress.[54] Substantial debate has occurred over how Mayhew and others have measured gridlock, but to date there is no convincing evidence that over time, as divided government became more common, Congress was afflicted by lower productivity.[55]

Using the data from the 205 case studies, I looked at the specific charge that increasing numbers of interest groups have made legislating more difficult. With just three sessions of Congress, this study cannot answer the question of whether there is gridlock. But by making the unit of analysis the 205 hearings, the relationship of group participation to the passage of legislation can be tested. The computations specified the likelihood that legislation will pass when (theoretically) no groups participated and when ten groups participated.[56] Under conditions where no groups participate, the probability of a bill passing is .66. When ten groups participate, the probablility is .64, obviously a trivial difference in the likelihood of passage. Disaggregating the data by year, there were no substantial differences between no groups and ten groups in any of the three sessions of Congress. In other words, by 1991, when the growth of interest groups was said to have already debilitated the political system, getting legislation passed when there was a high level of interest group conflict was just as likely as when there was no interest group conflict.

Those who have written about gridlock or Congress's capacity to solve the nation's problems have often singled out citizen groups for particular blame. Not only have citizen groups added more demands on Congress—demands that are not easily met—but they are also said to be unusually contentious participants in policymaking. John Gilmour notes that these groups are difficult for legislators and other groups to negotiate with because citizen groups find it advantageous to be moralistic and uncompromising. Says Gilmour, "The language of moderation and compromise does not appear to generate many memberships."[57] When the impact of citizen group participation on the likelihood of passage was calculated, however, it made no difference how many citizen groups were involved. In short, citizen group lobbying is unrelated to gridlock.[58]

That the conservative citizen groups' poor showing in comparison to that of the environmentalists in the 104th Congress was due to their having to play offense is also questionable. That idea ignores the success of the liberal citizen groups when they were playing offense. If it is more difficult to get legislation passed than to defeat it, the same rules of the game apply to liberal lobbies. Liberal citizen groups and their allies in the House and Senate have been responsible for a torrent of legislation when they were on offense—that is, when the Democrats controlled

Congress. Greater difficulty in playing offense didn't suddenly become the case in January 1995 when the Republicans took over both houses.

The performance of the conservative citizen groups can not be explained away by structural changes in American national government. The evidence for such a claim is weak. A more convincing explanation is that the conservative lobbies' disappointing record in the 104th Congress reflects strategic choices these organizations made about the allocation of their resources and their selection of issues.

Conclusion

Republican control of the 104th Congress did nothing to curb the trend toward postmaterialism in American politics. There were, of course, important differences in whose bills were marked up by committees, but the central conflicts between material and postmaterial values that characterized the earlier sessions of Congress studied were undiminished in the 104th. Without a similar measurement of the overall congressional agenda, no exact numerical comparison can be made with the pattern of postmaterialism documented in chapter 3. Yet in one key area, environmental policy, the number of important bills in the 104th Congress (as designated by *Congressional Quarterly*) is comparable to the amount of significant environmental legislation that the research uncovered for 1979 and 1991. Since the advocacy of the Christian Coalition and other conservative groups brought more postmaterial issues of the right onto the congressional agenda than was the case in 1991, it's entirely plausible that the proportion of issues with a postmaterial side was actually higher in the 104th than the 71.2 percent found for 1991.

There were, of course, other liberal postmaterial lobbies besides the environmental groups, and they may not have demonstrated the same prowess in the 104th as the environmentalists. Still, any suspicions that the rise of postmaterialism in Congress was an artifact of the control over the House and Senate by liberal Democrats should be laid to rest. In the 104th Congress, firmly controlled by a party committed to enhancing the material well-being of individuals and businesses, liberal postmaterialism proved remarkably resilient.

Since this study has no data on how conservative groups have done in other venues besides Congress, a comprehensive assessment of how they have influenced agendas and policymaking cannot be offered.

Some serious questions still remain about conservative citizen groups and how they have influenced Congress, the focus of my analysis here. As is true of liberal groups, the conservative lobbies have done exceptionally well in identifying potential members and donors and raising substantial financial resources.[59] The notoriety of a number of ideologically conservative PACs who raised huge sums of money, but not much more than their fundraising costs, should caution us in making assumptions about the effectiveness of groups' claims about ambitious public relations projects. Clearly, some of the leading conservative citizen groups like the National Rifle Association, the Christian Coalition, and the National Right to Life Committee have developed a strong capacity to work with state and local groups and to mobilize supporters. Broader research is needed to document just how many national conservative groups are able to fund significant advocacy projects aimed at influencing public opinion or election outcomes.

The most puzzling question is why the strategic orientation of the national conservative groups places so little value on Washington lobbying. Although the liberal groups have slogged in the legislative trenches for years, nurturing new issues onto the congressional agenda and engaging in the mundane, day-in, day-out lobbying of legislators and their staffs, conservative groups have expended far fewer resources on such efforts. Mobilizing the grass roots has much to commend it, and lobbyists attest to the value of activating the constituents back home. Why the conservative groups do not do more work to couple their grass-roots tactics with a more extensive Capitol Hill operation is a mystery. There are many steps in the policymaking process between trying to shape public opinion and the enactment of new laws. Interest groups wanting to influence legislative outcomes should have a strong Capitol Hill presence from the beginning of the process (before committees hold hearings) until the final stages with the conference committee and floor votes.[60]

With their connections to the Republican leadership, these organizations may feel that they have sufficient access to accomplish their goals. An alternative explanation of the conservative groups' surprisingly low rate of participation in the legislative process is that conservative groups have never developed the kind of organizations that have the capacity to draw on a full range of effective advocacy tactics. Conservative citizen groups differ from liberal ones not only in their choice of political strategies but in the type of political organizations they have built. Let us now turn to that subject.

CHAPTER SIX

Rich in Resources

IN EVERY MEASUREMENT taken so far, liberal citizen groups have demonstrated that they are effective and tenacious Washington lobbies. Their increasing success over time is substantive: these groups have influenced the agenda of Congress and succeeded in gaining many of their important policy objectives. The liberal groups have achieved their objectives in the face of formidable opposition from business on a range of issues pitting postmaterial values against material ones. Even if business remains more powerful, liberal citizen groups have proved that they are worthy adversaries capable of influencing policymakers.

Just how have these groups succeeded in a highly competitive environment? Although Americans' embrace of postmaterial values lies at the foundation of the changes observed, this explanation is hardly sufficient. As pointed out earlier, value change does not automatically yield new policies. Political organizations must mobilize those who embrace new attitudes and then work to influence policymakers, who are also hearing from those who hold conflicting views. To evaluate how interest groups work to build on any attitudinal support they may enjoy, let us look at three attributes critical to most lobbies' success. The first is attention. Interest groups want policymakers to recognize their issues as vital. This is a prerequisite for getting some kind of response from government. Consequently, I look at media coverage of interest groups.

Second, lobbies seek credibility. For an interest group, getting its message across means more than just communicating it to people who are paying attention. Every interest group has its own set of the facts. One lobby looking at a legislative proposal might conclude that it will cost jobs while another might determine that it will create jobs. Whom should policymakers and citizens believe? Why are some groups more credible sources of information than others?

Finally, lobbies' ability to succeed is affected by their organizational capacity. There is no one measure of the organizational capacity of interest groups, but key variables include size, membership, stability, and, as discussed in chapter 5, effective allocation of available funds.

Although this approach doesn't cover all the factors that are pertinent to understanding the relative success of different types of lobbies, it does offer an opportunity to think systematically about how groups mobilize and use resources. Interest group resources are not just quantities that have been accumulated in different amounts by different organizations. The status of groups and the wealth they possess also reflect the skill of the leaders in making choices about what issues to pursue and what strategies to employ in building their organizations.

The Nightly News

For interest groups, the long process of getting government to respond to their priorities frequently requires them to build public awareness of the problems they are concerned about. With the intense competition among lobbies for a spot on the congressional agenda, media coverage has become increasingly crucial as each group tries to rise above the din to gain the attention of policymakers and of the public.[1] For scholars, media attention has proved to be a good tool for understanding agenda change. Increasing media coverage of different interest group sectors is usually followed by increasing attention to them by government.[2]

With the explosion of "new media," gaining attention may seem easier than ever. With diverse options, all groups can presumably find an outlet. Yet for all the discussion and excitement about Web sites on the Internet, chat rooms, cable television, and talk radio (a rather old technology), there is not much evidence showing that these venues have enhanced the prowess or even the visibility of interest groups. Furthermore, although these new media may qualify as "media," what interest groups really crave is coverage by respected and widely followed news organizations. No interest group in Washington would prefer coverage in a top-notch Web site to coverage on the CBS *Evening News*.

To see how all types of interest groups compare in news coverage, data were gathered from both network news shows and from newspapers. The network news shows were chosen because of their large, national audiences, prestige, and perceived importance among Washingtonians. Obtaining copies of the network news shows for the three years used for the legislative case histories was not a practical option, so the data set that was created used 1995 as the window on TV coverage of lobbying groups. For 295 days during that year, I watched a network news broadcast, alternating among ABC, CBS, CNN *Headline News*, and NBC. No year can be said to be typical, and how usual or unusual this one was is not known. This was the year of the O.J. Simpson trial, the Oklahoma City bombing, and the Contract with America. It is hoped that the large number of observations—548 stories that included mention of at least one interest group—minimizes bias from any short-term anomalies in what made the network news in 1995.[3]

The results are striking (table 6-1). As with the data in chapter 2 on which groups received newspaper coverage of the issues on the congressional agenda, an enormous overrepresentation of citizen groups is found. Although they are but a small part of the lobbying population, citizen groups constitute 45.6 percent of all the citations by the network anchors and correspondents to specific interest groups or to interest group sectors. It was not possible to code each story on whether the policy dispute involved postmaterial concerns. The stories were often so brief that many times assumptions would have to be made about what was being advocated. There is nothing in these stories, however, that seemed out of line with the distribution of issues found in other tests in earlier chapters. Citizen groups were largely featured commenting on environmental and consumer issues, and there were numerous stories on abortion and civil rights.

In evaluating the stories that ran, I made an assessment of how citizen groups were treated in them. In a study of television network news coverage of interest groups between 1969 and 1982, Lucig Danielian and Benjamin Page found that half of all stories about citizen groups involved demonstrations or protests of some type. Such stories commonly cast the citizen groups in an unfavorable light because they came across as unruly, rebellious, radical, or simply just out of the mainstream. As Danielian and Page conclude, "Citizens' action groups can penetrate

Table 6-1. Television News Coverage of Interest Groups, 1995

Type of interest group	Percent of all interest group references
Citizen groups	45.6
Think tanks	4.3
Corporations	24.3
Trade associations	13.0
Professional associations	3.8
Labor unions	4.0
Other[a]	5.1
Total	100.1

Source: From 295 newscasts during 1995, alternating among broadcasts by ABC, CBS, CNN *Headline News*, and NBC. There were 847 references to groups. These references were contained in 548 distinct stories.

a. Veterans, nonprofits, churches, and other groups.

the media, but often only at the cost of alienating the public, corrupting the groups' purposes, and presenting only the most cryptic policy reasoning—with questionable persuasive effects."[4]

Danielian and Page's study included the years with the most serious protests against the Vietnam War. One would guess that the 1995 TV data would include fewer stories featuring protests and demonstrations. Still, some citizen groups continue to use demonstrations and some (like Operation Rescue and Act-Up) do outlandish things to attract media coverage. As it turns out, citizen groups—at least liberal citizen groups—were treated quite respectfully at this more recent point in time. Only 18 percent of the 1995 stories involving citizen groups included footage of some type of demonstrations. And even when they did, it was pretty tame stuff. A typical example was a group of senior citizens protesting proposals by congressional Republicans to cut back on Medicare. Over time, it's evident that journalists have come to view citizen groups as much more likely to be a part of the establishment. Citizen groups are not portrayed as radicals but as conventional, responsible interest groups.

When all references to citizen groups were divided into those where a group was advocating a conservative position and those where a group was advocating a liberal one, another strong pattern emerges. References to liberal organizations or generic references to sectors composed of liberal citizen groups were 60.5 percent of the total. For conservatives, the comparable figure is 27.6 percent. (The remainder were citizen groups that could not be coded as liberal or conservative.) This same pattern emerges when stories with the most frequently cited interest groups are isolated. Of the twenty-one lobbying organizations receiving the most coverage in 1995, eight are liberal citizen groups and four are conservative citizen lobbies. For comparison's sake, the top twenty from Danielian and Page's sample is set next to the 1995 leaders (tables 6-2 and 6-3). There are only four citizen groups in the 1969–82 period, and they are all liberal (the Moratorium Committee, the National Association for the Advancement of Colored People [NAACP], the American Civil Liberties Union [ACLU], and the constellation of groups operated by Ralph Nader).

For 1995 the differential between conservatives and liberals is greater than these statistics indicate. Virtually all of the references to liberal citizen groups had a neutral or positive spin. Not so for conservatives. The conservative citizen group receiving the most coverage was the National Rifle Association. Many of the references to the NRA had a negative connotation. A CBS story in October featured a Pasadena citizen group fighting guns on the street. The scenes of street crime clearly suggested that the citizen group was on the right track while the NRA, which was mentioned as an opponent of gun control, was cast in a less favorable light. Among generic references to interest group sectors or types, the greatest number were to state militias. In the wake of the Oklahoma City bombing, this coverage was negative to the extreme.[5] If the negative references to the NRA and all the references to state militias are removed from these calculations, the ratio of coverage becomes roughly three-to-one in favor of the liberal citizen groups. Clearly, when it comes to TV coverage, liberal citizen groups are the stars while other types of interest groups are supporting actors, or even worse, the villains.

Bias or Objectivity?

The severely disproportionate coverage of citizen groups in general and liberal ones in particular raises the obvious question of bias by the television networks. A small cottage industry of critics has long argued that the media are biased. Unfortunately, there is little agreement over just how they are biased. Some scholars have surveyed journalists and found that their political views are decidedly leftist. Journalists are seen as liberal elitists whose news judgment is influenced by their own ideology.[6] Other scholars see a conservative bias in the media. They look at news organizations as businesses and argue passionately that a capitalist class limits the news to stories that support the status quo. Dissent from the left is censored.[7]

Table 6-2. Lobbying Organizations Receiving the Most Television News Coverage, 1969–82

Organization	Number of appearances
1. AFL-CIO	40
2. Moratorium Committee	21
3. Exxon	18
4. American Petroleum Institute	16
5. Gulf Oil	15
6. United Auto Workers	14
7. OPEC	11
8t. U.S. Olympic Committee	10
8t. NAACP	10
10t. International Olympic Committee	8
10t. General Motors	8
12t. Quakers	7
12t. Texaco	7
12t. American Civil Liberties Union	7
15t. Palestine Liberation Organization	6
15t. Ralph Nader	6
15t. Teamsters Union	6
15t. U.S. Chamber of Commerce	6
15t. U.S. Steel	6
20. Mobil Oil	5

Source: Lucig H. Danielian and Benjamin I. Page, "The Heavenly Chorus: Interest Group Voices on TV News," *American Journal of Political Science*, vol. 38 (November 1994), p. 1068. "t" means tied.

Not surprisingly, this literature is subject to criticism that it is biased itself by the political orientation of the scholars.[8] Surveys of journalists are often difficult to interpret because the journalists working for the "Eastern Establishment" press are more liberal than those who work in the heartland of America.[9] Claims that the owners of the press structure the news are equally difficult to judge. Scholars have documented instances of managers who overrode journalists and editors on sensitive political matters.[10] The owners' influence may also be manifested in a subtle set of expectations that journalists come to accept about what management will like and what it won't. Other scholars, however, have found that the preeminent values in the newsroom are not those of liberals or conservatives but the values of journalism: to get the story first and to get it better than anyone else.[11]

This is not a debate that can be resolved in this book; no information has been collected on the networks' corporate managers, journalists, or

Table 6-3. Lobbying Organizations Receiving the Most Coverage, 1995

Organization	Number of appearances
1. National Rifle Association	17
2. Million Man March	15
3. Christian Coalition	13
4. American Civil Liberties Union	11
5. National Organization for Women	10
6. Philip Morris	9
7t. American Medical Association	8
7t. Major League Baseball (owners)	8
9t. American Airlines	5
9t. Catholic Church	5
9t. Dow Chemical/Dow Corning	5
9t. NAACP	5
9t. TimeWarner	5
14t. American Association of Retired Persons	4
14t. Center for Responsive Politics	4
14t. Consumer Federation of America	4
14t. Empower America	4
14t. Family Research Council	4
14t. Greenpeace	4
14t. Major League Baseball Players' Union	4
14t. Reynolds Tobacco	4

Source: From 295 newscasts during 1995, alternating among broadcasts by ABC, CBS, CNN *Headline News*, and NBC.

news gathering practices. Still, keeping this literature in mind, what might be reasonably inferred from this overrepresentation of liberal citizen groups? The common conservative complaint that journalists are out-of-step liberals can neither be embraced nor discarded. A Times Mirror survey found that journalists from the national broadcast media are not more liberal than the population at large. They are much less conservative though. Stated another way, the proportion of moderates is overrepresented among national broadcast journalists.[12] These journalists' background may make them less likely to develop stories about people's right to bear arms or alleged bias against Christian values in textbooks. Based on their own interests or values, stories about the environment (which were plentiful) may be more enticing.

There is certainly substantial opportunity for the values of editors, producers, and correspondents to influence the choice of which citizen groups gain network news coverage. No specific calculation was made, but a high proportion of the reports, including coverage of citizen groups, were secondary stories that came after the headlines and discussion of the important events of the day. Television journalists have a huge amount of discretion about which secondary stories gain a spot after the day's events and before the last "soft news" story that typically concludes each broadcast. When CNN *Headline News* ran a story in June on the ACLU's complaint about a baptism of forty people in a public swimming pool in Providence, Rhode Island, it was an entirely discretionary decision. It wasn't a big enough story to demand coverage. It would not have struck anyone as odd if the network had skipped it and run another story instead.

Even when important events dictate coverage of interest groups, there is often great discretion about which lobbies get covered. When ABC ran a story on the Contract with America about a proposal requiring compensation to private property owners whose land suffers a loss in value because of something the government does, the story included a critique of the bill by a Sierra Club spokesman. No other interest groups got to speak on camera, and no references were made to the views of other advocacy organizations. In terms of fairness, the ABC crew probably felt that they had presented both sides: congressional Republicans represented one side, and the Sierra Club represented the other.

Does such a story represent media bias? Several competing interpretations can be reached. One might generalize from this story to all of 1995: with the Republican juggernaut going through Congress, it was entirely appropriate for journalists to balance what Newt Gingrich and other congressional Republicans were saying with the views of liberals, whether they be liberals in Congress or representatives of lobbying organizations. In this respect 1995 might be anomalous because of the conservative control of Congress and the uniqueness of the Contract with America. In another year, in which the Democrats controlled Congress, the favoritism toward liberal citizen groups might have been less marked if TV correspondents used conservative citizen groups as the loyal opposition in their stories. Yet even if liberal citizen groups received more coverage than usual on stories on Congress in 1995, those stories were a distinct minority of all items involving citizen groups that were aired. The overrepresentation of liberal groups was consistent throughout the year, not just in those months when the Contract with America was a compelling feature story.

Conservatives might examine this story and argue that it was principally a piece about property rights, and who would be better to speak on the sanctity of property in a democracy than a conservative citizen group or think tank? Probably there was a conservative policy expert prepared to speak to this issue—what conservatives call "takings"—at the Cato Institute or the Heritage Foundation, the two most visible conservative think tanks in Washington. Shouldn't a balanced story incorporate the views of experts on both sides of the issue rather than juxtaposing the views of a seemingly dispassionate expert on one side with a politician on the other?

Part of the overrepresentation of liberal citizen groups may simply reflect the reality that there are more viable liberal citizen groups in Washington than conservative ones. Moreover, the liberal lobbies' coverage of issues is far broader. The 1995 newscasts featuring conservative citizen groups focused largely on just two issues, abortion and guns. Conservative groups may claim to be working on just as wide a variety of issues as the liberals, but in actual resources devoted to pushing legislation forward, the figures on lobbying in chapter 5 suggest that the liberal groups surely do more work on a much larger array of issues than their conservative counterparts.

Charges of liberal bias by the networks may also be leveled because of the negative coverage of some of the conservative groups. Yet this coverage seems justifiable. The state militias are truly radical in their political orientation, and the negative tone of these stories largely reflects the groups' extreme rhetoric condemning American government. Most would regard it as irresponsible of the press to run stories that treated these organizations as if they were in the mainstream of American life. Stories on the NRA, while not as negative, were colored, too, by the unbending views of leaders who reject virtually any regulation of guns. There is great support among Americans for the right to own a gun, but overwhelming support for various forms of gun control also prevails. In contrast to this negative coverage of the extreme right, there was no measurable coverage of radical groups of the left. Leftist groups received the unkindest cut of all: they were simply ignored.

Bad for Business

The news for liberal citizen groups is doubly good. Not only are they strongly favored in comparison to conservative citizen groups but business lobbies receive the worst treatment of all. The greatest proportion of lobbying by liberal citizen groups is on consumer and environmental policies—issues on which their natural adversaries are corporations and business trade associations. In fully two-thirds of the 1995 network news stories involving corporations, the corporation was responding to some kind of accusation. Business trade groups did somewhat better as they were responding to an accusation only 44 percent of the time.

The prototypical business story with a public policy context was something like CBS's March report on the safety problems in Chrysler minivans, complete with grisly footage of accidents. A December story on CBS told viewers that Costco was being sued by the Consumer Product Safety Commission for selling unsafe baby cribs. ABC ran a story in October that noted that Citibank and Chemical Bank had lowered the minimum due on credit payments. The story warned that this action led to more interest being assessed on consumers when they paid only the monthly minimum.

The companies listed among the most newsworthy during 1995 illustrate the relentlessly negative coverage of business by the television networks. Of the five companies listed in table 6-3, two (Philip Morris and Reynolds) are cigarette manufacturers that, unsurprisingly, are consistently portrayed in a bad light. Of Dow's five stories, four dealt with its liability for Silicon breast implants. The five appearances of American Airlines included stories on airline safety, which raised questions about the company's reliability.[13] Another, on American Airline's use of foreign workers to replace U.S. citizens, was also uncomplimentary. The least hostile reporting on the business groups in table 6-3 were the stories on Major League Baseball, which is essentially the trade association for team owners. (The team owners are included because the strike that year involved the National Labor Relations Board [NLRB], and the owners and players also testified before Congress. Anytime the owners and players act naughty and show a lack of respect for the sanctity of the national pastime, Congress gets huffy and says it's time to reconsider the game's antitrust exemption.) Occasionally there were stories that were favorable to business, such as an ABC story on Coca Cola's contributions to an antipoverty program. Seldom, however, were there neutral or positive stories simply involving garden-variety lobbying by business for policy changes. Most of the time, business was responding to someone else's agenda.[14]

The coverage of business in 1995 stands in stark contrast to the way business was treated on the nightly network news between 1969 and 1982. Business organizations were the subject of 36.5 percent of all types of interest groups mentioned in the stories for those years, comparable to the 1995 percentage (37.3) for corporations and trade groups combined. Danielian and Page found that business was treated respectfully. One striking finding was that 99.2 percent "of straight statistical material in interest group source stories came from business groups."[15] Business was often presented by the networks as if it was offering an unbiased opinion on policy. "All this suggests," write Danielian and Page, "that business sources were portrayed as presenting sober, factual, dispassionate positions in contrast to the emotional and often disorderly demonstrations by citizens' action groups."[16]

By 1995 citizen groups were being presented as sober and factual sources of information about public policy, while business was no longer to be trusted. This unfavorable coverage of business fits with a larger pattern of television journalism that has developed over the years. As media expert Thomas Patterson writes, "The notion that 'bad news makes for good news' has long been a standard of American journalism, but the media have raised it to new heights in recent decades. Negativity in the news increased sharply during the 1970s, jumped again during the 1980s, and continues to rise."[17] Emphasis is often placed on failure, scandal, and ineptness. Journalists especially like to emphasize conflict, and thus stories about competing interest groups are often framed as good guys versus bad guys. This works to the disadvantage of business groups, who are often the heavies fighting public spirited citizens who have organized to fight to protect their community. Business is also hurt by the brevity of reporting in an age in which public policy is so complex. In his study of reporting on environmental issues, Robert Entman notes, "The real media biases favor simplicity over complexity, persons over institutional processes, emotion over facts, and, most important, game over substance."[18] Such a system of journalistic norms favors environmental and consumer groups who can warn of dire health and safety consequences, putting the onus of proof on corporations to show that the charges are false. And that "proof" is often quite complicated and unsuited for a ninety-second report on a network news story.

Although business was treated harshly, labor unions were systematically ignored. The only union to get any extensive coverage was the baseball players' union, an organization hardly representative of America's working class. A strike by a major union will gain attention, but beyond that the networks evince little curiosity about the role of unions in contemporary society.

The treatment of business and labor by the network news offers powerful support to Inglehart's argument that postmaterialism is a function of affluence.[19] It is a luxury for a society's news media to portray business executives as villains and incompetents. The economy was very strong in 1995 and had been strong since a recovery began at the tail end of the Bush administration. Americans, of course, have become increasingly affluent over decades—literally since the end of the Great Depression. When the United States crossed the economic threshold that freed sizable numbers of people to value quality of life over material gains cannot be determined with any certainty. What is clear is that between 1969 and 1982, the period of Danielian and Page's research, and 1995, there was a shift in the underlying values that guided the public's attitude toward business. Those values, embraced by TV journalists, reflected a retreat from faith in the promise of economic growth to a healthy skepticism about the motivations of those in business and a higher regard for those who want to limit the freedom of corporations.

Whom Do You Trust?

Groups work hard to gain attention so that they can publicize their views and get their issues onto the agenda. As Danielian and Page's study demonstrates, however, attention is not always positive—the citizen groups between 1969 and 1982 often got the wrong kind of attention from the TV networks. Consequently, lobbyists work hard to give journalists a reason to seek them out or at least return their phone calls when they're trying to spin a story. They want journalists (and policymakers) to seek them out when they have questions about an issue.

Lobbyists' chances of being sought out by journalists, or having the news media publicize their group's views, are enhanced immeasurably when they are perceived as credible sources of information.[20] In general terms, credibility is the belief by others that what you say is true and that you stand by your word. In the context of interest group politics, credibility is the judgment by others that the policy analysis you offer is reliably factual and accurate and that a commitment made will be a commitment kept. (Since this study has no data on the propensity of different kinds of groups to keep their word in their political deal making, it focuses only on their credibility as policy analysts.)

Although all lobbies crave it, credibility is a resource that only citizen groups possess in abundance. They are blessed with it, not by luck, but because they have skillfully exploited the public's distrust of interest groups in general and business in particular. One study of public attitudes found that only 12 percent of the respondents regarded testimony on energy matters by representatives of public utilities as "very believable." Executives from the nuclear power industry scored only 8 percent. Ralph Nader, who is a lawyer with no training in this field, was regarded as very believable on energy questions by 24 percent. A second study found that in television coverage of the nuclear industry, Ralph Nader and the Union of Concerned Scientists, a liberal citizen group, received the most coverage of all those offering expert opinion.[21] Content analysis of press coverage of environmental regulation reveals that those people and groups who want to loosen environmental regulation are much more likely to be fixed with the pejorative terms "lobby," "lawyer," and "special interest" than were advocates working to protect environmental regulation.[22]

More systematic evidence comes from the data on press coverage of the issues included in the legislative case histories gathered for this study. The same data base used in chapter 2 is drawn on, but a more refined measure of press coverage is used to calculate which lobbyists were quoted in these stories in the *New York Times*, the *Wall Street Journal*, and *Congressional Quarterly Weekly Report*. This facilitates an assessment of journalistic judgments about who speaks for each side in a dispute. Such journalistic decisions are to some degree a judgment about who is most authoritative. Above all else, reporters want to get a story accurately. Which lobbyists do they trust the most?

The percentages in table 6-4 are based on the number of times each type of lobbying group's representatives was quoted in the stories reviewed for 1991. Not surprisingly, citizen group lobbyists dominate the accounting of who is quoted by print journalists. This finding is consistent with all our other measures. What is striking, however, is how journalists disregard lobbyists for corporations. Corporate representatives are a mere 1 percent of all lobbyists quoted by the reporters for these three outlets. It is not that the business point of view is absent. Lobbyists from trade associations received 30.3 percent of these oppor-

Table 6-4. Authoritative Lobbyists according to Print Media

Type of group	Percent of all quotations of lobbyists, 1991
Citizen groups	46.2
Think tanks	0.5
Corporations	1.0
Trade associations	30.3
Professional associations	15.4
Labor unions	5.6
Other[a]	1.0
Total	100.0

Source: Various stories in the *New York Times*, *Wall Street Journal*, and *Congressional Quarterly Weekly Report*. There were 195 quotations from press accounts reviewed for the 1991 case histories.

a. Veterans, nonprofits, churches, and other groups.

tunities to express a group's point of view. Since it was demonstrated earlier that conservative citizen groups were all but invisible on these issues, the 46.2 percent for citizen groups in table 6-4 is, for all intents and purposes, space allotted to spokespersons for liberal citizen lobbies. Since the study estimated that citizen groups of all stripes were less than 7 percent of all interests represented in Washington by 1991, the over-representation of liberal lobbyists quoted in these articles can only be described as extreme.

Importantly, however, credibility is not political power in and of itself. The Sierra Club got the most coverage in the fight over fuel efficiency standards for cars in 1991, but the bill it favored failed to pass. Still, for groups grabbing the initiative on an issue and then having the press give their representatives a disproportionate amount of coverage along with great deference is a potent mixture of political resources.

A major reason citizen lobbies are so highly regarded is their reputation for technical expertise. This is a common characteristic of effective lobbies, and interest group scholars have long emphasized the role that technical expertise has played in giving lobbies access to policymakers.[23] Business trade groups are typically well staffed with researchers and industry experts who provide lobbyists with whatever data they need in their dealings with policymakers. Citizen groups, convinced that the truth is on their side, have also built organizations rich in information resources. Liberal lobbyists like Michael Jacobson of the Center for Science in the Public Interest and Bob Greenstein of the Center for

Budget and Policy Priorities made themselves attractive sound bite dispensers because of the technical expertise they possess, which, in turn, is based on the original research conducted by their organizations.

Roughly two-thirds of all Americans regard lobbying organizations as a threat to America's democracy.[24] Citizen groups stand out, of course, because many of them are able to project themselves as free of self-interest, while business, labor, and professional groups are commonly perceived as having a selfish interest in the issues they pursue. Even though these private sector groups may be right that the policies they are pursuing will benefit the country by creating jobs, providing better services, or offering an expanded choice of products, the public is not being overly cynical to regard their arguments as self-serving. Although policymakers may regard such groups with great respect, these organizations may find that journalists and the public are a more skeptical audience.

Although affluence may be an important foundation of the public's changing attitudes toward business, business has also contributed to its lack of credibility. Americans have witnessed decades of cigarette company chief executive officers repeatedly denying that cigarette smoking causes cancer. A litany of the products that have been exposed as dangerous to consumers could go on for pages. American journalism, with an emphasis on investigative reporting, has relished dishing out the dirt on companies that have strayed from the straight and narrow. Business is so often the villain that it should come as no surprise that its credibility has been damaged. As Robert Durant notes, reporting on public policy frequently takes on a "soap opera-like plot structure." Within this structure "Someone is in trouble, someone heroically intervenes, and public health and safety are restored."[25] More often than not, the calvary on the white horses are lobbyists from liberal citizen groups.

Research

During the contentious debate over the sweeping Clinton administration health care proposal in 1994, the liberal citizen group, Families USA, sent each member of Congress a report, "Better Benefits, Millions Helped by Clinton Reform." The Heritage Foundation, which opposed the plan, also sent members of Congress a report warning that the Clinton plan "has huge hidden costs." Ironically, both organizations contracted out their research to Lewin-VHI, a highly respected health care consulting firm. Said one health care lobbyist, "I don't go anywhere in this town without being armed with a Lewin-VHI study. You can't win without it."[26] It is certainly unusual for opposing sides to use research reports prepared by the same consulting firm. The story, however, illustrates just how vital lobbyists believe it is to be able to carry highly credible research into battle with them. Lobbyists hope to persuade journalists and policymakers that they are bringing something new and important to the debate at hand. To accomplish this goal—that is, to develop a reputation for expertise and a strong research capability—lobbies must expend a significant portion of their scarce resources on a research support staff, outside consultants, or both.

Sometimes what groups take with them to Capitol Hill or an administrative agency is a synthesis or repackaging of research done elsewhere that the group really had nothing to do with. In dealing with staffers who are highly expert in the policy area, lobbyists would prefer to bring something that is entirely new as they know that will attract the most attention. And offering up original work is critical to gaining press attention for research. A summary of what academics have said over the years is not nearly as likely to generate a story in the *New York Times* as is a brand new study of the subject. Advocacy groups try to design studies that are not only substantively important but rigorous enough to get past an educated, skeptical audience who will rightfully wonder if the findings are compromised by a research design structured to produce specific results. Presenting research to policymakers is, however, a ubiquitous interest group tactic. Kay Schlozman and John Tierney's survey of Washington lobbies found that 92 percent of all lobbies use it, the fourth most widely used tactic out of twenty-seven.[27] (No data are available showing the percentage of all interest groups that conduct truly original research.)

How the press treats interest group research is an excellent test of a group's credibility. Although each research report released to the press and the public merits a separate judgment, measuring the broader pattern of whose research makes the papers offers an indication of how successful different sectors are in preparing studies judged as scientifically (or social-scientifically) credible. Again, the *New York Times* and the *Wall Street Journal* were used, and the time frame is identical to the research on interest groups on television. For the 295 days included in the 1995 media research, the daily and Sunday *Times* and weekday *Wall Street Journal* were read with an eye toward identifying stories where research was a central topic of the article.[28] Research from any source was included and, as table 6-5 indicates, the government, with its enormous

Table 6-5. Research Featured in Newspapers

Type of organization	Percent featured in newspapers
Citizen groups	19.4
Think tanks	5.6
Corporations	9.3
Trade associations	2.8
Professional associations	.9
Labor unions	.9
Other advocacy groups[a]	2.8
Academe	17.6
Independent research institutions	10.2
Government	30.6
Total	100.1

Source: From 108 stories in the *New York Times* and the *Wall Street Journal* that appeared during the 295 days in 1995 that the media research was conducted.

a. Veterans, nonprofits, churches, and other groups.

resources, not surprisingly produces the greatest volume of newsworthy research. When, for example, a Labor Department report concluded that "glass ceilings" and "concrete walls" still block women and minorities from positions in top management, it stimulated considerable news coverage.[29] More surprisingly, perhaps, is that colleges and universities are only the third largest producer of newsworthy research. Research is their business, though in fairness much of it is basic research, not specifically intended to have immediate relevance to policy questions. Still, there are many professional schools, especially those in public policy, public health, and business, where newsworthy, policy relevant research is highly valued. Citizen groups are responsible for roughly one out of every five research-related stories. Again, they do better than business. Combining corporations, professional associations, and trade groups, business accounts for 13 percent of all research. Labor is all but invisible.

In examining the citizen group stories in greater detail, the familiar pattern of liberal groups doing much better than conservative groups emerges. Conservative citizen groups are responsible for a mere 5 percent of the stories concerning research conducted by citizen lobbies. In contrast, liberal groups are responsible for 86 percent. This is a huge disparity, and it is implausible to believe it is all because of journalistic bias. Bias may be a contributing factor, but given that one of the two papers examined is the *Wall Street Journal*, which is sympathetic to the goals of many of these conservative citizen groups, it is unlikely that bias is the

major reason. There are, again, more viable liberal groups than conservative ones, so there is a larger producing sector on the left. Another reason for a difference in research output is that some of the largest and
most prominent conservative lobbies are motivated to act on the basis of
biblical precepts. Of what relevance is empirical research when the purpose of the organization is to bring God's word to Washington? More
broadly, the evidence in chapter 5 demonstrates that conservative citizen
groups are not oriented toward Capitol Hill lobbying. Since their
Washington representatives do not spend much time lobbying individual legislators or staffers, they do not have the pressing need for research
to bring along.

The prominence of some key conservative think tanks may also
reduce pressure on the nonreligious conservative citizen groups to produce research of their own. They may perceive that those organizations
are generating what is necessary. Finally, class differences between the
constituencies of typical conservative groups and typical liberal groups
may explain some of this disparity. The highly educated liberals who are
the financial backbone of most of the liberal membership lobbies would
certainly be more supportive of organizations that emphasize research.
It's not that members closely monitor how an organization allocates its
funds, but through a group's magazine, fundraising appeals, and public
"persona," individuals are able to match themselves with organizations
that reflect their values. Conservative groups often embody what Alan
Crawford calls the "politics of resentment." In this view, middle-class
conservatives who are angry at Washington for one reason or another,
donate money in the hope that a lobbying group will raise hell about the
issue.[30] Conducting scholarly studies isn't exactly raising hell. For all of
these reasons, conservative citizen groups do not appear to allocate any
significant amount of their scarce resources to original research.

The more intellectual tradition of the liberal groups certainly seems to
pay off in press coverage of their research, though it isn't known what
level of resources was needed to yield the coverage the groups received.
Whether the investment is cost effective or not, research released by liberal citizen groups produced the most coverage of all types of lobbying
organizations. Whether it be Public Citizen's report finding that the
North American Free Trade Agreement (NAFTA) isn't producing the
jobs promised, the Fair Housing Alliance's study concluding that insurance companies were redlining even middle-class black and Hispanic
neighborhoods, the ACLU's documentation of spying by the FBI on gay

and lesbian groups, or Children Now's study of how children are portrayed on television, liberal advocacy groups were able gain coverage for their work.[31] The articles focus on the content of the research, not on the political motivations behind the sponsorship. The ultimate impact of these studies is not known, but clearly liberal citizen groups have a significant influence on what people read when they read about politics.

Think Tanks

If corporate America is disadvantaged in the competition for public support by relatively low credibility, that handicap is more than offset by other crucial political resources. Corporate lobbyists in Washington certainly have the ear of government officials who welcome their involvement in the policymaking process. In terms of lobbying, what's particularly significant for corporations is that they have multiple avenues of representation. Besides their own lobbying offices, individual corporations are often represented by several different trade associations as well as by larger peak associations like the Chamber of Commerce and the National Association of Manufacturers. Many large companies also have political action committees, so they can channel campaign funds to legislators on the committees that are critical to their business. Yet business leaders express frustration at the attention that citizen groups get, and one survey of business elites showed that they regard consumer groups as more influential in politics than themselves.[32]

Given their great financial resources, it is understandable that many corporations use their money to try to buy credibility. Some companies purchase image advertising in political magazines like *Congressional Quarterly* and *National Journal* to convey the idea that they are responsible, serious observers of the world and have concerns that extend far beyond their own parochial interests.[33] A more substantive effort, however, has been the generous donations by corporations and corporate-based foundations to support think tanks in the nation's capital.[34] Think tanks are nothing new in Washington—the Brookings Institution was founded in 1916 and the American Enterprise Institute in 1943—but in the 1970s a new type of activist think tank emerged. With the founding of the Heritage Foundation (1973) and the Cato Institute (1977), the established think tanks modeled in Kent Weaver's words as "universities without students" were joined by think tanks who were avowedly interested in influencing public policy in a specific direction.[35] Said

Burton Pines of Heritage, "We are on one side and we make that clear.
We are not just for better government and efficiency, we are for particular ideas."[36] Advocacy-oriented think tanks could help corporations gain
policymakers' attention for the ideas cherished by those in the business
community. And those ideas could be associated with institutions possessing the credibility that business lacks. As David Ricci notes,
"Washington think tanks grew because their sponsors believed that people in the city would pay special attention to policy advice tendered by
researchers whose words would seem more valid and reliable than those
of lobbyists, designated representatives, spokespersons, or special plead-
ers by any other name."[37]

The new think tanks are often described as part of some massive new
movement that has overtaken Washington, but the numbers of these
organizations are rather modest. There are about 100 think tanks of all
types in and around Washington and about 1,000 across the nation. Most
"are tiny and often ephemeral operations."[38] Still, Heritage and Cato captured the imagination of many and have served as a model for activist
conservative think tanks that have followed, such as the Competitive
Enterprise Institute and the Progress and Freedom Foundation.

Advocacy-oriented think tanks muddy the distinction between
"interest group" and "think tank." Both interest groups and activist
think tanks conduct research, try to influence the public, and lobby the
government. Citizens for a Sound Economy spent hundreds of thousands of dollars in advertising in support of the Contract with America.[39]
Such activity has much more in common with the tactics of the Christian
Coalition than with the approach of the American Enterprise Institute.
The important distinction between activist think tanks and citizen
groups is not in their strategies and tactics but in their financing. More
precisely, what is significantly different is the way that *conservative* advocacy-oriented think tanks are supported. With such substantial corporate
funding, it is difficult to consider them as representatives of citizen interests.[40] Many conservative think tanks are really just another vehicle for
corporate advocacy. Citizens for a Sound Economy's lobbying unit gets
53 percent of its funding from business interests like CIGNA and the
American Petroleum Institute. Its research office, a separate organization, gets 37 percent of its support from corporations and another 49 percent from foundations, some of which are connected to corporations.[41]

Business donations and targeted advocacy campaigns by activist think
tanks are sometimes tightly linked together. For example, when the

Progress and Freedom Foundation undertook an effort to try to alter fundamentally the way the Food and Drug Administration operates, it received substantial gifts from companies regulated by the agency, like Burroughs Wellcome, Genzyme, Glaxo, and G.D. Searle.[42] Cigarette manufacturers who, of course, have no credibility of their own, regard conservative think tanks as excellent allies. The *Wall Street Journal* found that Philip Morris and R.J. Reynolds have made "lavish donations" to think tanks who are fighting to shrink government regulation by the FDA.[43]

For those who have invested in think tanks, have they offered a decent return? Each year the twenty-five largest think tanks produce 250 books and more than 1,000 reports, conference proceedings, papers, and the like.[44] This is certainly a prodigious output. As with the research reports issued by citizen groups, gauging the impact of the think tanks' scholarship is difficult. There are some notable successes. Brookings and the American Enterprise Institute are credited with spurring the deregulation of the 1970s and 1980s with the research they conducted beginning in the 1960s.[45] For conservatives, the proof of what think tanks could do came with the publication of Charles Murray's *Losing Ground*, a book sponsored by the Manhattan Institute.[46] Published in 1984, Murray's scholarly book amassed a great deal of quantitative evidence in support of his argument that welfare programs had not only failed but that they made things worse for the poor. The book became a cause célèbre as liberals venomously attacked it for its methodological shortcomings while the Reagan administration embraced it as an intellectual justification for its attack on the welfare state. Whatever its faults, *Losing Ground* was a forceful reminder of the power of ideas.

The new activist think tanks have deemphasized the book-length monographs that have been the staple of the older-style think tanks like Brookings and the Urban Institute and instead have focused on what can be done in short reports, backgrounders, and op-ed pieces. Coupled with aggressive marketing, activist think tanks like Heritage and Cato have tried to fashion their research to fit the real-life reading habits of busy Washington policymakers.[47] In this vein, op-ed essays in top newspapers are highly valued by advocacy organizations because they assume that elected officials and policy wonks from government read them. The *Wall Street Journal* is especially prized by conservatives because it is truly a national paper and is read by business leaders and policymakers alike.

To see how successful think tanks are in this arena, my study examines the op-ed pages of the same issues of the *New York Times* and the

Wall Street Journal used in the review of research-related articles.[48] The results demonstrate that op-eds are, in fact, one venue where think tanks do well: more than half of the essays from advocacy organizations came from think tanks (table 6-6). Conservative advocacy organizations also do better on op-ed pages than they have in the study's other tests of participation or visibility. Seventy percent of all op-eds in the *Wall Street Journal* written by someone from an advocacy organization came from a conservative citizen group or think tank. This might have been expected given the relentlessly ideological nature of their editorial page, but conservatives also did well in the more liberal *New York Times*. Of the op-ed essays written by representatives of a citizen group or think tank, about 40 percent came from conservative organizations and approximately 50 percent from liberal ones.[49] Kent Weaver, using a broader data base, found that conservative think tanks gain more visibility in the press than liberal ones. He demonstrates that the greater success of the conservative think tanks is linked to their considerably greater resources. Centrist, nonideological think tanks like Brookings, Rand, and the American Enterprise Institute do the best of all in media attention and in credibility.[50]

In terms of op-eds, it would be unwise to generalize from these two papers to all newspapers across the country—they are hardly typical of what lands on most people's doorstep each morning. Few papers are as rigidly ideological on their op-ed page as the *Wall Street Journal*. Many papers rely almost exclusively on syndicated columnists on their opposite editorial page rather than using guest editorialists who submit their work in the hopes of being published. Some use a point-counterpoint format to ensure that both sides of an issue are heard.

Just what should be made of the think tanks' success with op-ed placements? When Bruce Bartlett of the National Center for Policy Analysis, a conservative, Dallas-based think tank, published his essay "Will the Flat Tax KO Housing?" in the *Wall Street Journal*, did it make a difference in the debate over reforming national tax policy?[51] It was a learned, intelligent piece that responded to an attack on the flat tax by the National Association of Realtors. The association was touting a study demonstrating that a flat tax without a mortgage deduction would result in a 15 percent drop in housing prices and, consequently, a $1.7 trillion decrease in homeowners' equity. Although acknowledging that there would be some impact on housing, Bartlett countered many of the claims of the association and argued that the overall benefits to the economy would outweigh any negative impact on the housing sector. For

Table 6-6. Advocacy Organizations on the Op-Ed Page

Type of organization	Percent of all op-ed columns written by someone from a lobby or think tank
Citizen groups	22.8
Think tanks	54.8
Corporations	15.4
Trade associations	3.3
Professional associations	.4
Labor unions	.8
Other[a]	2.5
Total	100.0

Sources: All issues of the *New York Times* and *Wall Street Journal* for 295 days during 1995.

a. Veterans, nonprofits, churches, and other groups.

partisans of the flat tax, it was surely a useful essay to be clipped from the paper and stuck in a file folder. In its own small way, the article contributed to an extensive and ongoing debate about the flat tax.

If the data on op-eds demonstrate that the "art of the short" has flourished in this one venue, it is also true that the broader research done for this study suggests that the Heritage and Cato model has been only a modest success. The activist think tanks have created organizations that have mavens on call, ready to write op-eds and backgrounders, and offer sound bites to journalists. Yet in table 6-4, based on who is quoted in the *New York Times*, the *Wall Street Journal*, and *Congressional Quarterly*, staffers from think tanks score just one-half of 1 percent. At least for 1991, beat reporters on Capitol Hill weren't buying what the activist think tanks were selling. The think tanks do a bit better in getting their research cited (5.6 percent), but this figure is hardly impressive given that the production of newsworthy, policy-related research is their raison d'etre. More seriously for the activist think tanks, the 1991 legislative case histories found them active on just two issues and in rather marginal roles.[52] Apparently the activism of the activist think tanks is pretty limited.

At the outset of this study I thought, perhaps naively, that think tanks were the intellectual companion to the citizen groups of the left and right and that they had helped to enhance the growing presence of citizen groups in national politics. This turned out to be wrong for both sides. On the left, the activist think tank model never took hold. A few groups claimed to be a liberal version of Heritage or Cato, but they have modest budgets and none has achieved the notoriety or visibility of the conservative organizations.[53] For the advocacy think tanks on the right, they have worked not in tandem with conservative citizen groups but in partnership with business lobbies. Given the thousands of business lobbyists, and the deep pockets of the corporations that employ them, one might wonder what a small number of activist conservative think tanks adds to the business sector in Washington. The answer is simple: the think tanks offer credibility.

Strong Organizations

Citizen groups are often discussed in the context of social movements. Analyses of American politics speak of the environmental movement, the consumer movement, the women's movement, the civil rights movement, and the Christian right movement. These movements encompass most of the organizations that are the subject of this book. Sociologists who study social movements even have a special term, SMOs (social movement organizations), to label these groups. Why sociologists don't call them "interest groups" is a bit puzzling since SMOs do what interest groups do: organize, educate, and lobby.[54]

Viewing these groups as part of movements does not do them justice. Social movements are usually perceived as episodic and unstable and focused on challenging the existing political order on behalf of those who are "marginalized" in society.[55] Certainly all these movements had their origins in challenges to the political system. Yet most of them quickly passed from the stage of representing marginalized interests and became full and conventional participants in the policymaking process. Far from being episodic and unstable, citizen groups—in particular the liberal lobbies—have proved to be stable organizations with long and admirable track records.

Some may regard "stable liberals" as an oxymoron, but the argument is that the liberal citizen groups have thrived not simply because they have championed popular ideas that have caught the fancy of the media and affluent suburbanites but because they have built strong, well-managed organizations. The extensive participation of the liberal citizen groups in the legislative process has been well documented in the previous chapters. Importantly, considerable continuity has prevailed in the leadership of this liberal sector. Table 6-7 lists all the organizations cited by the media in their coverage of both the 1979 and 1991 issues.[56] These

Table 6-7. The Liberals' Staying Power

Conservative citizen groups involved in 1979 and 1991	Liberal citizen groups involved in 1979 and 1991
National Rifle Association[a]	American Association of Retired Persons
National Right to Life Committee	American Civil Liberties Union[a]
	Children's Defense Fund
	Common Cause
	Congress Watch
	Consumer Federation of America
	Consumers Union[a]
	Friends of the Earth
	League of Conservation Voters
	League of Women Voters[a]
	NAACP[a]
	National Audubon Society[a]
	National Wildlife Federation[a]
	Natural Resources Defense Council
	Sierra Club[a]
	Union of Concerned Scientists
	Urban League[a]
	Wilderness Society[a]

a. Organization was active in the 1963 issues too.

are not groups that merely testified or participated at the margins. They were seen by journalists as significant players in the issues they were writing about. There are not a huge number of organizations on this list, but they are organizations that have ample resources.

Since there were so few issues that conservative groups lobbied on in any of the three years, it is not surprising that we would find only a few who were significantly involved on issues in Congress in both 1979 and 1991. The two that do show up, the National Rifle Association and the National Right to Life Committee, have certainly proved to be forceful, stable fixtures in policymaking in their respective issue areas. Since any one session of Congress is unique, and its agenda may not significantly engage any particular lobby in a single year, conceivably some key conservative organizations in existence during this period were not picked up in either the 1979 or 1991 case histories. Yet my earlier survey of eighty-three Washington-based public interest groups during 1972–73 suggests that conservative citizen groups have not had the same staying power as the liberals. As noted in chapter 5, the survey identified eight conservative advocacy organizations. Only two of them—the American

Conservative Union and the Young Americans for Freedom—remain viable Washington lobbies, though neither group plays an especially prominent role today.[57] The conservative groups now active in Washington may turn out to be different and experience long organizational lives lobbying the government, but their predecessors don't inspire confidence that this will be the case.

A follow-up study of the entire set of eighty-three organizations conducted by Ronald Shaiko in 1985 found that more than 80 percent were still in operation.[58] Since the seventy-five lobbies that weren't conservative were almost all on the liberal side of the ideological spectrum, Shaiko's update of the survey indicates that liberal citizen lobbies were remarkably stable during this period. Given that these groups must overcome the collective action problem—getting people to voluntarily donate money to an organization that in most cases will not give them any significant selective benefits—such stability is an impressive achievement.

As table 6-8 demonstrates, many of the leading environmental groups have been in existence for more than fifty years. The Sierra Club was founded in 1892 and Audubon in 1905. Several of the more recent environmental groups have developed into large, wealthy, and stable lobbies. Although the environmental groups have suffered an occasional small drop in membership, over time they have grown tremendously, even as new environmental lobbies emerged to compete for members.[59] Among all policy areas, the environmental sector has the greatest concentration of large, long-standing citizen groups. Liberals have also been able to look to other large and successful citizen groups who have played an enduring leadership role in the areas of good government (League of Women Voters, Common Cause), civil rights (NAACP, Urban League), civil liberties (ACLU), and consumer protection (Consumer Federation of America, Consumers Union, and Ralph Nader through a variety of groups in his empire).[60]

The collective membership of the national environmental groups is striking. Although some overlap exists among the memberships since ardent environmentalists may belong to more than one lobby, these groups together represent millions of people. These large memberships are a great counterweight to trade groups that continually tell legislators that environmental legislation will be harmful to job creation. Members of Congress know that a significant number of their constituents may be informed by an environmental lobby as to how their legislators voted on

Table 6-8. Membership Trends among Environmental Lobbies, 1970–92

Group	1970	1980	1985	1990	1992
Sierra Club (1892)	113,000	181,000	364,000	630,000	650,000
National Audubon Society (1905)	105,000	400,000	550,000	575,000	600,000
Izaak Walton League (1922)	54,000	52,000	47,000	50,000	53,000
Wilderness Society (1935)	54,000	45,000	147,000	350,000	313,000
National Wildlife Federation (1936)[a]	540,000	818,000	900,000	997,000	975,000
Defenders of Wildlife (1947)	13,000	50,000	65,000	75,000	80,000
Nature Conservancy (1951)	22,000	n.a.	400,000	600,000	690,000
World Wildlife Fund (1961)	n.a.	n.a.	130,000	400,000	940,000
Environmental Defense Fund (1967)	11,000	46,000	50,000	150,000	150,000
Friends of the Earth (1969)[b]	6,000	n.a.	30,000	9,000	50,000
Environmental Action (1970)	10,000	20,000	15,000	20,000	16,000
Greenpeace USA (1972)	n.a.	n.a.	800,000	2,350,000	1,800,000

Source: See Christopher J. Bosso, "The Color of Money: Environmental Groups and the Pathologies of Fund Raising," in Allan J. Cigler and Burdett A. Loomis, eds., *Interest Group Politics*, 4th ed. (Washington: Congressional Quarterly Press, 1995), p. 104. Reprinted by permission of Congressional Quarterly.

Note: All figures rounded.

n.a. Not available.

a. Full members only. The Federation in 1992 also had affiliated memberships (for example, schoolchildren) of 5.3 million.

b. Merged in 1990 with the 30,000-member Oceanic Society and the nonmember Environmental Policy Institute.

relevant legislation. There are, of course, large liberal groups in other policy areas (for example, Common Cause at 250,000 members and the ACLU at 275,000), but the environmental groups dwarf all the other liberal sectors.[61]

One important caveat must be kept in mind when membership figures are being analyzed: groups on both the left and the right tend to exaggerate their actual dues-paying memberships. In 1995 the Christian Coalition's publicly stated membership was 1.7 million. Yet U.S. Postal Service records for 1995 indicated that the group mailed out only 310, 296 copies of its magazine, *Christian American*. The magazine goes to those who pay $15 or more to the organization.[62] This is an extreme example, and other organizations fudge a great deal less, but citizen group membership figures are not the most reliable of numbers. "Phantom" members may come from a variety of sources. People may be counted as members if they're affiliated with an organization that, in turn, is affiliated with the lobby. (Individual church members might be counted this way.) Anybody who has ever contributed money, or signed a petition sponsored by the group, or written to the organization to ask for information may be counted as a member. The National Wildlife Federation counts school children who receive its environmental magazine for kids as members. (The figures for the group in table 6-8 are for adult members only.) Groups use the most liberal standard in calculating their membership because they want to appear as formidable as possible. It's not clear that this fudging has any practical consequence, however, because legislators have such keen political antennae that they usually have a clear sense of what kinds of groups are important to constituents.

Membership dues are the main source of revenue for the vast majority of citizen groups.[63] Funding can also come from large individual gifts, foundations, corporations, government, and sales of goods (such as books) and services (such as conferences and training institutes). Despite the variety of possible funding sources, it is difficult for a citizen group to prosper over the long run without a significant and relatively stable dues-paying membership. Serious fluctuations in funding cause serious operational problems. Washington is surely the largest small town in America, where everyone in a policy field not only knows the juiciest gossip but knows it in a nanosecond. When the NAACP ran into financial difficulties in 1994, it was a major story in the newspapers.[64] Since a number of competing organizations are usually in the same policy area, a group that is damaged can find that matters easily go from bad to worse. Further

decline may come not so much by migration of members making a strategic decision to go with a competing organization but by the injured
group's lack of funds to search aggressively for new members to replace
the ones that they constantly lose through normal attrition.

Interest group resources are difficult to measure in any meaningful
way. Knowing their overall budgets or staff size is a crude indication of
a group's resources, but such figures can be very misleading. A citizen
group's budget does not reveal how much money is actually available
for political advocacy and what is spent on fundraising. As discussed
earlier, fundraising costs can be an enormous proportion of all expenditures. Staff size is a better indicator for citizen groups since those groups
who rely on direct mail usually use outside consultants for the mailings.
For trade or professional groups, knowing the budget reveals little about
the resources available for political purposes as well. Trade and professional associations spend far less on fundraising than citizen groups, but
they spend much of their budget on membership services having nothing to do with politics. With staff size too, the overall number of staffers
in a trade group is difficult to interpret because many employees will be
working on nonpolitical tasks such as organizing the complex logistics
of the annual trade show. Further complicating matters is that when
trade associations engage in lobbying campaigns, they can draw on the
resources of their member corporations. Corporate executives can be
sent to Washington, assessments can made for special public relations
campaigns, and corporate staffs can provide trade group lobbyists with
data or research reports. Thus, corporations provide a large reserve
account of resources that never show up in a trade group's budget.
Corporations also bolster the trade groups' resources through their own
PAC donations, which can be contributed independently of any contributions made by a trade association.

Given these difficulties with data on budgets and staffs, it is impossi-
ble to make any rigorous comparisons between citizen groups and business trade groups. But one simple point needs to be emphasized: the
large citizen groups have substantial financial resources at their disposal.
The entire environmental movement generated $4 billion in revenues
during 1996. Between 1987 and 1996, donations to environmental groups
increased by 91 percent. All other charitable giving grew by just 67 percent during the same period.[65] For the ten environmental groups that
show up in the 1991 case histories and had their budget listed in the
Encyclopedia of Associations for that year, the average annual budget was

approximately $40 million. Research by Robert Lowry on sixteen national environmental groups offers some insight into how they spend their money. On average they spend just 17 percent on fundraising and recruitment. Their costs for lobbying, other advocacy efforts, and private activities aimed at improving the environment average 43.5 percent. Given the size of their overall budget, this means that the large environmental groups were spending on average upward of $17 million a year in the early 1990s on lobbying and these other endeavors. (The remainder of these groups' budgets went for administration, magazines and other communications to members, and membership services.)[66]

A look at twenty-four liberal citizen groups (not just environmental groups) active on the 1991 issues studied, and for which budgetary information was available, shows that the average annual budget of each group was about $14 million. Twenty-two liberal citizen groups had an average of 132 paid employees. Forty-two business trade groups had an average staff of 120. Of course, many smaller citizen groups lobby in Washington as well and don't have the imposing resources of the larger citizen lobbies like the Sierra Club ($35 million, 300 staffers) or the National Wildlife Federation ($90 million, 800 staffers). Business trade groups also vary greatly in size, ranging from giants like the American Bankers Association ($62 million, 470 staffers) or the American Petroleum Institute ($56 million, 400 staffers), to the National Agricultural Chemicals Association and the National Association of Wholesale Distributors, which had annual budgets in 1991 of about $7 million. Again, this comparison of staffs really does not indicate who has the most resources available for political purposes. These figures do, however, tell us that the leading liberal citizen groups are not reenacting David meeting Goliath when they square off against business groups. As discussed in chapter 4, citizen groups do respectably when they are pitted against business lobbies. The overall financial resources that they have at their disposal may not be the equivalent of what the business coalition that they face has available, but citizen groups are not typically "outgunned" by an opponent with a vastly superior arsenal.

Although the conservative citizen groups have demonstrated that they, too, are capable of raising large sums of money, why have their lobbies failed to show the same staying power as the liberal citizen groups? One of the reasons was discussed in chapter 5: conservative citizen groups appear to be less efficient in their fundraising than liberal groups and more reliant on expensive direct mail prospecting. Beyond that, though, the development of conservative organizations in the strongest area in terms of rank-and-file citizen support for lobbying, specifically family values issues, was hampered first by the dominance of the Moral Majority and then by its collapse. It never developed a grass-roots capacity or much organizational strength at all beyond its fundraising prowess. Falwell pleaded for money through increasingly shrill direct mail, telling recipients of one solicitation, "Moments ago I was told my family and home would be blown up today." Among those threatening his life, he said, were "militant homosexuals" and "communist terrorists."[67] Over time, as revenues diminished, it began to cost Falwell too much to raise funds that way. Falwell also used television to preach and to raise money, and he took on the public persona of a TV evangelist. It wasn't too long after he became a public figure that opinion polls showed him to be very unpopular with the American people. The group's fundraising woes finally forced Falwell to close the Moral Majority in 1989. Coming on the heels of TV evangelist Jim Bakker's sexual and financial scandals, the Moral Majority's problems seemed part of a larger collapse of the marriage between television and evangelical Christianity.[68]

The Moral Majority so dominated the Christian right during the 1980s that it became difficult for other groups to grow and to take a leadership position among conservative citizen groups. The Reagan administration treated Falwell with great respect, and Christian conservatives were seen as a major component of the Republicans' electoral coalition. Even when the Moral Majority went into decline, other Christian right groups like the Eagle Forum and Concerned Women for America were not dynamic or entrepreneurial enough to emerge as a replacement for Falwell's organization. The Reverend Pat Robertson filled the vacuum. The Christian Coalition, which was founded the same year the Moral Majority folded, was consciously designed to avoid Falwell's mistakes. It has been a much more secular organization, symbolized by leaders of the organization who are not preachers (though Roberston has stayed involved in the background). From the beginning it has had a grass-roots orientation and focused some of its efforts on local politics such as school board elections. As a spokesman for the Christian Coalition put it, "We think the Lord is going to give us this nation back one precinct at a time, one neighborhood at a time, and one state at a time."[69] To their credit, Robertson and Ralph Reed built a political organization that draws on the fervor, imagination, and skills of committed Christians and their churches across the country. The Christian Coalition is one of the few conservative citizen groups that has placed a primary emphasis on issues of organizational development beyond immediate fundraising concerns.

If there is a single, critical flaw in the organizational design of conservative citizen groups, it is that too many of them are personal vehicles for the political activism of their founding patron saints. As noted in chapter 5, many of the most prominent conservative citizen groups are headed by leaders who see themselves as Republican strategists and focus their lobbying on working with the party's congressional leadership. Expending resources to build a strong organization with a thick layer of lobbyists and other political operatives may seem superfluous to these leaders when they have such good relations with party leaders. A less charitable interpretation is that they have built their organizations around themselves rather than developing strong organizational entities whose ongoing success will transcend any changes in leadership. An example is Grover Norquist, who founded Americans for Tax Reform in 1985. Norquist is a confidant of former House Speaker Newt Gingrich, and he is fiercely committed to Gingrich's vision of the Republican revolution. Because of his closeness to Gingrich, Norquist became a leader of conservative activists who began to hold strategy sessions at the group's headquarters after the GOP's sweep in the 1994 elections. Yet Norquist did not use his new prominence to build an organization whose political capacities extended much beyond his personal ties to Gingrich. Oddly, he has taken on private clients like Microsoft and Albert René, the Marxist dictator of the Seychelles, for whom he lobbies.[70] Technically, his private lobbying work is carried out through a separate organization, but whatever the mixture of his two roles, Norquist hardly seems to have fashioned an appropriate strategy for building a strong and enduring citizen group.

Paul Weyrich is another case in point. The founder of the Free Congress Foundation and its PAC, the Committee for the Survival of a Free Congress, he launched National Empowerment Television (NET), a cable outlet devoted to promoting his brand of hard-right conservatism. It reaches just 10 percent of all households (few of whom watch it) and has been a $20 million indulgence. Weyrich acknowledges that he took $2 million in funds from the Free Congress Foundation in 1995 alone to keep the cable network afloat.[71] (In November 1997, he was fired by the board of NET.)

These examples demonstrate how little accountability there can be for citizen groups, whether they be from the left or right. This problem is most acute among those organizations still led by a founder who, only in the most symbolic manner, reports to a board of directors or membership assembly. One of the marks of success of the liberal citizen groups that appear in table 6-7 is their successful transition from their founder to their next stage of development and leadership. Common Cause, for example, easily survived John Gardner's retirement, and the organization was subsequently guided over the years by effective leaders like David Cohen and Fred Wertheimer. There is no comprehensive inventory of citizen groups that have failed, and no statistics can be cited on the comparative survival rates of liberal and conservative organizations. Overall, however, the available evidence indicates that the liberals have done a better job of organizational development. They have been more successful in allocating their scarce resources, developing a strong lobbying capacity, raising money over the long haul and raising it at a reasonable cost, and in making the transition from founder to leaders who are employees.

Conservative groups are not without substantial resources. Collectively, they have millions of contributors, and many of these groups are closely tied to the Republican Party, which genuinely values them. The GOP's leadership has been highly accessible to the heads of these groups. Yet in the battle of resources, in terms of media attention, credibility, and organizational strength, the liberal groups win hands down. Indeed, when it comes to this range of resources, the liberal groups are loaded.

Conclusion

Not all important interest group resources have been investigated in this book. PAC donations, which are given in abundance by corporations, labor unions, trade groups, and professional associations, were not included because citizen lobbies, the primary focus of this study, are not usually affiliated with PACs. There is, however, a voluminous literature on PACs, and, clearly, at the very least campaign contributions purchase access to legislators and their staffs.[72] Interest group leaders believe that PAC donations are well worth it because the money is converted into more face time with legislators and key aides, and they think that this interaction increases the chances that these congressional offices will do something on the group's behalf.

Another critical resource that could not be captured by the methods used in this book is the importance that policymakers attach to the business climate and the need to keep America prosperous.[73] As discussed in chapter 4, business leaders always have access to officials in both the legislative and executive branches because business provides the jobs, wages, and dividends that the nation depends on. The greatest resource for business may simply be the belief that America has the most successful economic system invented. Thus, it is government's responsibility to respect its workings—and thus to respect and to listen to those who make it work.

What does the liberal citizen groups' decided advantage over the conservatives in attention, credibility, and organizational strength mean? Does their edge over business in some respects make them as powerful as business? Political scientist James Q. Wilson wisely cautions against equating resources with power: "One cannot *assume* that the disproportionate possession of certain resources (money, organization, status) leads to the disproportionate exercise of political power. Everything depends on whether a resource can be converted into power, and at what rate and at what price. That, in turn, can only be learned by finding out who wins and who loses."[74] If who wins and loses is the standard, then it's clear from earlier chapters that liberal citizen groups have been successful at converting their resources into power. The same is true of business. Conservative citizen groups did not compete enough during the three years studied for a measurement of how well they convert resources into legislative victories.

How is it that the liberal groups' resources are converted into properties that lead to bills being considered by committee, being sent to the floor, and eventually passing Congress? The most significant step in converting resources is to allocate them in such a way as to develop the organizational capacities that will maximize the group's ability to influence public policy. Strategically, the liberal lobbies have made effective choices in organizational development. A large number of the groups have built a strong and steady resource base that has enabled them to maintain themselves while funding large staffs of skilled lobbyists and researchers. This deployment of assets has nurtured policy expertise, neutralizing an advantage long held by business, which provided policymakers data and information that only it possessed. Coupled with the shifting values of the American people, the sustained efforts of these groups contributed to the shift toward postmaterialism in Congress.

CHAPTER SEVEN

Liberalism Transformed

CITIZEN GROUPS HAVE transformed liberalism in America. The center of gravity within the Democratic Party has shifted and citizen groups advocating postmaterialist concerns have become much more powerful than those groups focused on issues pertaining to economic equality. This is not a recent development or a short-term trend. Indeed, a primary reason citizen groups have been so successful is that they have been at it for a good long time. Of the leading environmental groups, the most recently formed is Greenpeace USA, which was started in 1972, more than a quarter of a century ago.

Not all the separate branches of postmaterialism have roots as deep as the environmentalists, though the women's movement and the civil rights movement also have rich and lengthy histories. Still, by the 1990s, virtually all the important liberal citizen groups had already been in existence at least two decades. The initial prosperity enjoyed by the groups begun in the 1960s or early 1970s was not squandered on overexpansion, ill-fated forays into Democratic Party politics, or excessive fundraising endeavors. These newer groups broadened their funding base while building up the political capacities of their organizations.[1] Ideas have power, but ideas are even more powerful when coupled with effective political organization.

Resource Mobilization

The surge of the new groups founded in the 1960s produced a critical mass of liberal citizen groups that, collectively, became a significant force in American politics. The 1960s were, of course, a time of turmoil, and there was little reason to expect that this period of intense political divisions would lead to a large and stable set of citizen groups oriented toward conventional Washington lobbying. As the fervor of the antiwar movement wound down, and American politics began to return to a more normal pattern, it might have been expected that the new environmental and consumer lobbies would begin to lose steam. But the attractive vision of the Ford Foundation's public interest law program, the liberal activists' disillusionment with the Democratic Party, and the movement of government into many new areas of social policy worked in favor of the ongoing development of citizen lobbies.

The broad success of entrepreneurs in organizing the liberal groups may make it seem that it was relatively easy to build these groups before the "market" for them became saturated with competing organizations. When he was forming Common Cause, John Gardner took out full-page ads in leading newspapers and exhorted Americans to join his group so that ordinary citizens would be represented before government. Americans quickly responded to Gardner's request and, with a membership of 230,000 signed up in a little over a year, Common Cause quickly became a player in Washington.[2] Gardner's accomplishment notwithstanding, it is difficult to organize even those citizens who are interested in politics into lobbying groups. Political scientists would not have been optimistic about these groups' chances for long-term success. The dominant scholarly explanation of interest group mobilization—then and now—is Mancur Olson's selective incentive theory of collective action.[3] Olson, using orthodox economic analysis, rejected the line of thinking stretching from Alexis de Tocqueville to Robert Dahl, which argues that people organize when an issue affects them. Olson's great insight was that interest groups exist because they are organized for some reason other than lobbying. For example, a trade group offers members a chance to make connections and do business with others in the same industry. With the money the group receives, however, it is able to use some of those resources to fund its lobbying. The efforts to influence public policy are thus a by-product of these selective incentives for membership. It is not rational for people to join a group for the collective goods it might win in the political arena. If a group wins a tax change beneficial to its members, that benefit also goes to those who are not members.

The typical citizen group has no significant selective incentives to offer members, so they attract members in defiance of this theory.[4] In Olson's mind, those who join such groups are irrational because all they can obtain in return for their membership fees are collective goods. He tells readers that they would be better served by turning to "psychology or social psychology" for an explanation of why these kinds of groups manage to attract members.[5]

Olson's original work was done in the early 1960s, when there were far fewer citizen groups than today. In light of the number of groups that now exist, and the size of their memberships and budgets, it may seem surprising that political science sticks tenaciously to his theory. At the same time, Olson's theory reminds us just how much citizen group leaders must overcome to build successful organizations. Potential members must be convinced that they can't wait for others to take up arms. Rather, individuals must come to believe that they need to join if the organization is going to be able to lobby the government. The only real return most members of citizen groups will get is the ideological satisfaction that they are fighting some injustice.

Citizen group leaders of both the left and the right have been extremely skilled at identifying constituencies that have the potential to be organized and, more important, in fashioning the kinds of appeals that persuade people to join. Beyond that, however, as already discussed, liberal and conservative citizen groups develop into different kinds of organizations, especially in the way they allocate their resources. The liberals have done a far superior job in organizational development. The leaders of these groups have kept their eyes on the prize, focusing their efforts on building large, capable staffs of lobbyists and researchers, public relations specialists, and other professionals.

It is not just the lack of selective incentives or the competition for members from other like-minded groups that makes long-term success for citizen groups problematic. The public policy problems that first lead people to join may dissipate over time or simply become less visible as other issues rise to the surface. There may be no apparent progress in solving the problems that members are concerned about, and over time they may desert the organization.[6]

Yet the liberal citizen lobbies proved adept at solving the organizational maintenance dilemmas that voluntary organizations must face after the initial burst of interest that brings members into the group. With the exception of the antiwar movement, the liberal activism of the social movements of the 1960s was quickly brought under the umbrella of Washington-based lobbies. For all the romantic notions of taking it to the streets, in forcing the system to confront unconventional political participation, the liberal postmaterial groups succeeded precisely because they quickly emerged as well-functioning bureaucracies. The watchword of these organizations was not "power to the people" but "policy expertise." The citizen lobbies were built around the most conventional of political assumptions: information is power.

The mobilization of resources and their conversion into political assets by liberal citizen groups has had a profound effect on the political agenda. The clearest case is in environmental politics. Evaluating the shift toward a political agenda much more concerned with environmental protection, Frank Baumgartner and Bryan Jones found that "whether we study group numbers, staff sizes, or budgets, our conclusions are identical. A massive shift in the mobilization of bias has occurred."[7] As we have seen, this mobilization of resources and shift in attention toward citizen groups extends far beyond environmental politics. Advantages once held exclusively by business must now be shared with citizen lobbies.

It is far easier to analyze the manifestations of a shifting agenda than to pin down the process by which it takes place. Policymakers are attuned to public opinion, and as they sense shifting attitudes they surely become interested in finding ways of addressing their constituents' new concerns. Public opinion, of course, is both a cause and a consequence of citizen group advocacy, but it is difficult to assess its impact on policymaking in the sessions of Congress studied because there are reliable opinion data on only a handful of the issues on the agenda in those three years.

We do know that periodically Congress senses an important change of direction in public attitudes and turns sharply one way or another, passing a lot of legislation that moves the country in a new direction.[8] Most of the time, however, Congress is slow and methodical, and legislators, staffers, and lobbyists work on issues that might not come to fruition for years if at all. Agenda building is a process that rewards expertise, steady accumulation of research, and long-term commitment. These qualities, possessed in abundance by liberal citizen groups, certainly don't guarantee anything for them. They do, however, increase any group's chances that its issues will eventually receive serious consideration. Over time, lobbyists develop relationships with staffers and work with them to develop proposals that have a chance of passage. A group's stability, long-term track record, and reputation for doing good research and running effective lobbying campaigns make it a good "investment" for a congressional office that must allocate its own scarce resources among competing demands from constituents and lobbies. Long-term stability also helps a group gain the confidence of potential coalition partners. Lobbies are hesitant to invest their scarce resources in a joint effort unless they have confidence that the groups they will be working with are highly respected on Capitol Hill.

The liberal lobbies' conversion of their resources into large staffs devoted to lobbying and research has, in turn, helped them to generate two other resources, attention and credibility. Their investment in high-quality research has enhanced their reputation, and the press has given their work ample exposure. The citizen groups with large budgets and stable funding have been able to use staff to work on new issues, which is a luxury for smaller interest groups that must use their limited resources to fight on more immediate concerns actively being considered by Congress or an administrative agency. This long-term horizon helps citizen groups to influence the policymaking agenda.

While liberal citizen groups and business lobbies are rich in resources, labor's resources have declined. Unions still have access to very large sums of money, but their most precious resource, members, has declined sharply. As a percentage of the work force, union membership has dropped to about half of what it was in the 1950s, from about one in three workers to about one in six.[9] Interest group influence has never been strictly a function of the size of members or constituents, but the diminishing size of labor unions has been too visible and too dramatic not to alter the way that politicians view them.

Labor's waning clout was amply illustrated by the analysis of economic equality legislation in chapter 3. Over time the legislative activity aimed at improving wages, working conditions, or job opportunities dwindled and what actually passed shrank as well. Labor's declining membership is the consequence of many factors. The movement toward a service economy is well understood and does not need to elaborated upon. More complicated, perhaps, is the greater reluctance of lower-paid service workers to unionize than their blue-collar counterparts in manufacturing. Conservative critics of unions would argue that labor has simply outlived its relevance. Those touting the virtues of the free market have never been the fairest judges of the labor movement, but in broad terms the affluence of modern America has made it far more difficult for unions. Many workers just do not believe that what unions will gain for them will outweigh dues that must be paid. Finally, more aggressive antiunion efforts by business have also contributed to this trend.[10]

The pressure on wages from increasing international competition, the relentless drive by corporations to produce profits at an ever-increasing rate, the constant threat of downsizing, and the increasing tendency of companies to use part-time employees to reduce the need to pay health insurance and other fringe benefits point toward a continuing need for unions. Conceivably, an imaginative, revamped labor movement might find ways of convincing workers in hard-to-organize industries, professions, and service sectors to join revitalized unions. A more likely scenario, however, is a labor movement that continues to struggle, working hard to keep aggregate membership at current levels.

Not only does labor have trouble gaining attention for its issues in Congress but it fares even worse with journalists. To the degree that journalists reflect society's larger values, the news couldn't be worse for labor. The data on media coverage revealed that for every time labor unions appeared on the network news, citizen groups were on more than ten times. Between 1969 and 1982, the AFL-CIO received the most TV news coverage of any single interest group. The United Auto Workers Union was sixth. Neither was even in the top twenty in 1995. No union—unless one considers the baseball players' union part of the labor movement—made the list in 1995. Union representatives constituted just over 5 percent of all lobbyists quoted in newspaper stories in 1991. Union-supported research was only 1 percent of stories focusing on public policy research, and union officials penned only 1 percent of all the op-eds in the two newspapers monitored. This is understandable for the business-oriented *Wall Street Journal*, but the *New York Times* is a bellwether of American liberalism.

Liberal citizen groups command attention, and they are perceived as highly credible sources of information. In simple terms, people care what citizen groups have to say. The same doesn't appear to be true of labor unions.

Ineffective Mobilization

At virtually every step of the way in this analysis, conservative citizen groups have been found much less active or effective than liberal citizen groups. This conclusion is surprising because many pundits credit conservative citizen groups with playing a critical role in turning the country in a conservative direction. It was my expectation when developing the research design that the third period of the study would confirm that conservative citizen groups were a rising force in legislative policymaking. This did not turn out to be the case. They were active on just two issues in 1991. They did better in the study of legislation in 1995 reported in chapter 5, but their success was still modest and must be considered disappointing given the number of conservative Republicans in the 104th Congress.

Some might regard this book's conclusions as the political science equivalent of an optical illusion. Wasn't the period between 1981 and 1992 one of conservative success in cutting spending and cutting back services? Wasn't it a period of liberal disarray, with GOP candidates Reagan and Bush winning three elections by comfortable margins?

The Reagan and Bush years were, in fact, a time when conservatism did advance. It's important to be clear on what has been argued. The argument is not that conservatism in America was vanquished by liberal citizen groups. What has been argued can be summarized briefly. First, the data indicate unequivocally that conservative *citizen groups* have been generally ineffective in lobbying Congress. What success conservatives have enjoyed in recent years has stemmed largely from other sources. Conservative citizen groups have made a small contribution but only that.

Second, in an era when most people believed that business and the Christian right were ascendant, the liberal postmaterial lobbies had the most success of all interest groups in influencing the congressional agenda. The liberal citizen groups were highly effective not only in agenda building but also in influencing the legislation once Congress took the issues up. These groups enjoy extraordinary media attention and respect. Their success with the media is surely tied to their success in influencing the Congress.

Third, as just discussed, my argument is not that liberalism per se has fared well in an ostensibly conservative period but that one type of liberalism fared well while another faltered badly. Since traditional liberal concerns such as promoting social services, economic equality, and income support for the poor have suffered so grievously at the hands of conservatives in Congress, it is easy to jump to the conclusion that we are living in an era in which conservatives are dominant and liberals are in retreat.

These observations may seem contradictory. How could conservatives in Congress and liberal postmaterial citizen groups do well at the same time? American politics isn't like a fight to the death between two opposing armies, with a victor being crowned only after the other side is routed and the prisoners hanged. Rather, lots of separate battles are going on in different arenas. In a large and complex political system like ours, policy may not move in one consistent unified fashion across all levels and venues.

Not all aspects of public policymaking have been measured in this study. Most important, congressional appropriations were not part of this research. There's no question that conservatives accomplished a great deal in enacting the budget cuts for domestic programs that began in Ronald Reagan's first year in office. The budget deficits that were largely a consequence of the Reagan tax cuts were also a great victory for conservatives because they made it much more difficult for the Democrats to create new programs or increase spending for old ones. Just how much government was truly cut in the Reagan years is a subject of much dispute. But unquestionably budgetary policy favored the conservatives between 1981 and 1998 when the deficit gave way to a surplus. Besides budgetary issues, conservative policy was also furthered by the administrative actions of Reagan and Bush appointees in the bureaucracy. The judges appointed during this twelve-year period were another source of conservative power. In some policy areas a devolution of power from Washington to the states has taken place. Many states, for example, tightened welfare eligibility and put stiff work requirements in place before the major reforms were instituted on the federal level.

In an ideal world of limitless resources for researchers, all of these things could have been measured to paint a complete picture of politics since the 1960s. Still, what has been measured is not a small part of what goes on in national politics. There is nothing more concrete to study than the agenda of Congress if one is to understand political change. And the media coverage of interest groups is an invaluable source of data on societal values.

If both conservatism and liberal postmaterialism have succeeded in many ways in recent years, why haven't conservative citizen groups played the same role as the liberal citizen lobbies? Without going too far afield from the data collected for this study, it seems likely that the leadership of Ronald Reagan, elected in the wake of a disappointing Carter presidency and the inflation-ravaged economy of those years, is the key ingredient in the success of conservatism since 1980. The Republican revival also led to capture of the Senate in 1980, which they held for six years, and in 1994 the party won majorities in both houses. Whatever the objective conditions that led to voter preference for Republican candidates since 1980, the GOP has offered a strong, distinct conservative alternative to the Democrats. The Republican Party, revitalized by Reagan and led rightward by him, has been the leading edge of modern conservatism.

The greatest impact of the conservative citizen groups appears to have come in the electoral arena. In this context, the performance of conservative citizen groups in the 1994 congressional elections is impressive. It is difficult to isolate the impact of the Christian Coalition and other groups on the vote, and it was obviously a Republican year in which GOP candidates would have done well if no conservative citizen groups had been active. Nevertheless, the mobilization of volunteers was carried out on a scale unusual in American national elections. Among interest groups only labor has traditionally been involved in election campaigns at such an extensive level.

Conservative citizen groups have made a concerted effort to try to take over Republican Party organizations, and they have had great success in states like Texas, Minnesota, and Iowa.[11] At recent GOP national conventions conservative citizen groups have grabbed a disproportionate share of press coverage for their zealous efforts to make the party toe the line on abortion.[12] In possibly the Christian right's greatest show of strength in Republican Party politics, the presumptive 1996 nominee, Bob Dole, was forced to publicly retreat on his proposed abortion language for the party platform. Believing that George Bush had been hurt in the 1992 general election by the unyielding stand on abortion in that year's platform, Dole said he wanted a platform plank indicating that the party was committed to "tolerance" of those Republicans who did not favor a constitutional amendment to outlaw abortion. After the explosion of criticism from the Christian right, the Dole forces offered some compromises. Those were rejected too, and since antiabortion forces appeared to be solidly in control of the platform committee, Dole finally had to accept a face-saving gesture to have dissenting views placed in an appendix to the platform.[13] The platform committee's fight over this contentious issue added insult to injury. It helped to push Dole's newly unveiled tax cut proposal, which he planned as the centerpiece of his campaign, off the front page.

It is evident that the Republicans' state and national party organizations are pushed further to the right on abortion and a handful of other social issues than would otherwise be the case without these groups.

There are plenty of examples of candidates supported by these groups who gain the GOP nomination but who can not win the general election because they stand too far to the right. The conservative citizen groups' rejection of Dole's moderate language on abortion, despite his commitment on the basic policy stand itself, flew in the face of the conventional wisdom on winning elections. After the primaries, candidates should move to the middle of the electorate. The antiabortion groups demanded that Dole reaffirm that he was *not* a centrist and thus distance himself from the moderates and independents that he needed to attract to win the election.[14]

Whether the conservative citizen groups continue to be a factor in national elections remains to be seen. At this point in only one election, 1994, was there a clear demonstration of success by these groups. Moreover, their efforts didn't seem to do much for George Bush's reelection campaign or for Dole just two years after their great victory in the off-year elections. The Christian Coalition, the leading force in the mobilization of campaign volunteers, has an uncertain future. With new leaders and shrinking revenues it may not be able to provide the same leadership as it has in the past.

This electoral activity is obviously one way of trying to get the right policies enacted. Obtaining what these groups want is not possible without fervent Republican conservatives in control of Congress and the White House. Electioneering and lobbying are not mutually exclusive strategies, however, and what success a handful of citizen groups have had in helping conservative Republicans get elected to Congress has not been matched by success in legislative policymaking. Conservative citizen groups have attempted to sway Congress to move toward adoption of the policies they favor by lobbying the public with public relations, direct mail, and grass-roots letter writing campaigns. In the abstract, this strategy could be very effective. By first electing the right kind of people to Congress (Republican social conservatives), and then by getting the public worked up about key issues, policy goals could be achieved. Yet if this is the grand plan of conservative citizen lobbies, it has been a failure. Citizen group leaders place the blame squarely on the shoulders of Republican office holders, and some recognize all too well how little they have gotten in return for their staunch support of the GOP. Says Gary Bauer of the Family Research Council, "There is virtually nothing to show for an 18-year commitment."[15] "Nothing" may be a bit strong, but Bauer understands how poorly conservative citizen groups have done.

The problem, as outlined in chapter 5, is that public relations campaigns are very expensive and few of the conservative groups have enough operating capital to conduct an extensive effort. Paid advertising is an especially inefficient interest group tactic. Direct mail has more potential, but it is really used by conservative groups to raise money rather than to activate the grass roots. Working to stimulate media coverage can be effective too, though the conservative groups are not nearly as proficient at this task as are the liberal lobbies. Letter-writing campaigns are a reliable interest group tool and are used frequently by all types of membership groups, including citizen groups of the left and the right. The weakness of the conservative groups' direct Capitol Hill lobbying, however, renders the letter writing less effective.

Although many conservative citizen groups exist at the national level, not that many of them have substantial resources available after fundraising costs, a long-term, stable history, and a strong organizational presence with a cadre of lobbyists and researchers. The National Rifle Association, the National Right to Life Committee, and a small number of other organizations fit these criteria. For all the millions of dollars raised by groups on the right, they don't get a lot of bang for the buck. These groups need leaders who are more interested in organizational development and less interested in having the organization built around them; more interested in allocating resources for lobbyists, researchers, and organizers, and less interested in trying to solidify their own personal relationship with the Republican leadership; more interested in developing real grass-roots organizations instead of looking at members merely as donors and occasional letter writers; and more interested in working on the nuts and bolts of legislation and less interested in making sweeping recommendations about policy and hoping that the rest of the country will follow.

A Postmaterialist Future

At the beginning of the 88th Congress in 1963, Democratic Party leaders and committee chairs looked forward to a session that would be devoted to policies aimed at stimulating the economy, fine-tuning commodity support programs for farmers, and improving wages and working conditions for America's laborers. These were the type of economic issues that Congress always dealt with. Between the reauthorizations that came up, and new demands from businesss, farm, and labor groups, there was always a full agenda of material issues for Congress to chew over.

As for quality-of-life issues in the 88th Congress, a cluster of environmental bills were taken up and some of them, such as the Water Pollution Control Act Amendments and the National Wilderness Preservation Act, were significant. The most important bill of the session would turn out to be the Civil Rights Act, which President Johnson would sign into law in July of 1964. The environmental bills and the civil rights proposal were harbingers of what was to come for Congress. Increasingly, more legislation devoted to environmental protection and proposals to establish and define the rights of various groups in the population would take front and center stage in Congress. In 1963 bills with a postmaterial side constituted just one-third of all the significant legislation that came before Congress. By 1979 postmaterial issues were a little more than half, and by 1991, they had grown to fully two-thirds of the congressional agenda.

Enduring Values

With only three data points in the analysis of the congressional agenda, there is no way of knowing for sure that the growth of postmaterialism was gradual and steady or if it followed an erratic pattern. As noted in chapter 1, the three sessions of Congress examined in this study do not appear to be unusual in any significant way. It seems highly unlikely that the growth of postmaterialism took a shifting, unpredictable course. It is hard to think of any sessions of Congress since the 88th in which a decided movement away from postmaterialist concerns occurred. Even the first session of the business-oriented 97th (1981) produced a strong backlash against the antienvironmental agenda of the Reagan administration. As already discussed, the Republicans seized control of the initiative in the 104th Congress, but the liberal postmaterialists joined the battle, and they did well in protecting the laws and programs they valued.

Polling data show a direct link between the rise in postmaterialist values in the United States and generational replacement.[16] People who came of age in recent decades have experienced relatively secure times and have grown up in a culture in which the desire for economic advancement competes with many attractive nonmaterial values. These new entrants in the political system replace older citizens who have known hard times and even the perils of war.

The issues that have brought people into citizen lobbies have proved highly enduring. Environmental protection, minority rights, the status of women, Christian family values, and consumer affairs have become hardy perennials of American politics. Although the specifics change from Congress to Congress, and some issues even get resolved or die—the Equal Rights Amendment, for example—the broader concerns remain persistent fault lines in American politics. Organizations promoting postmaterialist concerns will continue to attract large numbers of members because people will continue to search for meaning in their lives. Drawing on Abraham Maslow, Ronald Inglehart makes a compelling argument that in affluent, modern societies, people will search for ways to make their lives more fulfilling. For some individuals, work and professional advancement may be enough. For most individuals, though, there needs to be more to life than their jobs or family. It is our fundamental nature, whether we are religious or not, to ask why we are on this earth and what our obligations as citizens are. However we articulate these questions, we try to find answers that will allow us to believe that we give as well as take from our neighborhoods, communities, and nation. This search can lead down an endless number of paths. Some are nonpolitical—collecting for the cancer society, volunteering at the elementary school library—but other paths lead to efforts to influence public policy. Changes in policy can improve our lives and the lives of others, and working toward that goal can make us feel that we are doing something purposeful, something personally enriching.

When people ask, "How do I help influence policy on this issue which I think is so important?" the answer for millions of Americans has been joining a citizen group. Ironically, the enormous popularity of these groups comes when Americans are said to be increasingly disengaged from civic activities. Harvard political scientist Robert Putnam hit the rawest of societal nerves when he said that more and more, Americans are choosing to bowl alone.[17] His evocative image of the decline of community in America ignited extensive debate, and although his evidence has been disputed by some, Americans do feel that they live in a society in which people are less involved in civic affairs than they once were.[18]

Membership in national-level citizen groups has not figured prominently in this debate, though there is good reason to look at these organizations as their fortunes over time are a mirror of changing interests and values.[19] A primary reason why social scientists have discounted the growth of national citizen lobbies in their critiques of American democracy is that there is a strong tradition in political theory that values participatory democracy over representative democracy. To the most feasible degree possible, we should engage in face-to-face democracy, working with our neighbors to govern ourselves rather than relying on elected representatives to make decisions on our behalf.[20] Face-to-face participation will make us better citizens, educating us about our communities and teaching us to be tolerant and cooperative. These benefits from participation do not just come from what is overtly political but from all types of cooperative civic activity in which the goal is to make the neighborhood or city a better place to live. In this sense, declining community participation represents more than loss of interest in civic affairs; it also reflects a weakening of the very foundation of democratic politics.

Another reason the growing mobilization of people by national citizen groups has received little attention in this debate over the health of American democracy is because membership in one of these groups is seen as almost incidental in comparison to more demanding forms of participation. After all, one's participation in a national interest group might not require more than a few minutes a year—the time it takes to write a check for one's annual dues. In Benjamin Barber's terms, such participation is characteristic of "thin" democracy rather than "strong" democracy.[21] Thus, we must ask, does membership in one of these organizations truly make people's lives more meaningful, more enriching?

By itself, joining one of these groups is a modest form of participation and is certainly limited in the impact it has on people's sense of wellbeing. People who join these groups, however, are likely to participate in other ways in the political process. For an individual joining the National Organization for Women, there is no requirement that she do anything more than pay her annual dues. That same individual, however, may be part of a group that meets regularly to discuss issues pertaining to women in their profession, may also donate to EMILY's List, may work for an occasional woman running for office, may only vote for pro-choice candidates, and may sometimes respond to communications from NOW asking her to write to her members of Congress. As part of this larger array of feminist activism, membership in NOW is no trivial act—it's part of a larger political identity.

Although these organizations may not be building blocks of a participatory democracy, they should not be quickly dismissed as manifestations of thin democracy. In their own ways, they serve as a means by which we search for community. National groups don't offer the same sense of community one receives from directly participating in face-to-face group activities at the local level, but when we identify with a cause, we also identify with the people who join the same group. Even if we are not personally acquainted with other people in these national groups, we believe we know the type of people who join such an organization, and it is with those people that we want to try to turn government in the right direction.

The greatest virtue of these groups is that they *represent* us in the political process. With the criticism that is heaped on these groups for not being participatory, for pursuing the narrow interests of their members, for weakening the political parties, for exaggerating the problems we face, for offering simple solutions to complex problems, and for a thousand other alleged sins, this simple and obvious point is often overlooked: these groups speak for us in national politics. We can't be in Washington ourselves. We can't call press conferences, issue policy statements, coalesce with other interest groups, meet with committee staffers, testify at hearings, or lobby senators.

As attractive as the model of democracy idealized by de Tocqueville (and espoused by Putnam) is, the reality is that most governing in America is done by representatives who act on citizens' behalf rather than by participatory institutions. Although our active participation in local communities can make our neighborhoods more vibrant and our cities more democratic, some issues must be fought on the national level. When we think of representatives in national politics, it is usually in the context of members of Congress and the role they play in working on behalf of their constituents. But representation in the political process takes many forms, and theorists have cast a wide net in analyzing how representation is transacted.[22] The representation that is carried out by interest groups on our behalf is more than a minor complement to what we receive from our members of Congress. Our own members of Congress may, in fact, stand in diametric opposition to what we believe in. Interest groups are a vehicle for articulating what we care the most intensely about. Citizen groups, with their ideological zeal and strong issue focus, offer members a loud, passionate, and aggressive voice in Washington politics.

Postmaterialist Parties

Interest groups are one voice, political parties are another. As noted, postmaterialist politics have had a strong influence on the two major political parties. The pressure from both public opinion and citizen groups has pushed candidates to talk more about these issues, and many races are fought around competing stands on abortion, the environment, and family values.[23] The parties have been influenced differently by postmaterialist politics, though each has been affected significantly.

Generally, the Christian right has coexisted peacefully with the economic conservatives who have been the traditional backbone of the GOP. The conservative postmaterialist groups are not hostile to business, and no sustained friction has occurred between lobbies representing business and those representing Christian social conservatives. There have been some conflicts, though, such as strong opposition by business lobbies to the movement backed by the Christian right to institute economic sanctions against countries that permit religious persecution. More problematic is tension between Christian conservatives and the moderate wing of the Republican Party. The antiabortion, Christian fundamentalist outlook of these postmaterialist lobbies has often come into conflict with the views of Republican office holders who are more moderate on social policy. These Republicans also worry that the Christian right makes the party less appealing at election time to independent, moderate voters.

For the Democrats, conflict has emerged because the postmaterialism of liberal citizen groups does not fit benignly alongside of the party's traditional base of support. In comparison to the moderates in the GOP, material interests form a much larger constituency within the Democratic Party. Most important, the Democrats' traditional constituency includes those at the bottom rungs of the economic ladder. This is the constituency most underrepresented by lobbying groups and thus the most dependent on vigorous representation by a political party.

It would be unfair to say that the Democrats have abandoned these constituencies, but there is no doubt that they've become less important to the party. The conservative welfare reform bill signed by President Clinton in 1996, with its restrictive limits on the time people can receive benefits, was a watershed in the history of the Democratic Party. Symbolically, it seemingly marked an end to the party's commitment, begun during the New Deal, to provide income support for all those who cannot provide for themselves. For organized labor, the North American Free Trade Agreement was a shocking transgression by the administration. Labor was bitterly opposed to NAFTA because it saw a net loss of jobs to our trading partners, and when President Clinton committed all the resources of his administration to getting it passed, it seemed as though the Democratic Party was telling unions that it no longer needed them.

Many saw an administration that was lurching to the right in a desperate attempt by Clinton to shed the liberal label before the 1996 election. Others saw not so much Clinton, but the evil hand of Dick Morris, the president's Machiavellian political adviser who wanted to steal all the Republicans' issues. The *New Yorker*, angry at the president for turning his back on liberal principles, denounced him for taking "a hard right turn."[24]

There is no shortage of confusion about what the modern Democratic Party stands for or where it is headed, but it would be wrong to describe Clinton as a secret conservative.[25] Rather, Clinton will be recorded as the first postmaterialist president. Often accused of not having any firm principles, Clinton turned out to be steadfast in his support of civil rights, women's rights, environmental protection, education, and consumer protection. These are postmaterial concerns, which have taken center stage in legislative policymaking. When Clinton abandoned traditional liberalism on bills like welfare reform and NAFTA, he turned away from the party's material interests.[26] The previous Democratic president, Jimmy Carter, would have never signed the welfare bill, and he felt indebted to labor for the help some unions gave him in his race for the Democratic nomination in 1976. But Clinton saw the fork in the road.

Although Clinton pursued his postmaterialist agenda, it was an agenda that congressional Democrats had already adopted. The Democratic leadership of Congress professes support for both strands of liberalism, but the postmaterial agenda has emerged as dominant. The bottom line for the working class, the working poor, and the nonworking poor is that they are the losers in the transformation of the Democratic Party.

Earlier we found that it is not so much that postmaterial groups have worked against those Democratic Party constituencies concerned about issues of economic equality as that they have ignored them. There does not seem to be much common ground where both sets of liberals can work together. Hostility has come from the Republicans, and their attacks (and stereotyping) of people on welfare have raised the costs to Democrats who want the party to do more work on behalf of those who need the help of government. The poor have the worst of both political worlds—they are despised by the Republicans and have been devalued by the Democrats.

Although the values underlying the rise of postmaterialism will endure, how these values are manifested in the party politics of the future is less certain. The relationship between postmaterial and material interests within each of the parties could be altered by a variety of factors. A pro-choice Republican who wins the party's presidential nomination would spark a firestorm within the GOP. A prolonged economic downturn could weaken environmentalists within the Democratic coalition. In some fashion, though, postmaterialist interests will remain an important part of party politics.

The rise of postmaterialism has generated change in American politics. In a system often criticized for being static, and for serving the same large economic interests, the postmaterialist citizen groups have fundamentally changed the nation's political agenda. As noted in chapter 2 some students of social movements see these groups' participation as dependent on a sympathetic regime willing to tolerate their demands.[27] Yet the citizen groups studied have flourished regardless of who has controlled the White House or Congress. These are social movements all grown up. Citizen groups participate in the governmental process not because government has been eager for these organizations to be involved but because they mobilized millions of Americans whose values lean in a postmaterialist direction. These groups represent large constituencies, and their success is the mark of a system that is open, democratic, and responsive to its citizens.

Methodology

MANY OF THE important decisions about the methodology for this study are described in chapter 1. I expand on those decisions and offer additional information in this appendix for those who want to know more of the specifics about the research design, data collection, and coding used in this study. One item raised in chapter 1 but only mentioned in passing was the choice to study domestic social and domestic economic issues while excluding appropriations, oversight hearings, nominations, and foreign and defense policy. Also excluded were hearings before joint committees, special (select) committees, the Rules Committee in the House of Representatives, and the District of Columbia committees.

The reasons for inclusion and exclusion were driven largely by pragmatism rather than theory. The primary research for this study—the case histories of legislation—was labor intensive. At the outset it was anticipated that when the primary research was brought to an end, the number of completed case studies would be in the neighborhood of 200 to 225. Given the limits to analysis with this size "n" it was not desirable to have a highly diverse set of bills or other legislative actions. To maximize the chances that meaningful statistical analysis could be conducted, some limits had to be placed on the diversity of what was studied. The expectation was that foreign and defense policy would be characterized by a considerably different mix of material and postmaterial concerns. I also assumed that citizen groups as a whole are not as active on foreign and defense policy. For those reasons, the decision was made to exclude those areas. I hope that future scholarship will determine if citizen group advocacy is, in fact, significantly different in foreign and defense policy.

Beyond the constraints imposed by the number of cases in the data base, there were further limitations on what could be included. For the other types of legislative actions—appropriations, oversight, and hearings on nominations—the additional problem arose of finding an adequate record of what went on. Only the most controversial hearings in these areas receive much press coverage. Whereas the press covers many mundane authorizations, the same cannot be said of these other legislative activities.

By concentrating the available resources on domestic social and domestic economic issues (including foreign trade), it was possible to fully develop a data set for three separate years of congressional policy-making. A preliminary examination was done for 100 percent of the eligible Congressional Information Service's hearings index entries for 1963 and 1979 and for more than 99 percent in 1991. Although it was not known at the time that the study would end up sampling the universe of congressional hearings on the domestic side, it was anticipated at the outset that a large share of each of the three yearly agendas would be included. The goal was to get a picture of what the agenda of Congress looks like in a given year.

A legitimate question can be raised about what might be missing or how it might be misleading to focus on hearings as the unit of analysis. What of those issues that don't receive hearings? Some bills proceed to the floor without a hearing, but they surely represent a small percentage of those issues usually considered politically significant. Hearings are difficult to bypass because of committee prerogatives and because committee deliberations are an efficient way of resolving disagreements within and among parties. Clearly, the more controversial a proposal, the more likely it is to receive a hearing. But what of issues that are routine and noncontroversial? If one read through the narratives and coding sheets of all 205 cases, one would quickly come to the conclusion that many of the issues were fairly routine and that there was a great range among all of them in the degrees of controversy and salience. The completed case studies were divided into two levels of press coverage. The less covered issues, unsurprisingly, turned out to be less significant policy matters. The hearings excluded from the research (those with no substantive press coverage) also appeared to be the least consequential of the policy proposals brought before committees.

Both House and Senate hearings are used, but for each legislative proposal only one or the other is included. If, for example, an economic development issue before a Senate committee in one of the years was successfully researched, any House hearings on the same economic development proposal would not be included as a separate case study. Data collection that is specific to the hearings would only come from the Senate hearings. A handful of completed cases were subsequently thrown out because it was decided that some House and Senate bills, which were ostensibly on different legislation, were too closely related to be considered distinct. If there were hearings on the same proposal in both houses, the first hearing drawn—if successfully researched—was included and the other hearing put aside. House and Senate hearings had an equal chance of coming up first in the selection procedure, and hearings that took place at the beginning of the legislative year had no more chance of being drawn first than those held in the later part of the year. (Appendix B contains the full list of hearings used in the study.) Data derived from the press coverage were collected for only the calendar year the hearing was held in, though we did follow what happened to legislation still unresolved by year's end by tracking its outcome in the subsequent year through coverage in *Congressional Quarterly Weekly Report*.

Hearings are used rather than bills introduced for a number of reasons. Most important, it is simply not practical to try to examine a sample of the thousands of bills introduced into Congress each year. A large proportion are relatively trivial private bills, and there is little hope of uncovering information in the press or through congressional documents on them. Hearings have the advantage of being an unambiguous indicator that a policy proposal has reached the agenda of Congress.

To meet the minimal threshold to be included in the study, at least two articles had to appear in *CQ*, the *New York Times*, or the *Wall Street Journal*. These articles had to appear in at least two different points in time. Thus, articles in two of the sources on the same event (such as the hearing or a vote) would only count as one article. The cases have frequently been referred to as narrative case histories. An effort was made to develop the story of what happened to each bill that came before a committee for a hearing. However, data collection followed a set of specific questions to be answered about the participating interest groups, the coalitions that formed, the press coverage of the lobbies, subsidiary issues that became important, who won and who lost, and other matters. For a case to be included in the high-salience subset, the press coverage, whatever the number of articles, had to contain sufficient information so that all the questions in the full coding sheets could be answered. The legislative case histories for the high-salience issues were typically built around a considerable number of articles from these sources. Most of the statistical analysis in the text uses only this set of full case histories.

Three different sessions of Congress were used so the investigation could track change over time. An alternative was some form of time series analysis in which rather than using hearings from this limited number of sessions, each session of Congress between 1963 and 1991 would be sampled and a small number of hearings for every year would be placed into the data base. Using appropriate statistical techniques, changes over time could be measured along the same set of variables used in the three session method.[1] Using all the years in the time frame eliminates the problems that can stem from picking specific years to study. Relying on only three years out of a period of close to thirty certainly presents some risks. If only one of those years is anomalous, true trend lines will be confounded. Another possibility is that there could be three or four basic prototypes of sessions of Congress. By the luck of the draw, I could have gotten three sessions that were all of one kind or a mix that included no years representative of one particular type. Although using sessions that were the third year of first-term presidencies and sessions that took place under Democratic Party control provides some commonality, it did not eliminate these risks.

In thinking about this problem during the research design phase, I specified some commonsense criteria providing guideposts on whether sessions of Congress stand apart from the norm. As noted in chapter 1, the first is determining if there was unusual movement away from basic, ongoing policy orientations. For 1963, 1979, and 1991, there was no broad-scale movement in Congress toward a new policy direction. Second is the question of whether there was an unusual election preceding the session. Clearly, this was not the case for the three years.

Third, were there unusual outside events that could have broadly influenced Congress across a range of issues? There are always events and trends that Congress takes note of, but it seems unlikely that the results were seriously biased by Congress's external environment those years. The assassination of President Kennedy surely influenced passage of the Civil Rights Act, which was held up as a tribute to the slain president. Conceivably, it could have had some impact on the passage rate of legislation in 1964 (the only one of the variables that could have been influenced since all the other data pertain just to 1963). The rate of passage of the bills in the 1963 data set was not unusually high, but it is possible that it would have been lower if Kennedy had not been killed.

Another possibility was that concern about high inflation and continuing energy supply problems in 1979 strongly shaped the agenda that year. A review of all the 1979 cases indicates that certainly more hearings were related to energy than is normally the case. At the same time, there are some economic problems that are almost always troubling to Congress, and the level of attention to the economy was not unusual in 1979. In terms of the material-postmaterial framework used, the external environment created pressures on Congress in both directions. On the one hand, legislators surely felt pressure from business and consumers to formulate policies that would lead to the development of more energy. On the other hand, pressure came from environmentalists to "produce" more energy through conservation. This is not to say that everything evened out in the end but rather to suggest that the degree and type of conflict between material and postmaterial interests in the 96th Congress did not seem atypical. There may be other criteria that one could apply, but in studying the issues from these three years, there was simply no strong evidence to indicate that these sessions of Congress were unusual in comparison to the sessions around them.

The greatest advantage of using the three years is that the entire universe of domestic social and domestic economic issues that warranted coverage by the press could be included. Thus, there is no sampling error. In comparison, a time series analysis using the entire time period would have been able to include only a small number of hearings from each year. In turn, the sampling error for each year would have been large. Aggregated into an overall sample equal to the same number of cases used here, the error term would be smaller but would still be a concern.

For this study, being able to use a data set with the entire domestic agenda of individual years had the principal advantage of facilitating analysis of the interest group population. Since a primary focus was the participation of lobbies in the legislative process, using entire sessions allowed for measurement of interest group activity across a relatively comprehensive set of possible legislative targets. Resources for any one group are limited, and from these three sessions of Congress it was possible to learn which lobbies were most extensively involved in the legislative process. The use of complete years turned out to be critical in determining that the conservative citizen groups were relatively inactive in legislative lobbying. If a small number of issues from each session had been sampled, a plausible interpretation would have been that low rates of participation by the groups simply reflected a random draw of hearings that failed to come up with the issues that constituted priorities for these groups.

A critical assumption was that 1963 would serve as an adequate baseline for measuring change in interest group politics. Since concern about interest groups in America can be traced back at least as far as the *Federalist* (1787–88), it may seem somewhat capricious to choose this particular year as a starting point. A broader concern is that the trend line for quantitative data can often be manipulated by choosing a particular year as the first point on the graph.

The hypotheses I generated about the rise of liberal and conservative groups were not conceived of in relation to what might have happened in any particular year. If the trends I envisioned did take place, the results would have emerged at the later data points because there was sufficient time for such developments to materialize. Still, since there would surely be some citizen group advocacy at any time chosen as the first data point, the decision on how far back to go could have influenced the degree of growth that we measured at the subsequent intervals. The decision to begin with 1963, however, was far from arbitrary. To maximize the comparability of the data, whatever years were to be selected, roughly equivalent intervals were desirable. At the same time, the decision to make each data point the third year of a first-term president restricted the choice. Since the research commenced just after President Clinton took office, the last data point could be no later than 1991 (the third year of Bush's single term in office).

Even if it had been decided that it would have been useful to go back further in time, either to include a fourth data point or to begin at an earlier starting point, it would not have been possible with the methodology used. A trial run for 1961 (using a somewhat different methodology) demonstrated that the available historical resources were insufficiently comprehensive to provide what was needed. When 1963 was considered, sources proved adequate (in particular, an evolving *Congressional Quarterly Weekly Report* was more helpful for the study's purposes).

The main questions asked in this research concerned the nature of the congressional agenda and the participation of interest groups on the most important domestic issues of the day. There are certainly other ways that the agenda of Congress could be measured, but the method used captured the agenda at that stage of the legislative process (hearings) in which proposals were being taken seriously. This is the position taken by George Edwards and his colleagues in their study of legislative gridlock: "If a committee or subcommittee in at least one house of Congress held hearings on the bill, we counted it as seriously considered."[2] This is also a stage at which there is still no assurance that anything more will happen. Interest groups and their legislative allies can be successful in getting their proposals heard but could be stymied from going any further by opposition. Consequently, this method of delimiting the agenda tells us about success in getting Congress to pay attention but presupposes nothing about any subsequent movement toward passage.

The single greatest shortcoming with this research design is that it does not enable us to understand what didn't make it on to the congressional agenda. As pointed out in chapter 1, this is a significant methodological problem that political scientists have yet to solve. What doesn't get to the formal agenda stage of congressional hearings is not a complete mystery.[3] Interviewing lobbyists, legislators, and congressional staffers could certainly yield a list of problems that they had done some work on. The problems that they had yet to make any progress on could then be distinguished. For the purposes of this study, though, research to document efforts to push proposals forward that did not succeed would be difficult to do retrospectively. It would also be difficult to do on a sizable number of cases since there are no easily accessible data that provide an explanation.

It was possible, however, to take legislation that had gained a spot on the agenda by 1991 and examine its history in an effort to identify what forces initiated it. This was no simple process, and the research on each issue was extensive. Trial efforts proved that the approach used to monitor the legislation in the three years studied was less effective when directed at tracing legislation back in time. The newspapers were of limited use; coverage in the two papers used tends not to commence until an issue comes front and center in Congress. *Congressional Quarterly Weekly Report* was, of course, instrumental in researching the legislation back in time, as were congressional hearings, which could extend over a number of years on the same basic policy proposal. For legislation that moved beyond the hearings stage, the legislative reports published by committees were helpful. For bills that reached the floor the *Congressional Record* helped, but floor debate usually revealed little about interest group participation.

The critical decision in working back through time was the determination of what qualified as an appropriate antecedent to the 1991 legislation. The coding rules that were established did not require that previous proposals be the same legislation as the 1991 bills. This standard would have been far too strict. Instead, the requirement was that such legislation deal with the same general issue. This guideline worked well, though in some instances a 1991 issue may first have appeared as a subsidiary part of a somewhat different issue and thus was missed at that particular stage. In such cases the data would show a proposal emerging at the session of Congress in which it first evolved as a discrete and primary issue. There is no pretense of having traced any piece of legislation in 1991 back to the point at which the *idea* behind the legislation first took hold in Congress. As John Kingdon points out, "An idea doesn't start with the proximate source. It has a history. When one starts to trace the history of a proposal or concern back through time, there is no logical place to stop the process."[4]

The purpose of the historical research on the 1991 bills was to determine if citizen groups were working at earlier stages to initiate the proposals eventually taken up in 1991 rather than opportunistically seizing issues already moving forward. As explained in chapter 4, it could be true that for strategic reasons the liberal postmaterial groups became active on legislation only because they realized that it was going to come forward because of pressure from business or labor. Knowing that the time was ripe for such bills, these liberal lobbies might have taken the initiative and worked with their friends chairing the appropriate committees so that the legislation considered would be framed around quality-of-life concerns. Yet no pattern of this kind of strategic behavior was uncovered. As with the legislation for the three years in the primary data base, there is no assumption that only interest groups were responsible for initiating bills. Legislators are partners in this enterprise. Groups pushing the legislation at any one stage in each proposal's history could be identified through the sources used, and this facilitated the judgments made in chapter 4.

Identifying which groups participated was important information, but the focus was on determining which lobbies were the leading advocates and making the greatest effort to move the legislation forward at the earliest stages in each bill's history. On occasion, the legislative reports would credit a particular group or groups with bringing the issue to the committee's attention. More commonly, a pattern was uncovered in *CQ's* coverage and in the hearings. That is, certain groups over the years were not only there at the beginning but remained highly active on the legislation over time. Discussion of groups in *CQ*, sponsorship of rallies or advertising campaigns, the time allowed and position accorded to groups testifying at the hearings, and the sheer persistence of groups were all factors that contributed to the decisions about which groups were most important in agenda building.

In doing research both on the issues before committees in 1963, 1979, and 1991, and on the antecedents for the 1991 set, the hearings transcripts provided one record of interest group participation. In chapter 2 the summary statistics for groups testifying before committees were offered as evidence of interest group involvement on the issues before the committees in the three years studied. Some may wonder which groups might not testify at hearings but would be otherwise active in the legislative process. As noted in the text one survey showed that 99 percent of interest groups participate in congressional hearings, so it would appear that the answer is not many.[5] Yet that does not mean that lists of those who testify are not biased in favor of some types of groups and against others. The witness list is influenced by the committee's composition and is especially sensitive to the goals of the legislation's sponsors in the majority party.

The data on interest groups derived from the hearings transcripts were supplemented by coverage of lobbies in press accounts. This approach draws on journalists' firsthand knowledge of each issue. The press accounts are less comprehensive than the published hearings, but they have the virtue of selecting out those groups judged the most important. But does the journalists' choice of which groups to mention, which lobbyists to quote, and which groups' research to highlight constitute some type of bias? By selecting out groups that they thought most important, were reporters conferring status on those groups which for one reason or another, they found most interesting, most colorful, or that they personally felt most comfortable with? Finally, were they rewarding those groups who were most aggressive in seeking them out?

There is no way of telling if the reporters' collective judgments biased the results reported in chapters 2 and 6. And it is not only the reporters' personal bias that may be a problem. It would be naive to think that newspaper companies do not have points of view that can seep into their news coverage. Where would Richard Nixon's career have gone without the enthusiastic and highly biased coverage of the *Los Angeles Times*?[6] In thinking about what kinds of bias, if any, might be present, the two sources of data—the 205 issues before Congress and the 1995 media coverage of citizen groups—must be considered separately. For the issues that came before congressional committees in 1963, 1979, and 1991, there is ample reason to believe that the data on which groups were cited or whose representatives were quoted are not seriously flawed by journalistic bias. Although a primary intent of using *CQ Weekly Report,* the *New York Times,* and the *Wall Street Journal* was to create some balance and diversity in the coverage, the three publications were not strikingly different in whom they covered. *CQ,* which is widely respected because of its objectivity, was the greatest source of information among the three, while the *Wall Street Journal* provided the least coverage. The trend toward coverage of liberal citizen groups was found in all three publications. That this source of data, and the data on participation in the hearings, shows essentially the same patterns allows for greater confidence in the trends they demonstrate.

The data on research conducted by interest groups and given coverage by the *New York Times* and the *Wall Street Journal* and the frequencies of op-ed appearances in the same two papers reflect different kinds of editorial judgments. For purposes of this study op-ed pieces were defined as those appearing on the editorial page (*Wall Street Journal*) or opposite editorial page (*New York Times*). As mentioned in a footnote accompanying the appropriate text, any guest editorials appearing in other parts of the paper were not included. Anything written by columnists or by regular contributors and appearing on the same page as other op-eds was excluded. Humor, reminiscences, poetry, and short sidebars to an op-ed were also ignored.

Since op-ed pieces are editorials, the question is not so much whether there is a bias but its degree and direction. The *Wall Street Journal* uses its editorial page almost exclusively to publicize the conservative causes it backs. Rare was the op-ed by a representative of a liberal lobby. The *New York Times* is less doctrinaire, and its op-eds presented more of a kaleidoscope of political views.[7] What's important is not how representative these papers are of other papers' op-eds—most other papers rely on syndicated columnists rather than original op-eds—but that these two papers and the *Washington Post* are the most widely read papers by Washington policymakers. It is for that reason that these guest editorials are of interest.

Determining what kind of biases might characterize the selection of stories on policy-related research that appears in the *Times* and the *Wall Street Journal* is difficult. Because only 5 percent of all such articles features the work published by conservative citizen lobbies, a bias of sorts against these conservative organizations may seem self-evident. As discussed in chapter 6, however, it seems likely that this disparity largely reflects the lack of production of truly original scholarship by conservative organizations. This impression remains to be verified empirically.

The method of reviewing these two papers for articles featuring research by citizen groups was certainly less precise than the other media-related data collection. In reading these papers during 1995, I consciously looked for articles that might be discussing policy-relevant research. There had to be some hint in the headline. Headlines did not, however, have to explicitly mention "research" or "report" or "new findings" or some such term, though that was often the case.

Periodic government reports, such as the release of the monthly unemployment figures, were excluded. Also disqualified were articles on basic medical research, though articles on the health care industry or on health care policy were included. For a research report mentioned in an article to qualify, its content needed to be described in such a way that there was an obvious link to public policy questions. The research reported on did not have to have any immediate relevance to a bill before Congress or some other imminent policy decision. Interest groups commonly conduct research with an eye toward influencing the political agenda, so it was important to include reports that might not influence the current Congress, but a Congress down the road. If a report did not deal with an issue currently on the front burner of government, the following question was posed: "Does this report offer information that would be useful to policymakers if and when they do take up the related policy question?" If the answer was yes, the case was included.

Certainly some research reports discussed in articles were missed. Using a search engine in a computerized data base might seem to be a way of solving this problem. Difficulties would arise, however, in fashioning a succinct set of key words to yield the kind of data desired without also producing an excessive amount of other material. Although it is conceptually clear to political scientists what an "interest group" is, newspaper articles use a wide variety of labels to describe the diverse organizations that lobby the government. The data ultimately reported on research are hardly the final word, but the strong patterns uncovered are in line with other findings in this study.

The final piece of the media research was the analysis of the nightly news on television. For a story on one of the network newscasts to be included, there had to be a group context. A businessman complaining about interest rates is not a group. Both references to specific interest groups and to interest group sectors were included. That is, I coded stories not only about Ford or General Motors but also stories in which the reference from the correspondent was to automobile manufacturers (or farmers, seniors, insurance companies, and so on). The reason for this decision was that news stories are so brief and cover so much territory with so few words that much of what TV news does to cover the conflict of competing interests before government would be lost if coding were restricted to stories in which proper organizational names are mentioned. What is important, of course, is not what organizational name is mentioned but that some interest group sector's issue gets exposure. The viewer at home doesn't really care (or conceptually distinguish) between a story about "prolife groups" and a story about the "National Right to Life Committee."

There had to be an obvious public policy context in the story for any groups involved to be counted. If there was a story on price cutting on diapers that mentioned Procter and Gamble, this story would not be included, and Procter and Gamble would not be coded as an interest group in this instance. If a story ran on disposable diapers as an environmental problem, and a Procter and Gamble spokesperson appeared on camera to defend the company, then that story would count and the company would be coded as one of the interest groups involved in the story. The data do not distinguish between national lobbies and those on the state and local level because differentiating a national story from a state or local one was frequently difficult to do. A typical story might start with a correspondent reporting from Washington on some action the EPA was contemplating. Then, after the issue was described, it would be illustrated by offering an example of a conflict in Denver or Albuquerque or Duluth. Spokesmen for the environmentalists and the business interests might come from this local conflict, or they might be mixed in with advocates from Washington. From the viewers' point of view, it really makes no difference since what is politically meaningful is which sides of the controversy get articulated, not where a group is headquartered.

The documentation is of interest group involvement rather than of specific instances of lobbying. The TV stories do not usually show or describe a group's efforts to influence policymakers. Rather, usually a group spokesman gives an opinion to the network correspondent (which, of course, constitutes lobbying public opinion). Finally, unlike the rest of the data, foreign and defense issues were not excluded. This probably could have been done without too much loss of accuracy, but because of the brevity of the reports, I was concerned about being always able to judge whether foreign trade issues were involved. (Again, foreign trade was counted as domestic policy in the primary data collection effort.)

The data collection for the network news broadcasts and for the research reports and op-eds in the newspapers was conducted on 295 days between February 1, 1995, and December 31, 1995. These were all the days that I was not traveling or on vacation during this eleven-month period.

List of Cases

House/*Senate*

1963

Hours of Work
Maritime Labor Legislation
Amendments to the Federal Coal Mine Safety Act
National Wilderness Preservation Act
Interstate Shipment of Firearms
Vocational Education Act
Quality Stabilization
Kinzua Dam (Seneca Indian Relocation)
Uniform Time Legislation
Wheat (Voluntary Acreage Retirement)
SEC Legislation
Criminal Justice Act
Revenue Act of 1963
Area Redevelopment Act Amendments
Youth Conservation Corps, Local Area Youth Employment Program
Urban Mass Transportation
Export-Import Bank Amendments
Extend the Mexican Farm Labor Program
Fire Island National Seashore, New York
National Service Corps

Manpower Retraining
Fourth-Class Mail Rates
Equal Pay Act
Transportation Act Amendments
Domestic Cotton Price Equalization
Health Professions Educational Assistance
Migratory Labor Bills
Marketing of Imported Articles
Silver Legislation
Civil Rights Act
Political Broadcasts—Equal Time
Oregon Dunes National Seashore
Mental Health
Feed Grain Act
National Arts Legislation
Education Legislation 1963
Dairy Legislation
Further Amend the Federal Civil Defense Act of 1950
Proposed Canyonlands National Park
Medical Care for the Aged
Private Ownership of Special Nuclear Materials
Water Pollution Control Act Amendments
Broadcast Advertisements
Truth in Lending
Clean Air
Pesticide Controls
Water Resources Research Act
Insurance of Deposits and Share Accounts
Veterans Organizations Legislative Objectives
Intermediate Care for Veterans
Library Services Act
Amending the Railroad Retirement Act of 1937
Central Arizona Project
Increased Flexibility for Financial Institutions
Organization of the Public Health Service
Training of Foreign Affairs Personnel (National Academy)
Federal Aid to Airports Program
Potato Marketing Quotas
Sleeping Bear Dunes National Lakeshore

Coast Guard Personnel Legislation
Extension of the Juvenile Delinquency Act
Presidential Transition Act
Cold War GI Bill
Lead-Zinc Stabilization
Puerto Rico
Outdoor Recreation Act of 1963
Fishing Vessel Construction
Small Business Legislation
Land and Water Conservation Fund
Sale, Without Regard to the 6-Month Waiting Period Prescribed, of
    Cadmium
Pacific Northwest Power Preference
Federal Grants for Collection of Documentary Source Material
VA Legislative Policy—Administrator of Veterans' Affairs
Miscellaneous Peanut and Rice Legislation

1979

Amendments to the Council on Wage and Price Stability Act
President's Hospital Cost Containment Proposal
Speedy Trial Amendments of 1979
Revisions in the Federal Crop Insurance Program
Fair Housing Amendments
Food Stamp Program
Veterans' and Survivors' Benefits Adjustment Act
Domestic Violence Prevention and Services
Child Health Assurance Act of 1979
Economic Regulation of the Trucking Industry
Consumer Checking Account Equity Act
Federal Highway Beautification Assistance Act
Coal Pipeline Carriers
Proposals Related to Social and Child Welfare Services, Adoption Assistance,
    and Foster Care
ERISA Improvements Act
Labeling of Alcoholic Beverages
Disability Insurance Legislation
Nuclear Waste and Facility Siting Policy
Refugee Act of 1979
Equal Employment for the Handicapped Act

Drug Abuse Prevention, Treatment, and Rehabilitation Act
Federal Reserve Membership
Milk Price Supports
Railroad Transportation Policy Act
U.S. Export Control Policy and Extension of the Export Administration Act
Alaska National Interest Lands
Amendments to the Communications Act of 1934
Reclamation Reform Act of 1979
Priority Energy Project Act
Aviation Safety and Noise Abatement
Mental Health Systems Act
Drug Regulation Reform Act
U.S. Sugar and Sweetener Policy
Chrysler Corporation Loan Guarantee Act
Health Planning and Resources Development Amendments
Saccharin Moratorium
Department of Education Organization Act of 1979
To Establish a Solar Energy Development Bank
Proposed Energy Tax Legislation
Domestic Energy Resources
Public Disclosure of Lobbying Act of 1979
Employee Contributions to IRA's and Other Pension Plans
Emergency Medical Services System
Law of the Sea
Nurse Training Amendments
University and Small Business Patent Procedures Act
Increase Target Prices of 1979 Crops
Small Business Development Center Act of 1979
FIFRA Extension
Federal Courts Improvement Act of 1979
Martin Luther King, Jr., National Holiday
Extension of Authority to Waive Countervailing Duties
Home Energy Assistance Act
Higher Education Act Amendments
Antitrust Procedural Act of 1979
Law Enforcement Assistance Reform
Magistrate Act of 1979

1991

Admission of O and P Nonimmigrants
Water Pollution Prevention and Control Act
Striker Replacement Legislation
AT&T Consent Decree's Manufacturing Restriction
Insurance Competitive Pricing Act
Product Liability
Wetlands Conservation
Audio Home Recording Act
Amend the Federal Black Lung Program
Tax Treatment of Intangible Assets
Fast Track Authority and North American Free Trade Agreement
Strengthening the Supervision and Regulation of the Depository Institutions
Healthy America: Affordable Health Care for All Americans
Milk Supply Reduction and Food Donation Act
America 2000 Excellence in Education Act
Selected Crime Issues: Prevention and Punishment
Telemarketing/Privacy Issues
Civil Rights Act of 1991
Surface Transportation
National Biological Diversity Conservation and Environmental Research Act
Veterans Compensation, Including Radiation Exposure and Hospice Care
Prohibiting State-Sanctioned Sports Gambling
Highway Fatality and Injury Reduction Act
Bentsen-Roth IRA
National Energy Security Act of 1991
Federal Lands and Families Protection Act
Family and Medical Leave Act
Generic Drug Enforcement
Reauthorization of the Higher Education Act
Cable Television Consumer Protection
Child Labor Amendments
Resource Conservation and Recovery Act Amendments
NIH Reauthorization
Campaign Advertising
Motor Vehicle Fuel Efficiency Act
Emerging Telecommunications Technologies
Modifying the Honoraria Prohibition for Federal Employees
Establish Limits on Prices of Drugs Procured by the Department of
Veterans Affairs

Notes

Chapter 1

1. Readers of my earlier book, *Lobbying for the People* (Princeton University Press, 1977), may wonder why I use the concept in this book of "citizen group" rather than "public interest group," which I use in that work. The two are not synonyms. Public interest groups are citizen groups, but not all citizen groups are public interest groups. My definition of a public interest group is that it "is one that seeks a collective good, the achievement of which will not selectively and materially benefit the membership or activists of the organization" (p. 7). Since a primary purpose of my latest study was to analyze the mix of material and postmaterial concerns and to determine which groups were pushing different kinds of issues forward, it was important to include those citizen groups that advocate material policies as part or all of their lobbying efforts. The practical consequence of this concern was to include civil rights groups and women's groups and some other citizen lobbies with the environmental and consumer groups that were the predominant focus in *Lobbying for the People*. In chapter 3 I discuss how public interest groups pursuing collective but material benefits to the poor qualify as advocates of postmaterial goods because of their philanthropic orientation.

2. This account is taken from Walter A. Rosenbaum, *Environmental Politics and Policy*, 3d ed. (Washington: Congressional Quarterly, 1995), pp. 162–63.

3. Rosenbaum, *Environmental Politics and Policy*, p. 162.

4. Laura Jereski, "Oprah Knocks Beef, and a Big Rancher in Texas Has a Cow," *Wall Street Journal*, June 3, 1997, p. A1.

5. E.E. Schattschneider, *The Semisovereign People* (Hinsdale, Illinois: Dryden Press, 1975), pp. 34–35. Ironically, since the membership of the liberal citizen groups is disproportionately composed of wealthy professionals, Schatt-

schneider's observation of an "upper-class accent" may describe these groups as well, even though he had in mind business and professional associations. Schattschneider's next sentence is, "Probably about 90 percent of the people cannot get into the pressure system" (p. 35). This remark illustrates just how much interest group politics has changed. Although no summary figure is available, it's certainly true that a majority of Americans have entered "into the pressure system" and not merely 10 percent.

6. Among the works in this growing literature are Berry, *Lobbying for the People*; Anne W. Costain, *Inviting Women's Rebellion* (Johns Hopkins University Press, 1992); Andrew S. McFarland, *Common Cause* (Chatham House, 1984); and David Vogel, *Trading Up* (Harvard University Press, 1995).

7. An insightful and systematic analysis of the interplay and conflict between business and citizen groups is David Vogel, *Fluctuating Fortunes* (Basic Books, 1989).

8. The literature cannot be summarized here, but an excellent review is Frank R. Baumgartner and Beth L. Leech, *Basic Interests* (Princeton University Press, 1998).

9. Ronald Inglehart, *The Silent Revolution* (Princeton University Press, 1977); and Ronald Inglehart, "The Trend toward Postmaterialist Values Continues," in Terry Nichols Clark and Michael Rempel, eds., *Citizen Politics in Post-Industrial Societies* (Westview Press, 1997), pp. 57–66. He has also extended his work beyond the industrialized Western democracies. See Paul R. Abramson and Ronald Inglehart, *Value Change in Global Perspective* (University of Michigan Press, 1995); and Ronald Inglehart, *Modernization and Postmodernization* (Princeton University Press 1997).

10. See Theodore J. Lowi Jr., *The End of Liberalism*, 2d ed. (Norton, 1979).

11. Charles E. Lindblom, *Politics and Markets* (Basic Books, 1977).

12. Lindblom, *Politics and Markets*, p. 170.

13. Bob Woodward, *The Agenda* (Simon and Schuster, 1994), p. 165.

14. See J. Craig Jenkins, "Social Movements, Political Representation, and the State: An Agenda and Comparative Framework," in J. Craig Jenkins and Bert Klandermans, eds., *The Politics of Social Protest* (University of Minnesota Press, 1995), p. 15; and Sidney Tarrow, *Power in Movement* (Cambridge University Press, 1994), pp. 3–4.

15. Doug McAdam, *Political Process and the Development of Black Insurgency, 1930–1970* (University of Chicago Press, 1982); and Costain, *Inviting Women's Rebellion*. A more expansive view of political opportunity can be found in Tarrow, *Power in Movement*.

16. See V.O. Key Jr., *Politics, Parties, and Pressure Groups*, 5th ed. (Thomas Y. Crowell, 1964); and David B. Truman, *The Governmental Process* (Knopf, 1951).

17. See, for example, Douglass Cater, *Power in Washington* (Vintage, 1964), pp. 26–48.

18. David McCullough, *Truman* (Simon and Schuster, 1992), pp. 639–40.

19. See Berry, *Lobbying for the People*; Kay Lehman Schlozman and John T. Tierney, *Organized Interests and American Democracy* (Harper and Row, 1986); and Jack L. Walker Jr., *Mobilizing Interest Groups in America* (University of Michigan Press, 1991).

20. Jeffrey M. Berry, *The Interest Group Society* (Little, Brown, 1984), p. 35.

21. See appendix A for a detailed discussion of how outside events or conditions may have influenced the results.

22. See Virginia Gray and David Lowery, *The Population Ecology of Interest Representation* (University of Michigan Press, 1996); and Walker, *Mobilizing Interest Groups in America.*

23. See Frank R. Baumgartner and Bryan D. Jones, *Agendas and Instability in American Politics* (University of Chicago Press, 1993); and John W. Kingdon, *Agendas, Alternatives, and Public Policies*, 2d ed. (HarperCollins, 1995).

24. Some approaches to this problem can be found in David R. Mayhew, *Divided We Govern* (Yale University Press, 1991); and George C. Edwards III, Andrew Barrett, and Jeffrey Peake, "The Legislative Impact of Divided Government," *American Journal of Political Science*, vol. 41 (April 1997), pp. 545–63.

25. Peter Bachrach and Morton S. Baratz, "Two Faces of Power," *American Political Science Review*, vol. 56 (December 1962), pp. 947–52.

26. The agenda building process has been oversimplified, and a more complex analysis follows in the text. It should be pointed out, though, that citizen groups do not initiate policies on their own. As will be discussed later in the book, distinguishing the influence of interest groups from that of legislators in relation to agenda building is exceedingly difficult.

27. Five entries in the 1991 index could not be reviewed, though it is not clear that any of them would have yielded a completed case study. The 1991 research covered at least 99 percent of the index entries while the other two years included 100 percent.

Chapter 2

1. See Russell J. Dalton and Manfred Kuechler, eds., *Challenging the Political Order* (Oxford University Press, 1990).

2. Jeffrey M. Berry, *The Interest Group Society*, 3d ed. (New York: Longman, 1997), pp. 45–51.

3. Jack L. Walker Jr., *Mobilizing Interest Groups in America* (University of Michigan Press, 1991); Kay Lehman Schlozman and John T. Tierney, *Organized Interests and American Democracy* (Harper and Row, 1986); Berry, *The Interest Group Society*; and Jonathan Rauch, *Demosclerosis* (Times Books, 1994).

4. Unfortunately, the definition of lobbying under the new law is relatively narrow and does not correspond to the academics' conception of advocacy. See Scott R. Furlong, "Interest Group Lobbying: Differences between the Legislative and Executive Branches," paper delivered at the annual meeting of the American Political Science Association, August, 1997.

5. Schlozman and Tierney, *Organized Interests and American Democracy.*

6. Arthur C. Close, ed., *Washington Representatives—1981* (Washington, D.C.: Columbia Books, 1981).

7. I've combined their categories for "citizens' groups," "civil rights groups-minority organizations," "social welfare and the poor," and "new entrants"

(elderly, women, handicapped). Some of these organizations would be closer to what I consider to be nonprofits (which were eventually put into my residual category for "other" in the tables). Still, this grouping of their data is roughly comparable to my classification of citizen groups for the three years of Congress.

8. Schlozman and Tierney also try to estimate change in the interest group community by using the same coding scheme to classify all lobbies listed in the *Congressional Quarterly Almanac* for the 1960 session of Congress. Although their 1981 figures are a pure population estimate, the *Congressional Quarterly* figures are presumably a rough measure of the participation of groups on issues before Congress that year. Since data collected for this study offer a more clearly unambiguous measure of group participation, these data are used in comparison with Schlozman and Tierney's population figures for 1981 rather than their *CQ* data.

9. John P. Heinz and others, *The Hollow Core* (Harvard University Press, 1993), pp. 3–7.

10. Schlozman and Tierney, *Organized Interests and American Democracy*, p. 150.

11. Tracing the population dynamics of different interest group sectors is a complex undertaking, requiring data on organizational deaths as well as births. See Virginia Gray and David Lowery, *The Population Ecology of Interest Representation* (University of Michigan Press, 1996), pp. 111–36.

12. Frank R. Baumgartner and Bryan D. Jones, *Agendas and Instability in American Politics* (University of Chicago Press, 1993), p. 186.

13. Rauch, *Demosclerosis*, p. 91.

14. If individuals and government officials are included, the average numbers for testimony rise to 30.5 in 1979 and 22.6 in 1991.

15. As shown in table 2-2, the rate of change for citizen groups over time is not statistically significant from that of all noncitizen groups. However, our primary concern is not with the rate of change between citizen and noncitizen groups but with the magnitude of difference between the rate of citation for citizen groups and their actual proportion of the population of interest groups. Since that comparison is indirect (with a summary statistic for the 1981 population and an estimate for 1991), there is no significance test to be used.

16. David Vogel, *Lobbying the Corporation* (Basic Books, 1978), pp. 23–68.

17. *The Public Interest Law Firm* (New York: Ford Foundation, 1973), p. 39.

18. *Public Interest Law: Five Years Later* (New York: Ford Foundation, 1976), p. 39.

19. Charles McCarry, *Citizen Nader* (New York: Saturday Review Press, 1972), pp. 3–29.

20. Walker, *Mobilizing Interest Groups in America*.

21. *The Public Interest Law Firm*, p. 39.

22. Michael S. Greve, "Why 'Defunding the Left' Failed," *Public Interest*, vol. 89 (Fall 1987), pp. 91–106. One exception to the failure of the defunding strategy was the handful of poor people's lobbies. See Douglas R. Imig, *Poverty and Power* (University of Nebraska Press, 1996), pp. 49–54.

23. Jeffrey M. Berry, *Feeding Hungry People* (Rutgers University Press, 1984).

24. Gray and Lowery, *The Population Ecology of Interest Representation*, pp. 219–42.

25. James T. Bennett and Thomas J. DiLorenzo, *Destroying Democracy* (Washington: Cato Institute, 1985), pp. 424–25.

26. *Fortune* identified close to sixty activists with a "public interest" background in top positions in the Carter administration, including Joan Claybrook (Nader protégé), Carol Tucker Foreman (Consumer Federation of America), and Peter Schuck (Consumer's Union). See Juan Cameron, "Nader's Invaders Are Inside the Gates," *Fortune*, October, 1977, pp. 252–60. Clinton would later follow the same pattern. Berry, *The Interest Group Society*, p. 198.

27. Walter A. Rosenbaum, *Environmental Politics and Policy*, 3d ed. (Washington: Congressional Quarterly Press, 1995), p. 138.

28. See *Office of Communication of the United Church of Christ* v. *FCC*, 359 F. 2d 944 (D.C. Cir. 1966).

29. Greve, "Why 'Defunding the Left' Failed," p. 91.

30. Steven S. Smith and Christopher J. Deering, *Committees in Congress*, 2d ed. (Washington: Congressional Quarterly Press, 1990), p. 126.

31. Robert F. Durant, "The Democratic Deficit in America," *Political Science Quarterly*, vol. 110 (Spring 1995), p. 37.

32. Doug McAdam, *Political Process and the Development of Black Insurgency* (University of Chicago Press, 1982).

Chapter 3

1. Daniel Bell, *The Coming of Post-Industrial Society* (Basic Books, 1973), p. 44.

2. Postmaterialist attitudes have been found to be positively associated with strong partisanship. See Howard L. Reiter, "The Rise of the 'New Agenda' and the Decline of Partisanship," *West European Politics*, vol. 16 (April 1993), pp. 89–104; and Réjean Pelletier, "Are Political Parties in Decline?" paper delivered at the conference on Party Politics in the Year 2000, January 1995.

3. Ronald Inglehart, *The Silent Revolution* (Princeton University Press, 1977).

4. Paul R. Abramson and Ronald Inglehart, *Value Change in Global Perspective* (University of Michigan Press, 1995); and Ronald Inglehart, *Modernization and Postmodernization* (Princeton University Press, 1997).

5. Inglehart, *The Silent Revolution*, p. 28. Later surveys incorporated a longer battery of questions.

6. Inglehart, *The Silent Revolution*, pp. 31–37; and Abramson and Inglehart, *Value Change in Global Perspective*, pp. 12–15.

7. The literature is voluminous. See, for example, the symposium in *Comparative Political Studies*, including Inglehart's response to criticism. William M. Lafferty and Oddbjørn Knutsen, "Postmaterialism in a Social Democratic State"; James Savage, "Postmaterialism of the Left and Right"; Ferdinand Böltken and Wolfgang Jagodzinski, "In an Environment of Insecurity"; and Ronald Inglehart, "New Perspectives on Value Change," *Comparative Political Studies*, vol. 17 (January 1985), pp. 411–532.

8. Everett Carll Ladd, "Clearing the Air: Public Opinion and Public Policy on the Environment," *Public Opinion*, vol. 5 (February–March 1982), p. 20.

9. See Abraham H. Maslow, "A Theory of Human Motivation," *Psychological Review*, vol. 50 (January 1943), pp. 370–96; and Abraham H. Maslow, *Motivation and Personality* (Harper, 1954).

10. Abraham H. Maslow, *Toward a Psychology of Being*, 2d ed. (Van Nostrand Reinhold, 1968), pp. 25, 153.

11. Alan Marsh, "The 'Silent Revolution,' Value Priorities, and the Quality of Life in Britain," *American Political Science Review*, vol. 69 (March 1975), p. 29.

12. Hugh Heclo, "The Sixties' False Dawn: Awakenings, Movements, and Postmodern Policy-Making," *Journal of Policy History*, vol. 8, no. 1 (1996), p. 50.

13. There is no dispute about Americans' generosity when it comes to volunteering. On the trends for many other types of civic involvement, considerable disagreement occurs. See Robert D. Putnam, "Bowling Alone: America's Declining Social Capital," *Journal of Democracy*, vol. 6 (January 1995), pp. 65–78; and for an opposing view, Everett C. Ladd, "The Data Just Don't Show Erosion of America's 'Social Capital,'" *Public Perspective*, vol. 7 (June–July 1996), pp. 1ff.

14. Jeffrey M. Berry, Kent E. Portney, and Ken Thomson, *The Rebirth of Urban Democracy* (Brookings, 1993), pp. 71–98.

15. See Robert Booth Fowler, *The Dance with Community* (University Press of Kansas, 1991).

16. Robert N. Bellah and others, *Habits of the Heart* (Harper and Row, 1986), p. 202.

17. Sidney Verba, Kay Lehman Schlozman, and Henry E. Brady, *Voice and Equality* (Harvard University Press, 1995), p. 67.

18. Verba, Schlozman, and Brady, *Voice and Equality*, pp. 58–65.

19. Abramson and Inglehart, *Value Change in Global Perspective*, p. 19.

20. See Theodore J. Lowi, *The End of Liberalism* (Norton, 1969); and Charles E. Lindblom, *Politics and Markets* (Basic Books, 1977).

21. See Frank R. Baumgartner and Bryan D. Jones, *Agendas and Instability in American Politics* (University of Chicago Press, 1993); and Frank R. Baumgartner and Jeffery C. Talbert, "From Setting a National Agenda on Health Care to Making Decisions in Congress," *Journal of Health Politics, Policy and Law*, vol. 20 (Summer 1995), pp. 437–45.

22. Peter Bachrach and Morton S. Baratz, "Two Faces of Power," *American Political Science Review*, vol. 56 (December 1962), pp. 947–52.

23. Baumgartner and Talbert, "From Setting a National Agenda," p. 440.

24. See, for example, Lester W. Milbrath, *Environmentalists: Vanguard for a New Society* (State University of New York Press, 1984).

25. Abortion exemplifies a further difficulty in developing an operational definition: for a single group, material concerns may be intertwined with postmaterial ones on the same issue. The right to abortion has material implications as it can significantly alter the economic opportunities of the mother and the father. At its core, however, it is an issue of personal autonomy, rights, and, in the eyes of abortion opponents, a matter of morality and rights of the fetus. In such cases a judgment had to determine the central, driving force among those on each side of an issue.

26. See Jeffrey M. Berry, *Lobbying for the People* (Princeton University Press, 1977), pp. 7–9.

27. David S. Cloud, "Bush's 'Action Plan' May Be Key to Approval of Fast Track," *Congressional Quarterly Weekly Report*, May 4, 1991, p. 1124.

28. See, for example, David R. Mayhew, *Divided We Govern* (Yale University Press, 1991).

29. See chapter 4 for a more detailed analysis of which groups won and lost based on final outcomes.

30. Mancur Olson Jr., *The Logic of Collective Action* (Schocken, 1968).

31. Russell J. Dalton, *The Green Rainbow* (Yale University Press, 1994), p. 256.

32. William Tucker, *Progress and Privilege* (Anchor Press/Doubleday, 1982), p. 15. Emphasis in the original.

33. See Mark Dowie, *Losing Ground* (MIT Press, 1995).

34. Amory Lovins, *Soft Energy Paths* (Harper and Row, 1977); E. F. Schumacher, *Small is Beautiful* (Harper and Row, 1973); and Paul R. Ehrlich, *The Population Bomb* (Ballantine Books/Sierra Club, 1968).

35. There is a corollary of the elitist criticism and the fate of blue-collar workers that relates to environmental lobbies and inner city residents. The charge is that these groups concern themselves with the environment of parks and wilderness areas but ignore the environment in which poor urban dwellers live. It is difficult to know what standard to use in making a judgment about an appropriate balance between protecting parks, wilderness, flora, and fauna, and protecting people who live in the inner city. Clearly, however, a significant portion of these groups' advocacy efforts does go toward working on issues affecting the quality of the environment in the inner city. Surface transportation and clean air are the most obvious examples, and solid waste disposal, pesticide regulations, and water quality legislation are issues that affect the poor in rural and urban regions alike. This is a complicated question, though, and cannot be resolved with the data gathered for this study.

36. Jeffrey M. Berry, "The Changing Face of American Liberalism," paper delivered at the conference on the Politics of Inequality in the Twentieth Century, Kennedy School of Government, Harvard University, September 1996.

37. Douglas R. Imig, *Poverty and Power* (University of Nebraska Press, 1996).

38. Robert Cameron Mitchell, "From Conservatism to Environmental Movement: The Development of the Modern Environmental Lobbies," in Michael J. Lacey, ed., *Government and Environmental Politics* (University Press of America, 1990), as cited in Walter A. Rosenbaum, *Environmental Politics and Policy*, 3d ed. (Washington.: Congressional Quarterly, 1995), p. 28.

39. These figures are for whites only. Clyde Wilcox, *Onward Christian Soldiers?* (Westview Press, 1996), p. 48.

40. See the discussion in chapter 5.

41. Mark J. Rozell and Clyde Wilcox, eds., *God at the Grass Roots* (Rowman and Littlefield, 1995).

42. Jeffrey M. Berry and Deborah Schildkraut, "Citizen Groups, Political Parties, and Electoral Coalitions," in Anne N. Costain and Andrew S. McFarland, eds., *Social Movements and American Political Institutions* (Rowman and Littlefield, 1998), pp. 136–56.

Chapter 4

1. Ronald Inglehart, *The Silent Revolution* (Princeton University Press, 1977), pp. 4, 6.

2. John W. Kingdon, *Agendas, Alternatives, and Public Policies* (Little, Brown, 1984), pp. 134–37.

3. See David Rochefort and Roger W. Cobb, eds., *The Politics of Problem Definition* (University Press of Kansas, 1994).

4. Jeffrey M. Berry, *The Interest Group Society*, 3d ed. (Longman, 1997), pp. 235–36.

5. See Marc Howard Ross and Roger Cobb, "Cultural Strategies and the Politics of Agenda Denial," paper delivered at the annual meeting of the American Political Science Association, August 1997.

6. Roger W. Cobb and Charles D. Elder, *Participation in American Politics*, 2d ed. (Johns Hopkins University Press, 1983), pp. 64–67.

7. Frank R. Baumgartner and Bryan D. Jones, *Agendas and Instability in American Politics* (University of Chicago Press, 1993).

8. Kingdon, *Agendas, Alternatives, and Public Policies*, p. 30.

9. Gary Mucciaroni, *Reversals of Fortune* (Brookings, 1995).

10. If there were both material and postmaterial interests pushing the legislation forward, a judgment was made about whether one or the other was dominant based on congressional attention. If one was not clearly dominant, the case was coded "mixed."

11. David Vogel emphasizes the importance of economic conditions in determining the relative influence of business and citizen groups over the congressional agenda. *Fluctuating Fortunes* (Basic Books, 1989).

12. On such strategies see John B. Gilmour, *Strategic Disagreement* (University of Pittsburgh Press, 1995).

13. Kingdon, *Agendas, Alternatives, and Public Policies*, pp. 75–94.

14. Not all the 1991 cases had any identifiable antecedent before that session of Congress. For those bills without an antecedent, the coding decision for table 4-1 was used.

15. By themselves the similar percentages in table 4-2 do not disprove the hypothesis that citizen groups succeeded in getting their issues on the agenda by highjacking material issues that are poised to make it onto the agenda in the next Congress. Conceivably, if that did happen frequently, it could be counterbalanced by business groups stealing a similar number of postmaterial issues and transmuting them. However, earlier histories of the 1991 bills show no pattern of such opportunistic behavior. There were a handful of cases, but by and large the orientation of the bills does not change significantly over time.

16. David Price, *Who Makes the Laws?* (Cambridge, Mass.: Schenkman, 1972).

17. Sidney Tarrow, *Power in Movement* (Cambridge University Press, 1994).

18. Rachel Carson, *Silent Spring* (Houghton Mifflin, 1962).

19. Ronald J. Penoyer, *Directory of Federal Regulatory Agencies*, 3d ed. (St. Louis: Center for the Study of American Business, 1981), pp. 107–08.

20. Walter A. Rosenbaum, *Environmental Politics and Policy*, 3d ed. (Washington.: Congressional Quarterly, 1995), p. 34.

21. See Mark J. Rozell and Clyde Wilcox, eds., *God at the Grassroots* (Rowman and Littlefield, 1995).

22. If one business sector was fighting another, only the side that was initially pushing the legislation was coded as winning or losing. If a coalition crossed sectors—business and citizen groups, for example—a judgment was made as to whether one sector from that coalition had more at stake. If so, that sector was coded as the winner or loser. If it appeared that the stakes were equal, the issue was not included in these ratios.

23. Charles E. Lindblom, *Politics and Markets* (Basic Books, 1977).

24. Peter Bachrach and Morton S. Baratz, "Two Faces of Power," *American Political Science Review*, vol. 56 (December 1962), pp. 947–52.

25. Thomas Gais, *Improper Influence* (University of Michigan Press, 1996).

26. Robert H. Salisbury, "The Paradox of Interest Groups in Washington—More Groups, Less Clout," in Anthony King, ed., *The New American Political System*, 2d ed. (Washington: AEI Press, 1990), pp. 203–29.

27. It's conceivable that although the proportion of issues with conflict is stable over time, there are more groups in conflict on each matter. This does not turn out to be the case. For the high-salience cases the mean number of corporations and trade associations decreases from 1963 to 1979 and decreases further from 1979 to 1991. The number of professional associations decreases in 1979 but increases a bit in 1991.

28. On the lack of such central trade groups in contemporary issue networks, see John P. Heinz, Edward O. Laumann, Robert L. Nelson, and Robert H. Salisbury, *The Hollow Core* (Harvard University Press, 1993).

29. See Douglass Cater, *Power in Washington* (Vintage Books, 1964), pp. 26–48.

30. Berry, *The Interest Group Society*, pp. 196–215; and Heinz and others, *The Hollow Core*, pp. 247–367.

31. Hugh Heclo, "Issue Networks and the Executive Establishment," in Anthony King, ed., *The New American Political System* (Washington: American Enterprise Institute, 1979), pp. 87–124.

32. See, for example, H. Brinton Milward and Gary L. Wamsley, "Policy Subsystems, Networks, and the Tools of Public Management," in Robert Eyestone, ed., *Public Policy Formation* (JAI Press, 1984); and Jack Knott and Gary J. Miller, *Reforming Bureaucracy* (Prentice-Hall, 1987).

33. *The Federalist Papers* (New American Library, 1961), p. 79.

34. Typical of this view are Marver H. Bernstein, *Regulating Business by Independent Commission* (Princeton University Press, 1955), Lindblom, *Politics and Markets*, and Theodore J. Lowi, *The End of Liberalism*, 2d ed. (Norton, 1979).

35. Kay Lehman Schlozman and John T. Tierney, *Organized Interests and American Democracy* (Harper and Row, 1986), pp. 284–85.

36. David Hosansky, "Pesticide, Food Safety Law," *Congressional Quarterly Weekly Report*, September 7, 1996, p. 2546.

37. Cases where neither side won, or some other outcome took place were excluded. There were 10 cases (1963); 14 (1979); and 23 (1991).

Chapter 5

1. On the evolution of conservative political advocacy, see Jerome L. Himmelstein, *To the Right* (University of California Press, 1990).

2. Alan Crawford, *Thunder on the Right* (Pantheon, 1980), p. 145.

3. The coding was not restricted to coverage of any particular type of advocacy. Anything that a group was doing to try to influence legislation inside or outside of Congress or any mention of a group's views on an issue or on the related policymaking on the issue was included. References had to be to specific organizations rather than to movements or generic labels (such as, "environmentalists," "prolife movement").

4. Ronald G. Shaiko, "More Bang for the Buck: The New Era of Full-Service Public Interest Organizations," in Allan J. Cigler and Burdett A. Loomis, eds., *Interest Group Politics*, 3d ed. (Washington: Congressional Quarterly, 1991), p. 123; and Douglas J. Bergner, ed., *Public Interest Profiles* (Washington: Foundation for Public Affairs, 1986).

5. Jeffrey M. Berry, *Lobbying for the People* (Princeton University Press, 1977), pp. 298–300.

6. As noted in chapter 3, the rate of passage of bills with a postmaterialist side is not significantly different from the rate of passage of all bills. In 1991, 50 percent of all bills in the high-salience category passed.

7. Thomas Gais, *Improper Influence* (University of Michigan Press, 1996), pp. 63–68; "PAC Activity in 1994 Elections Remains at 1992 Levels," Federal Election Commission, March 31, 1995, pp. 30, 32; and "PAC Activity Increases in 1995-96 Election Cycle," Federal Election Commission, April 22, 1997, pp. 29, 31.

8. Gais, *Improper Influence*, pp. 66–68.

9. R. Kenneth Godwin, *One Billion Dollars of Influence* (Chatham House, 1988), pp.11–12.

10. Marilyn Werber Serafini, "Senior Schism," *National Journal*, May 6, 1995, p. 1091.

11. Serafini, "Senior Schism," p. 1093; and Erik Eckholm, "Alarmed by Fund Raiser, the Elderly Give Millions," *New York Times*, November 12, 1992, p. A1.

12. John C. Green, "The Christian Right and the 1994 Elections," in Mark J. Rozell and Clyde Wilcox, eds., *God at the Grass-roots* (Rowman and Littlefield, 1995), pp. 1–17.

13. Nancy L. Bednar and Alan D. Hertzke, "Oklahoma: The Christian Right and Republican Realignment," in Rozell and Wilcox, *God at the Grassroots*, pp. 91–107.

14. Jerry Gray, "Christian Coalition Offers Dole Both Cheers and Sharp Prodding," *New York Times*, September 15, 1996, p. 38.

15. Denise L. Baer and Julie A. Dolan, "Intimate Connections: Political Interests and Group Activity in State and Local Parties," *American Review of Politics*, vol. 15 (Summer 1994), pp. 257–89; and Réjean Pelletier, "Are Political Parties in Decline?" paper delivered at the conference on Party Politics in the Year 2000, January 1995.

16. EMILY's List solicitation, 1995; and Terri Susan Fine, "When EMILY

WISHes upon a Star, Do Her Dreams Come True?" paper delivered at the annual meeting of the American Political Science Association, September 1994.

17. See John W. Kingdon, *Congressmen's Voting Decisions*, 2d ed. (Harper and Row, 1981).

18. David Hosansky, "Christian Right's Electoral Clout Bore Limited Fruit in 104th," *Congressional Quarterly Weekly Report*, November 2, 1996, p. 3161.

19. Elizabeth MacDonald and Jacob M. Schlesinger, "Group Targets Politically Active Churches for Audits," *Wall Street Journal*, March 20, 1997, p. A18.

20. Darrell M. West, Diane J. Heith, and Chris Goodwin, "Harry and Louise Go to Washington: Political Advertising and Health Care Reform," *Journal of Health Policy, Politics and Law*, vol. 21 (Spring 1996), pp. 35-68.

21. Burdett A. Loomis and Eric Sexton, "Choosing to Advertise: How Interests Decide," in Allan J. Cigler and Burdett A. Loomis, eds., *Interest Group Politics*, 4th ed. (Washington.: Congressional Quarterly Press, 1995), pp. 193–214.

22. Eighty-four percent of interest groups report using letter writing campaigns. Kay Lehman Schlozman and John T. Tierney, *Organized Interests and American Democracy* (Harper and Row, 1986), p. 150.

23. Kenneth M. Goldstein, "Tremors before the Earthquake: Grass Roots Communications before the 1994 Election," paper delivered at the annual meeting of the American Political Science Association, September 1995, p. 4.

24. Goldstein, "Tremors before the Earthquake," p. 6.

25. Jeffrey M. Berry, *The Interest Group Society*, 3d ed. (Longman, 1997), pp. 116–38.

26. See William G. Mayer, *The Changing American Mind* (University of Michigan Press, 1993).

27. On lobbyists and congressional leaders, see Christine A. DeGregorio, *Networks of Champions* (University of Michigan Press, 1997).

28. John B. Bader, *Taking the Initiative* (Georgetown University Press, 1996).

29. *The Contract with America* (Times Books, 1994).

30. Catherine S. Manegold, "Some on Right See a Tactical Misstep on School Prayer," *New York Times*, November 19, 1994, p. A1.

31. Darrell M. West and Richard Francis, "Selling the Contract with America: Interest Groups and Public Policymaking," paper delivered at the annual meeting of the American Political Science Association, September 1995, p. 20.

32. John Harwood, "Religious Right Plans to Use Tax, Budget Battles to Start Reshaping the Nation's Moral Landscape," *Wall Street Journal*, January 17, 1995, p. A18.

33. Gustav Niebuhr, "The Religious Right Readies Agenda for Second 100 Days," *New York Times*, May 16, 1995, p. A1.

34. Annie Tin and Juliana Gruenwald, "'Contract with Family' Welcomed Cautiously by House GOP," *Congressional Quarterly Weekly Report*, May 20, 1995, p. 1448.

35. See Hosansky, "Christian Right's Electoral Clout Bore Limited Fruit in 104th."

36. Gerald M. Pomper, "The Presidential Election," in Gerald M. Pomper, ed., *The Election of 1996* (Chatham House, 1997), p. 185; and Marjorie Randon Hershey, "The Congressional Elections," in Pomper, *The Election of 1996*, p. 213.

37. Jerry Gray, "Gingrich Offers an Agenda, but the Christian Coalition Attacks Sharply," *New York Times*, March 5, 1997, p. A20.

38. Katherine Q. Seelye, "Christian Coalition Plans Inner-City Program," *New York Times*, January 31, 1997, p. A21.

39. Katherine Q. Seelye, "Lawmaker Proposes New Prayer Amendment," *New York Times*, March 25, 1997, p. A20.

40. Richard L. Berke, "Christian Coalition Reaffirms Its Strength," *New York Times*, September 15, 1997, p. A18.

41. Katherine Q. Seelye, "Christian Coalition's Reed Quits for New Political Role," *New York Times*, April 24, 1997, p. A28.

42. See John C. Green, James L. Guth, and Clyde Wilcox, "Less Than Conquerors: The Christian Right in State Republican Parties," in Anne N. Costain and Andrew S. McFarland, eds., *Social Movements and American Political Institutions* (Rowman and Littlefield, 1998), pp. 117–35.

43. In June 1998, the House voted on the prayer amendment for the first time in more than twenty-five years. The vote was 224 in favor and 203 against, 61 votes short of the two-thirds necessary for passage.

44. Mark A. Peterson and Jack L. Walker, "Interest Group Responses to Partisan Change: The Impact of the Reagan Administration upon the National Interest Group System," in Allan J. Cigler and Burdett A. Loomis, eds., *Interest Group Politics*, 2d ed. (Washington: Congressional Quarterly, 1986), p. 172.

45. *Contract with America*, pp. 131–32.

46. Stephen Engelberg, "Business Leaves the Lobby and Sits at Congress's Table," *New York Times*, March 31, 1995, p. A1.

47. Timothy Egan, "Industries Affected by Endangered Species Act Help a Senator Rewrite Its Provisions," *New York Times*, April 13, 1995, p. A20.

48. Jill Abramson and Timothy Noah, "In GOP-Controlled Congress, Lobbyists Remain as Powerful as Ever—and Perhaps More Visible," *Wall Street Journal*, April 20, 1995, p. A14.

49. Jeffrey M. Berry, "The Real Powers on Capitol Hill," *Boston Globe*, Sunday Focus section, December 15, 1996, p. C1.

50. It should be pointed out that *Congressional Quarterly's* list includes some appropriations bills. As noted in chapter 1, the legislative case histories for 1963, 1979, and 1991 exclude appropriations. In 1995–96, there appeared to be considerably more policymaking—aside from spending decisions—made in appropriations bills. There is no evidence to show that these three earlier years were characterized by unusual degrees of legislating substantive change through appropriations. However, no exact comparisons were made with 1995–96.

51. Samuel P. Huntington, "The Democratic Distemper," *Public Interest*, vol. 41 (Fall 1975), pp. 9–38.

52. Jonathan Rauch, *Demosclerosis* (Times Books, 1994).

53. Kevin P. Phillips, "The 1990's' Political Upheaval and the Pressures for Reform," in James L. Sundquist, ed., *Back to Gridlock?* (Brookings, 1995), p. 79.

54. David R. Mayhew, *Divided We Govern* (Yale University Press, 1991).

55. The literature as it pertains to gridlock and divided government is reviewed by Morris Fiorina, *Divided Government*, 2d ed. (Allyn and Bacon, 1996).

56. Although the choice of any particular number of groups was somewhat arbitrary, the data indicated that ten groups was toward the high end of participation. It was assumed with that number of lobbies active, the legislation was likely to be hard-fought, involve a range of groups, and be subject to a complex set of negotiations.

57. John B. Gilmour, *Strategic Disagreement* (University of Pittsburgh Press, 1995), p. 29.

58. This analysis of group participation and legislative productivity is fully developed in Jeffrey M. Berry, "Interest Groups and Gridlock," paper delivered at the annual meeting of the American Political Science Association, September 1998.

59. See generally, Jack L. Walker, Jr., *Mobilizing Interest Groups in America* (University of Michigan Press, 1991).

60. See John P. Heinz and others, *The Hollow Core* (Harvard University Press, 1993).

Chapter 6

1. Robert H. Salisbury, "The Paradox of Interest Groups in Washington—More Groups, Less Clout," in Anthony King, ed., *The New American Political System* (Washington: AEI Press, 1990), pp. 203–29.

2. See Frank R. Baumgartner and Bryan D. Jones, *Agendas and Instability in American Politics* (University of Chicago Press, 1993); and Anne N. Costain, *Inviting Women's Rebellion* (Johns Hopkins University Press, 1992).

3. Given the brevity of most stories, only a limited number of variables could be coded. I concentrated on which groups got covered either by specific organizations named or by general references to interest group sectors. Thus references to the "American Association of Retired Persons" and to "senior citizen organizations" were both recorded. See appendix A for a fuller explanation of the research and the coding decisions.

4. Lucig H. Danielian and Benjamin I. Page, "The Heavenly Chorus: Interest Group Voices on TV News," *American Journal of Political Science*, vol. 38 (November 1994), pp. 1072, 1074.

5. Some may wonder why these organizations, whose membership is composed of grown men who march around in the woods playing soldier, qualify as an interest group. They are certainly not conventional lobbies, but some of the state militias did testify before Congress after the bombing and they do make attempts, lame as they may be, to influence public opinion.

6. See S. Robert Lichter, Linda Lichter, and Stanley Rothman, *The Media Elite* (Adler and Adler, 1986).

7. See Ben Bagdikian, *The Media Monopoly* (Beacon Press, 1983); and Michael Parenti, *Inventing Reality: The Politics of the Mass Media* (St. Martin's Press, 1986), pp. 42–59.

8. See Herbert J. Gans, "Are U. S. Journalists Dangerously Liberal?" *Columbia Journalism Review* (November-December 1985), pp. 29–33.

9. G. Cleveland Wilhoit and David H. Weaver, *The American Journalist* (Indiana University Press, 1986), p. 27; and "The Political Views of Journalists," *American Enterprise*, vol. 7 (March-April 1996), p. 88.

10. Parenti, *Inventing Reality*.

11. Gans, "Are U.S. Journalists Dangerously Liberal?"; and Herbert J. Gans, *Deciding What's News* (Vintage Books, 1980).

12. "The Political Views of Journalists."

13. Stories on American Eagle were coded as stories about American Airlines.

14. Another reflection of business's adverse treatment at the hands of the networks was the opportunity business had to articulate its positions and goals. Each story was coded as to whether any interest group mentioned was given the chance to speak on camera or was just referred to by the correspondent or anchor. An organization that was allowed to speak usually had a greater chance to lay out what it was advocating, or in the case of business groups, to offer a defense of the accusation that was made in the broadcast. Getting to speak on camera usually meant that the lobbying group was featured for a longer period. Corporations were allowed to speak on camera 38 percent of the time and trade associations scored almost the same. It was often the case that something negative was said about a company, but the company was given no opportunity to offer a rebuttal. Citizen groups were treated more favorably, gaining speaking parts 58 percent of the time. Professional associations did the best, speaking 78 percent of the time.

15. Danielian and Page, "The Heavenly Chorus," p. 1072.

16. Ibid.

17. Thomas E. Patterson, "Bad News, Period," *PS*, vol. 29 (March 1996), p. 17.

18. Robert M. Entman, "Reporting Environmental Policy Debate," *Harvard International Journal of Press/Politics*, vol. 1 (Summer 1996), p. 78.

19. Ronald Inglehart, *The Silent Revolution* (Princeton University Press, 1977).

20. Jeffrey M. Berry, *The Interest Group Society*, 3d ed. (Longman, 1997), pp. 98–99.

21. Stanley Rothman and S. Robert Lichter, "Elite Ideology and Risk Perception in Nuclear Energy Policy," *American Political Science Review*, vol. 81 (June 1987), pp. 384, 393.

22. Entman, "Reporting Environmental Policy Debate," p. 82.

23. See, for example, John E. Chubb, *Interest Groups and the Bureaucracy* (Stanford University Press, 1983); and John Mark Hansen, *Gaining Access* (University of Chicago Press, 1991).

24. Alan Rosenthal, *The Third House* (Washington: Congressional Quarterly Press, 1993), p. 7.

25. Robert F. Durant, "The Democratic Deficit in America," *Political Science Quarterly* , vol. 110 (Spring 1995), p. 33.

26. Hilary Stout, "One Company's Data Fuel Diverse Views in Health Care Debate," *Wall Street Journal*, June 28, 1994, p. A1.

27. Kay Lehman Schlozman and John T. Tierney, *Organized Interests and American Democracy* (Harper and Row, 1986), p. 150.

28. If it was not directly mentioned in the headline, there at least had to be a

hint in the headline that research might be discussed in the body of the article. Stories did not have to have any immediate lobbying context, but they did have to have some public policy relevance. This is certainly not as exact a method as used for some of the other tests in the study, but despite a larger margin for error, any broad patterns that emerge from the data should reveal how different interest group sectors do in comparison with one another. Stories in the *Times* that were exclusively related to New York City were excluded.

29. Peter T. Kilborn, "Women and Minorities Still Face 'Glass Ceiling,'" *New York Times*, March 16, 1995, p. A22.

30. Alan Crawford, *Thunder on the Right* (Pantheon, 1980).

31. Helene Cooper, "Consumer Group Says NAFTA Claims Haven't Been Met," *Wall Street Journal*, September 5, 1995, p. B7B; Bob Herbert, "NAFTA's Bubble Bursts," *New York Times*, September 11, 1995, p. A15; John R. Wilke, "Study Finds Redlining Is Widespread in Sales of Home-Insurance Policies," *Wall Street Journal*, September 12, 1995, p. A6; David W. Dunlap, "F.B.I. Kept Watch on AIDS Group during Protest Years," *New York Times*, May 16, 1995, p. B3; and Tamar Lewin, "Children on TV out of Touch, Study Finds," *New York Times*, February 27, 1995, p. B8.

32. Sidney Verba and Gary R. Orren, *Equality in America* (Harvard University Press, 1985), p. 188.

33. Burdett A. Loomis and Eric Sexton, "Choosing to Advertise: How Interests Decide," in Allan J. Cigler and Burdett A. Loomis, eds., *Interest Group Politics*, 4th ed. (Washington: Congressional Quarterly, 1995), pp. 193–214.

34. On think tanks and credibility, see Andrew Rich, "Perceptions of Think Tanks in American Politics," Burson-Marsteller Worldwide, December, 1997.

35. See R. Kent Weaver, "The Changing World of Think Tanks," *PS*, vol. 22 (September 1989), pp. 563–78.

36. James A. Smith, *The Idea Brokers* (Free Press, 1991), p. 205.

37. David M. Ricci, *The Transformation of American Politics* (Yale University Press, 1993), p. 16.

38. Smith, *The Idea Brokers*, pp. xiv–xv.

39. Louis Jacobson, "Tanks on the Roll," *National Journal*, July 8, 1995, p. 1768.

40. Since the financial records of these organizations were not available, think tanks were simply defined as those organizations that consider themselves as such. One might wish for stricter conceptual clarity, but this self-definition at least tells us which groups believe they have chosen this particular organizational model.

41. Jacobson, "Tanks on the Roll," p. 1769. Corporations also contribute to centrist think tanks, though they tend not to be oriented toward advocacy.

42. Peter Stone, "Ganging Up on the FDA," *National Journal*, February 18, 1995, pp. 410–11; and Philip J. Hilts, "F.D.A. Becomes Target of Empowered Groups," *New York Times*, February 12, 1995, p. 24.

43. Timothy Noah and Laurie McGinley, "Tobacco Industry's Figures on Political Spending Don't Reflect Gifts to Think Tanks, Other Groups," *Wall Street Journal*, March 25, 1996, p. A16.

44. Smith, *The Idea Brokers*, p. 191.

45. Martha Derthick and Paul J. Quirk, *The Politics of Deregulation* (Brookings, 1985), pp. 36–37.

46. Charles Murray, *Losing Ground* (Basic Books, 1984).

47. Ricci, *The Transformation of American Politics*, pp. 161–62; Christopher Georges, "Conservative Heritage Foundation Finds Recipe for Influence: Ideas + Marketing = Clout," *Wall Street Journal*, August 10, 1995, p. A12; and John J. Fialka, "Cato Institute's Influence Grows in Washington as Republican-Dominated Congress Sets Up Shop," *Wall Street Journal*, December 14, 1994, p. A16.

48. Excluded were humorous pieces, reminiscences, poetry, and brief sidebars to an op-ed essay. Foreign policy essays were included. Only those pieces on the op-ed page were included, even though similar type essays by nonnewspaper staff sometimes appeared in other parts of the paper. Regular columnists whose work appears on the op-ed page (such as Anthony Lewis of the *Times*) were excluded. Essays written by individuals unaffiliated with any advocacy organization were also excluded from the calculations in table 6-6.

49. In his study of op-eds in the *New York Times* during the war with Iraq, Benjamin Page concluded that "much of this diversity" on the editorial and op-ed pages was an "illusion." On the op-ed page, he writes that "the vast majority of these column writers occupied positions in mainstream institutions and organizations associated with the foreign policy establishment." *Who Deliberates?* (University of Chicago Press, 1996), pp. 22–23.

50. R. Kent Weaver, "Private Think Tanks in the U.S. Political System," paper delivered at a conference on Think Tanks in the USA and Germany, University of Pennsylvania, November 1994; R. Kent Weaver and Andrew Rich, "Think Tanks, the Media, and the Policy Process," n.d.; and Rich, "Perceptions of Think Tanks in American Politics."

51. Bruce R. Bartlett, "Will the Flat Tax KO Housing?" *Wall Street Journal*, August 2, 1995, p. A10.

52. Think tanks do not score any better in the 1979 data, but one could argue that the new activist model was still in its infancy then, and it would be unfair to judge their performance that year.

53. Weaver, "Private Think Tanks in the U.S. Political System"; and Weaver and Rich, "Think Tanks, the Media, and the Policy Process."

54. Paul Burstein, "Interest Organizations, Political Parties, and the Study of Democratic Politics," in Anne N. Costain and Andrew S. McFarland, eds., *Social Movements and American Political Institutions* (Rowman and Littlefield, 1998), pp. 39–56.

55. See J. Craig Jenkins, "Social Movements, Political Representation, and the State: An Agenda and Comparative Framework," in J. Craig Jenkins and Bert Klandermans, eds., *The Politics of Social Protest* (University of Minnesota Press, 1995), p. 15.

56. These are the high-salience issues only.

57. Berry, *Lobbying for the People*, pp. 298–300.

58. Ronald G. Shaiko, "More Bang for the Buck: The New Era of Full-Service

Public Interest Organizations," in Allan J. Cigler and Burdett A. Loomis, eds., *Interest Group Politics*, 3d ed. (Washington: Congressional Quarterly Press, 1991), p. 112.

59. See Christopher Boerner and Jennifer Chilton Kallery, *Restructuring Environmental Big Business*, Occasional Paper 146 (Washington University, Center for the Study of American Business, December 1994).

60. The coding in table 6-7 did not aggregate all the Nader groups together, though a plausible case could be made they should be counted as one since most depend in one way or another on his fundraising. Congress Watch, which is listed in table 6-7, is a Nader organization.

61. Unless otherwise indicated, all membership and budget figures are from 1991, the last of the three years studied. The figures come from the *Encyclopedia of Associations* (Detroit: Gale Research, 1991).

62. Stephen Glass, "After the Fall," *New Republic*, May 26, 1997, p. 15.

63. Jack L. Walker, Jr., *Mobilizing Interest Groups in America* (University of Michigan Press, 1991), p. 82.

64. John H. Cushman, Jr., "Short of Cash, N.A.A.C.P. Stops Paying Its Employees," *New York Times*, November 2, 1994, p. A14.

65. Scott Allen, "The Greening of a Movement," *Boston Globe*, October 19, 1997, p. A1. See also Christopher J. Bosso, "The Color of Money: Environmental Groups and the Pathologies of Fund Raising," in Allan J. Cigler and Burdett A. Loomis, eds., *Interest Group Politics*, 4th ed. (Washington: Congressional Quarterly Press, 1995), p. 102.

66. The annual budgets for the groups in Lowry's data base varied, but most were for years in the late 1980s and early 1990s. I calculated the percentages by averaging the data he presents in table C-2. Robert C. Lowry, "The Private Production of Public Goods: Organizational Maintenance, Managers' Objectives, and Collective Goals," *American Political Science Review*, vol. 91 (June 1997), p. 322.

67. Jeffrey M. Berry, *The Interest Group Society*, 2d ed. (Scott, Foresman/Little Brown, 1989), p. 60.

68. Clyde Wilcox, *Onward Christian Soldiers* (Westview, 1996), pp. 4, 38.

69. Matthew C. Moen, *The Transformation of the Christian Right* (University of Alabama Press, 1992), p. 108.

70. Tucker Carlson, "What I Sold at the Revolution," *New Republic*, June 9, 1997, pp. 15–20; and Leslie Wayne, "Conservative Advocate and His G.O.P. Ties Come into Focus," *New York Times*, July 8, 1997, p. A10.

71. David Grann, "Robespierre of the Right," *New Republic*, October 27, 1997, pp. 20–24.

72. See John R. Wright, "Contributions, Lobbying, and Committee Voting in the U.S. House of Representatives," *American Political Science Review*, vol. 84 (June 1990), pp. 417–38.

73. Charles E. Lindblom, *Politics and Markets* (Basic Books, 1977).

74. James Q. Wilson, "Democracy and the Corporation," in Robert Hessen, ed., *Does Big Business Rule America?* (Washington: Ethics and Public Policy Center, 1981), p. 37. Emphasis in original.

Chapter 7

1. Jack L. Walker Jr., *Mobilizing Interest Groups in America* (University of Michigan Press, 1991).

2. Jeffrey M. Berry, *Lobbying for the People* (Princeton University Press, 1977), p. 29.

3. Mancur Olson Jr., *The Logic of Collective Action* (Schocken, 1968).

4. Berry, *Lobbying for the People*, p. 39.

5. Olson, *The Logic of Collective Action*, p. 161.

6. See Laura R. Woliver, *From Outrage to Action* (University of Illinois Press, 1993); and Lawrence S. Rothenberg, *Linking Citizens to Government* (Cambridge University Press, 1992).

7. Frank R. Baumgartner and Bryan D. Jones, *Agendas and Instability in American Politics* (University of Chicago Press, 1993), p. 189.

8. Baumgartner and Jones, *Agendas and Instability in American Politics*.

9. Jeffrey M. Berry, *The Interest Group Society*, 3d ed. (Longman, 1997), p. 27.

10. Richard B. Freeman and James L. Medoff, *What Do Unions Do?* (Basic Books, 1984), pp. 221–45.

11. Mark J. Rozell and Clyde Wilcox, eds., *God at the Grass Roots* (Rowman and Littlefield, 1995). See also John C. Green, James L. Guth, and Clyde Wilcox, "Less than Conquerors: The Christian Right in State Republican Parties," in Anne N. Costain and Andrew S. McFarland, eds., *Social Movements and American Political Institutions* (Rowman and Littlefield, 1998), pp. 117–35.

12. Jeffrey M. Berry and Deborah Schildkraut, "Citizen Groups, Political Parties, and Electoral Coalitions," in Costain and McFarland, *Social Movements*, pp. 136–56.

13. David E. Rosenbaum, "Accord Satisfies G.O.P. Moderates on Abortion Issue," *New York Times*, August 8, 1996, p. A1.

14. Liberal citizen groups have in the past also tried to move the Democrats away from the center on issues like affirmative action. Berry and Schildkraut, "Citizen Groups, Political Parties, and Electoral Coalitions."

15. Bauer was referring to the period between the time that Ronald Reagan took office and when Bauer was being interviewed (1998). Laurie Goodstein, "Religious Right, Frustrated, Trying New Tactic on G.O.P.," *New York Times*, March 23, 1998, p. A1.

16. Paul R. Abramson and Ronald Inglehart, *Value Change in Global Perspective* (University of Michigan Press, 1995); and Ronald Inglehart, *Modernization and Postmodernization* (Princeton University Press, 1997).

17. Robert D. Putnam, "Bowling Alone: America's Declining Social Capital," *Journal of Democracy*, vol. 6 (January 1995), pp. 65–78; and Robert D. Putnam, "Tuning In, Tuning Out: The Strange Disappearance of Social Capital in America," *PS*, vol. 28 (December 1995), pp. 664–83.

18. Robert N. Bellah and others, *Habits of the Heart* (Perennial, 1985); and *Citizens and Politics* (Dayton: Kettering Foundation, 1991).

19. Theda Skocpol, "The Tocqueville Problem: Civic Engagement in American Democracy," presidential address delivered at the annual meeting of the Social Science History Association, October 1996.

20. See Benjamin Barber, *Strong Democracy* (University of California Press, 1984); Jeffrey M. Berry, Kent E. Portney, and Ken Thomson, *The Rebirth of Urban Democracy* (Brookings, 1993); and Jane J. Mansbridge, *Beyond Adversary Democracy* (Basic Books, 1980).

21. Barber, *Strong Democracy*.

22. Hanna Fenichel Pitkin, *The Concept of Representation* (University of California Press, 1972).

23. Berry and Schildkraut, "Citizen Groups, Political Parties, and Electoral Coalitions."

24. Jeffrey Toobin, "Clinton's Left-Hand Man," *New Yorker*, July 21, 1997, p. 30.

25. See generally, William G. Mayer, *The Divided Democrats* (Westview, 1996).

26. Clinton has not drawn a perfect demarcation between material and post-material in choosing what to support. The *New Yorker's* attack on him centered on his retreat on civil liberties, which are postmaterial concerns.

27. See Doug McAdam, *Political Process and the Development of Black Insurgency* (University of Chicago Press, 1982).

Appendix A

1. An excellent study of Congress that samples issues over a long period of time is Mark A. Peterson, *Legislating Together* (Harvard University Press, 1990).

2. George C. Edwards III, Andrew Barrett, and Jeffrey Peake, "The Legislative Impact of Divided Government," *American Journal of Political Science*, vol. 41 (April 1997), p. 549.

3. See Marc Howard Ross and Roger W. Cobb, "Cultural Strategies and the Politics of Agenda Denial," paper delivered at the annual meeting of the American Political Science Association, August 1997.

4. John W. Kingdon, *Agendas, Alternatives, and Public Policies*, 2d ed. (HarperCollins, 1995), p. 73.

5. Kay Lehman Schlozman and John T. Tierney, *Organized Interests and American Democracy* (Harper and Row, 1986), p. 150.

6. See Roger Morris, *Richard Milhous Nixon* (Henry Holt, 1990).

7. For an oppposing view, see Benjamin I. Page, *Who Deliberates?* (University of Chicago Press, 1996), pp. 17–42.

Index

Printed in the United States
100098LV00002B/195/A